GROWING

Vegetables

Chief Executive: Juliet Rogers
Publishing Director: Kay Scarlett
Publisher: Lynn Lewis
Cover Design: Heather Menzies
Internal Concept Design: Mary Louise Brammer
Art Direction and Design: Alex Frampton
Production: Elizabeth Malcolm
Project Manager: Ariana Klepac

Metro Books
122 Fifth Avenue
New York, NY 10011

ISBN: 978-1-4351-2264-2

Printed and bound in Singapore

10 9 8 7 6 5 4 3 2 1

GROWING
Vegetables

grow, harvest, eat

METRO BOOKS
NEW YORK

contents

INTRODUCTION   6

GROWING VEGETABLES
first things first   18
garden design   34
cultivating   52
propagating   70
maintenance   94
extend the season   126

HARVESTING AND USING
harvest time   144
eat the garden   162

VEGETABLE DIRECTORY   198

Index   250
Acknowledgments   256

Growing, harvesting, preparing, and eating food from your own garden is all part of the same activity and a wonderfully rewarding experience. It should be a grand celebration from garden to table, and the purpose of this book is to show you just how easy it is to grow your own vegetables.

introduction

What is a vegetable?

A vegetable is the edible part of an herbaceous plant and includes all parts of the plant. Fruits that are used as vegetables include tomatoes, peppers, eggplants, cucumbers, and squash. Stems or shoots that are treated as vegetables include celery, asparagus, and leeks. Leaf vegetables, eaten either raw or cooked, include cabbage, spinach, lettuce, and endive. We eat the roots, bulbs, and tubers of carrots, parsnips, beets, turnips, onions, and potatoes. Seeds are eaten as vegetables, too, and include green peas, snow peas, corn, and fava beans. Flowers known as vegetables include cauliflowers, artichokes, and broccoli.

Your favorite vegetables will taste particularly flavorsome and be more nutritious when freshly picked just prior to eating or cooking.

Ruby chard.

And he gave it for his opinion, "that whoever could make two ears of corn, or two blades of grass, to grow upon a spot of ground where only one grew before, would deserve better of mankind, and do more essential service to his country, than the whole race of politicians put together".
Jonathan Swift, *Gulliver's Travels*, 1726

A tradition of vegetable gardening

Despite frequent claims to the contrary, professions such as law and prostitution were long preceded by horticulture. And even before the horticulturists came the botanists. In early hunter-gatherer communities, human survival depended on correctly identifying edible species, and bad or inattentive botanists were inclined to be short lived, for obvious reasons. This botanical knowledge was passed on and enlarged by progressive generations, so that thousands of plants with edible roots, leaves, fruits, and flowers could be identified and grown as food.

Ancient times

Prehistoric horticulture developed in the Neolithic era, which began around 12,000 years ago, arising independently in many centers of the world including Mexico, China, Egypt, Mesopotamia (within present day Iraq), in the areas now known as Turkey, Syria, Jordan, and Israel, and around ancient Macedonia, Thrace, and Thessaly.

Mesopotamia, "the land between the rivers," was located between the Tigris and Euphrates Rivers. The area to the east where the two rivers nearly converge was known as Babylonia, which in turn encompassed two areas, Sumer to the south, and Akkad to the north. Sumeria, which was destined to be the world's first civilization, invented written language and was extraordinarily advanced in both the arts and sciences, including horticulture. They carried out remarkable feats of engineering in order to create sophisticated irrigation systems that watered their dry, inland soils.

The writings of the Greeks, Romans, Hebrews, and Chinese in the following historical period indicate an era when horticulture was further refined and important edible plants were introduced into cultivation including cucumbers and onions, among many others.

The surviving descriptions and frescoes of the gardens of the upper classes during this period in the Mediterranean region reveal often well designed and beautiful spaces that were retreats from the hot climate, with formal, inward-looking walled gardens accessed from very substantial villas. Most vegetables, though, were cultivated beyond the villa garden on farmland.

Gardening was surely one of the greatest legacies Rome left England. The English diet was notoriously limited until the Roman occupation introduced onions, garlic, and leeks (and grapes for wine, of course). Rome also passed on its high level of horticultural knowledge.

After the demise of the Roman Empire, England gradually fell into disarray in the power vacuum that was left behind, with centuries of relentless struggles. During this long period of civil unrest, the monasteries became the keepers of learning, including horticulture, not only in England but throughout Europe.

Green oak leaf lettuce, leeks, and violas.

The Middle Ages

The vegetable garden of a medieval monastery, known as a hortus, was well planned and functional. The plans for a Benedictine monastery at St Gall in Switzerland, drawn in c. AD 820 show a central walk bordered with nine simple raised beds on either side, each allocated a single crop such as onions or dill. Although travel was dangerous, monks did travel between monasteries within their orders, and those who were assigned the role of priest-gardener ensured that new cultivars of vegetables were spread throughout Europe.

Poorer people often owned small pieces of land on which they grew vegetable crops, as well as raised animals. The Domesday book lists large numbers of such horti and hortuli (small production gardens). Their diet was monotonous, mainly a mess of potage, as uninteresting gastronomically as it sounds and consisting of a thick vegetable soup based on meat broth when available, and supplemented with barley. Cabbage, leeks, fava beans, and the white field pea were common ingredients.

The rich, living behind fortified castle walls, ate considerably better with a greater variety of protein derived from seafood, mutton, and beef. Simple salads were served. But vegetables were largely neglected in favor of an array of meats. Green peas were acceptable but fava beans were considered the food of peasants and monks.

Rise of the market garden

In the Middle Ages there was an increasing demand for more and more vegetables, as people could not produce enough food for themselves in their gardens alone. This brought about the creation of the market garden in towns and cities, where there was room enough within the town walls to build one.

The sixteenth century

The Elizabethan garden of the sixteenth century was a remarkable place. England had both stability and prosperity under the reign of Elizabeth I. Without the need for living under fortification, English gardens were able to expand and an appreciation of garden aesthetics and knowledge of horticulture and botany became a preoccupation of many Elizabethan gentlemen and an acceptable subject for social discourse.

European travel reinforced the fact that England had dropped well behind some other European countries in many civilized pursuits while it was occupied with its political struggles. Italy was far more sophisticated in both gastronomy and horticulture, and the newly affluent of England borrowed the Italians' ideas, as well as those of the French.

With rising prosperity came a concern for fine dining, and gentlemen of the era were likely to take a deep and well informed interest in all stages of food preparation from the raising of ingredients to their preparation. The vegetable garden or potager of rich houses was laid out in a sunny place within the overview of the home, protected and discreetly screened at ground level by quickset hedges. The beds were raised, and dug through with manure to maintain fertility. Each bed was devoted to a single crop, perhaps leeks or onions, carrots, turnips, beets, lamb's-quarters (fat hen), spinach, sorrel, or parsley. The potager was a place of pleasure, extensive, very neatly laid out, and filled with a rich array of vegetables and herbs. New crops were introduced at an astonishing rate, both from the New World and Europe. However, many of these new vegetables, such as the tomato, runner bean, and potato were regarded for over a century with the deepest suspicion.

The earliest English settlements in North America were organized by Sir Walter Raleigh. The gardens of very early English settlements such as those in Jamestown in Virginia were modest, functional, raised, rectangular beds, filled with vegetables and herbs, placed close to the house and protected by fencing.

No section of the garden makes more demands on the soil than does the vegetable garden with its need for constant, luxuriant growth.

Shall I not have intelligence with the earth? Am I not partly leaves and vegetable mold myself?
Henry David Thoreau, 1817–1862

Zucchini flower.

The seventeenth century

As settlement progressed, American gardens of the seventeenth century were similar in design to those of Europe with clipped box-hedged knot gardens and well managed home orchards. The soils of Virginia were hailed as very fertile by those advocating emigration to the new colony. A number of indigenous root crops, herbs, fruit vines, and salad flowers had also been incorporated into the kitchen gardens.

By 1705 Robert Beverley, an early promotions expert, wrote robustly of kitchen gardens in America in his book *History and Present State of Virginia* that they "don't thrive better or faster in the Universe than here. They have all the Culinary plants that grow in England, and in far greater perfection, than in England." He added that a number of indigenous root crops and salad flowers had also been incorporated into the kitchen gardens.

The nineteenth century

The nineteenth century was a period of great affluence when the British Empire was most influential. The grand houses of the era were serviced by huge walled kitchen gardens many acres in extent, and would have included at least one hothouse where the raised temperature allowed the culture of rare plants from the colonies, and an array of hotbeds, greenhouses, and cloches to protect outdoor crops from frost. Technology had entered the vegetable garden. As the century progressed, gardeners' magazines, garden knowledge, and garden societies proliferated. The garden show with its giant vegetables and greatly coveted awards became the testing grounds for cultivars, theories, and techniques.

A well-kept vegetable garden can be satisfying to the eye, whether you choose to plant in regimented rows or in more casual beds, as pictured here. Be sure to include paths between beds for easy access.

The humble potato was first cultivated around 2,000 years ago in Peru. Through the sophisticated plant-breeding technqiues of the Incas, potatoes developed from small, bitter, and misshapen wild plants, which grew at very high altitudes, into the dependable vegetable we know and love today.

The New World

When Europe first encountered the Americas, there was little perception that great empires had risen and fallen for thousands of years, that extraordinary knowledge in engineering, architecture, math, and astronomy had been accumulated, or that the native peoples of the Americas had become indisputably master plant breeders.

For more than 8,000 years before Columbus reached America, they had been actively engaged in cultivating and breeding plants, and collecting and testing new potential food species. By 1492, it has been estimated that the indigenous peoples had domesticated over 300 edible species, many of which had beeen subjected to intensive selection for thousands of years to improve their taste, size, yield, appearance, and to adapt them to particular climates or soils.

Corn never occurred wild in nature. It is a crop that was synthesized in Mexico perhaps as long as 7,000 years ago.

The Inca civilization that the Spanish military expedition of Pizarro and his soldiers encountered in Peru in 1532 was an empire comparable to that of Rome in size, stretching from central modern Chile in the south to southern Colombia in the north, with a population of fifteen million people. It is estimated that when Pizarro encountered them, Andean Indians were growing some 3,000 different cultivars of potatoes alone, and had developed the art of freeze-drying them.

According to legend, the Aztecs were told that they were to build their city in the place where they found an eagle perched on a cactus and eating a snake. They found this site in a place that was virtually uninhabitable, a snake-infested area of lakes and swamps studded with islands. However, they drained the land with canals, installed irrigation for crops, and created floating gardens—rafts anchored in the shallow areas of the lake and covered in soil on which they raised vegetables and flowers, which they do to this day. The roots grew downwards and were fed on the nutrients in the lake water, thriving in the hottest summers. They had created hydroponics.

Although in the end the great civilizations of the Aztecs of Mexico and the Incas of South America were no match for the muskets and introduced diseases of Europe, they left a gift to the world of more than half of our food resources, representing 10,000 years of skilled plant breeding.

some vegetable origins
The Americas: corn, jicama, potato, tomato
Asia: bamboo shoots, mung beans, bok choy, white radish (daikon), garlic, lotus root, onion, radish, shallot, soybean, spinach
Eurasia: celery, lettuce, mustard greens, turnip
Europe: asparagus, beet, Brussels sprouts, cabbage, carrot, endive, fennel, kale, kohlrabi, parsnip
Near East: alfalfa, leek

Vegetable gardens don't always have to be green. You can either plant colorful varieties of vegetables, or interplant your greens with colorful ornamental plants, as shown here.

Most **vegetables** are about 70 percent water, with about 3.5 percent protein and less than 1 percent fat. They are good sources of minerals, especially calcium and iron, and vitamins, mainly A and C.

Alternative vegetables

Heirloom vegetables

These old-fashioned types often have the best flavor. You can obtain low-acid, yellow-striped tomatoes, red-skinned eggplant, and rainbow chard to brighten up your dinner plate. Many other types are available, and seed-swapping or gardening clubs offer selections, too.

Perpetual vegetables

Most vegetables are annuals and need replacing each season. Look for perpetual varieties of beans, beets, and lettuce to save the effort of replanting.

Asian vegetables

Specialized regional cuisine has developed around the wide varieties of vegetables grown in Asia. Chinese kale, cabbage, radish, turnips, and lettuce-like greens such as tatsoi and mizuna are all delicious additions to stir-fries and salads.

Edible flowers

Appearance is an integral part of the enjoyment of food. Borage, calendula, elder flower, heartsease, nasturtium, and sage flowers don't just have pretty faces, they also taste great.

GROWING

VEGETABLES

One of the most liberating experiences is being able to provide food for yourself to eat. The simple and rewarding task of growing your own vegetables can easily be overlooked in today's busy and hectic lifestyle, but it can be an easy job undertaken by almost anyone anywhere.

first things first

Starting a vegetable patch

Even the tiniest space in your garden, or a pot or container, will yield some of your favorite vegetables once you know how easy it is to grow them.

The diversity of vegetables means that there is always a way possible for the young, fit, and healthy or the less mobile and elderly. Raised garden beds, hydroponics, and no-dig gardens have revolutionized the world of gardening, and are perfectly suited for the disabled as the working area can be at any level to suit and have easy access for wheelchairs around the crops. Many groups that provide horticultural therapy have established themselves and are worthwhile joining.

Bring your soil to life
Don't put all your efforts into life only above the soil. The secret to a healthy vegetable garden is healthy soil, prepared with plenty of organic material, such as compost.

Gardening this way is also the perfect way to overcome less than ideal sites that may have poor soils or climates, as weather screens, cloches, and so on can be fitted.

Many vegetable crops, such as lettuce and tomatoes, will grow hydroponically; many will grow as climbers, such as beans and peas, for use as screens; other crops will even cope in a polystyrene box, like spinach and Swiss chard.

It's also not often that one can say "money is no object," but as almost all vegetables are available by seed, from the local supermarket or nursery, even the cost of vegetable gardening is affordable, and indeed profitable, and the net product saves you buying many of your groceries.

Beet is a great vegetable to start with as it is easy to grow.

Peas that are tall-growing will need some kind of trellis to support them. Otherwise peas are fairly trouble-free plants. Just make sure to provide adequate moisture when they're in bloom.

Vegetable families

Vegetables come from a wide range of families. For example the lily family (Liliaceae), which asparagus belongs to; the grass family (Poaceae), which gives us corn; the palm family (Araceae) where taro root and palm hearts originate; and the hibiscus family (Malvaceae) from which okra and rosella are members. Most vegetables, however, are from the following five well-known families.

The daisy family (Asteraceae), apart from all those superb flowering shrubs and annuals, also boasts globe artichoke, Jerusalem artichoke, endive, lettuce, and dandelion.

The mustard family (Brassicaceae) includes ornamentals like wallflowers and stock, as well as very important commercial crops such as canola, cauliflower, broccoli, Brussels sprouts, cabbage, radish, turnip, watercress, and horseradish.

The pea family (Fabaceae) includes some beautiful flowering plants, such as wattles, cassias, brooms, and sweet peas, but it is the edible beans and peas that are our staples—legumes such as lima bean, fava bean, green bean, pea, snow pea, and soybean.

The deadly nightshade family (Solonaceae) is unusual in that many members are highly poisonous plants, such as tobacco, deadly nightshade, and Angel's trumpet. Edible fruit from eggplants, chilies, pepper, and tomato, as well as the favorite tuber, potato, have become important in the western diet.

The cucurbits (Cucurbitaceae) are popular summer vegetables with cucumber, marrow, cantaloupe, squash, watermelon, and zucchini among their members.

Tomatoes are part of the deadly nightshade (Solanaceae) family.

Easy-to-grow vegetables

Bean, green	Onion
Beet	Pea
Carrot	Pepper
Cucumber	Radish
Garlic	Squash
Lettuce	Tomato

Cucumbers are part of the Cucurbitaceae family.

Although classified as an herb, **fennel** has an enlarged leaf base that is cultivated and eaten as a vegetable. It has a slightly aniseed flavor that is used in seafood dishes, sauces, and liqueurs. Fennel is easy to grow but prefers sun and acid soil.

Soil is approximately 45 percent minerals, 25 percent water, 25 percent air, and 5 percent organic matter.

Soil pH

Gardening books often speak of the pH range. The pH is a measure of acidity and alkalinity, based on a scale of 1 to 14, with 1 being extremely acid and 14 being extremely alkaline.

Most soils contain some free lime, and the presence of this lime (or lack of it) will cause the soil to be either 'acid' or 'alkaline', depending on the amount present. The lime content within the soil will greatly influence the range of plants that can be grown, as well as the overall fertility of the soil, so it is important to find out the pH value before adding plants to it. Many plants will grow happily in a soil with a high lime content, but there are others that cannot tolerate it, and will die. Testing the soil will therefore save costly mistakes—both in terms of time and money.

Most vegetables do best in slightly acidic soils, so if you are serious about growing healthy crops, invest in an inexpensive pH testing kit. These can be purchased from garden centers. Gardens like regular applications of lime to maintain ideal pH levels. Lime contains an essential nutrient, calcium. This is easily lost from the soil, especially in areas of high rainfall and will constantly need replacing. An annual application of between 1¾ and 3½ ounces per square yard is usually sufficient to remedy this. If you are a keen organic gardener, it is not advisable to mix lime with animal manure. This causes a release of ammonia gas and consequent loss of nitrogen. Lime is returned to the soil by adding it or wood ash to the compost heap rather than digging directly into the soil.

These days, commercially available garden lime often contains quantities of trace elements as well. The uptake of trace elements and other nutrients will only occur within certain pH ranges. Nitrogen, phosphorus, calcium, and magnesium, for example, need a neutral to slightly alkaline pH range for their uptake, whereas iron, manganese, and boron prefer a slightly acidic soil. Nevertheless, even though pH levels may remain constant, remember that it is humus and other decaying organic matter in the soil that bacteria feed on which in turn makes nutrients and trace elements available to the plant. Diseases indicating these nutritional shortages will soon manifest themselves if the soil is not rich in humus.

Testing soil pH

1 Place the soil sample in a tube (the tube should be about one-fifth full).

2 Pour in water.

3 Shake.

4 Let the sample settle. The color change indicates whether the soil is alkaline or acidic. This test shows that the soil is alkaline.

For washing and storing the test kit, follow the manufacturer's instructions.

Plants such as climbing peas and beans support themselves by tendrils, which are specialized organs designed to move laterally and encircle any object. Tendrils are sensitive to touch. If you stroke them lightly on the underside, they will start to turn toward that side within a couple of minutes. As a tendril brushes against any object, it turns toward it and will start to wrap itself around it.

Comfortable conditions

Surprisingly little land is required to raise enough vegetables and herbs to keep an average family of two adults and two children luxuriously supplied with gourmet vegetables. Just 118 square yards would be more than sufficient to supply abundant harvests of delicious, chemical-free food like buckets of corn rushed from the garden to the saucepan, early season asparagus, vine-ripened juicy tomatoes, intensely fragrant armfuls of herbs such as basil, peas, and snapping fresh beans, new-season and heirloom potatoes, and winter squash that has been matured under the fall sun for thick winter soups. With intensive cultivation the amount of space needed could even be halved.

Many vegetables can be obtained as dwarf forms, which occupy less space. Clever use of vertical space and the use of large pots can also reduce the amount of land required. Replacing newly harvested crops with vegetable seedlings reduces both wastage of garden space and nutrient losses from the soil.

A well managed, organically enriched, mulched, raised garden that is continuously planted will yield far more than a larger one that is in continuous need of care. Companion planting can reduce the impact of pests and diseases without resorting to poisonous sprays, and will help to reduce crop losses. If you are using a sprinkler hose to water the garden, it is convenient to design the vegetable garden so that it does not extend beyond the reach of the sprinkler.

If space is very limited, imagine building one or more large, traylike, rectangular boxes with drainage provided, and filled with rich, well-composted soil. These can be rested on any surface including wooden decking, a strongly built balcony, or a brick patio, held above the surface by stacked bricks. Simply an enlarged version of a seed flat, such gardens can be enormously productive, and can be moved with the seasons to take advantage of sunlight. Drip irrigation can even further reduce the small effort in maintaining such gardens. Window boxes and potted gardens can also be employed to produce summer herbs, tomatoes, and salad greens.

Even if you just have a window box, you can grow a few leafy green salad vegetables for fresh flavor.

The **ornamental kale and onions** here are ready for harvest, but the onions won't keep unless you wait for the foliage to wither. Pick leaves from the kale as needed, and let the plant continue to grow for more harvests.

Analyzing the site

Take some time to become really familiar with a site before planning a vegetable garden. Good design always emerges from making the most of the opportunities a site offers and minimizing its defects. Perhaps surprisingly, the quality of the soil on the site is not a major constraint as it can be considerably improved. Vegetable gardens may be of any shape or size, but regardless of design, they must be in a position to receive sunlight for the greater part of the day and have protection against wind. Keep clear of trees and other garden plants that will compete for water and nutrients. If topsoil is shallow or of poor quality, beds should be raised and well drained to allow root growth and prevent waterlogging after heavy rains. The following topics need to be carefully considered before you start.

Aspect

Gardens facing the east are sunniest in the morning and offer milder conditions. In the northern hemisphere, south-facing gardens receive the greatest sunlight exposure and warmth in winter while in the southern hemisphere a north-facing aspect maximizes growth. Most gardens offer different aspects that can be exploited by sun-loving or shade-requiring plants. The presence of walls and

Raised bed gardening is a compromise between garden beds and containers. It can also solve the problem of localized poor soils and drainage. Beds can be constructed from railway sleepers, rocks, or other strong material. Moisture levels should be monitored, as raised beds tend to dry out faster than normal ground-level beds.

buildings can throw long shadows, particularly in winter. At night, sunny walls re-radiate the warmth absorbed during the daylight hours. Gardeners have long taken advantage of this effect by planting espaliered fruit trees and fruiting vines like grapes and cantaloupes against sunny walls. Rows that run east to west intercept the most light. In the northern hemisphere shorter plantings should be on the southern side, and taller plantings on the northern side. The converse holds for gardens in the southern hemisphere.

Climate

A very old adage warns novice gardeners to plant their garden to survive the extremes of the climate. But even the most experienced gardener is sometimes tempted to throw caution to the wind and plant some vegetables and fruits that will fail in an extreme season. This is fine, and fun, if only small gambles are taken but, generally, you will want the majority of your crops to succeed.

Some of the facts you need to know in planning are the maximum temperature extremes in the district, prevailing winds, rainfall and its distribution and historic extremes, first and last frost dates and their severity, and the length of the growing season. Soil in raised garden beds is better drained and warms more quickly in spring, so that gardens in cooler climates can be planted up to a fortnight earlier. Consider what kind of climate modifying structures might be needed on the site such as a greenhouse or polytunnel. These need to be sited in a clear sunny area that is protected from any severe winds.

Climate change is a reality for the superheated twenty-first century. Current predictions by the world's most respected

Corn likes it hot and is reasonably drought-tolerant, as it sends its roots deep into the soil, seeking moisture. Corn will be one of the last garden vegetables to wilt in the heat of the sun, but it does not fare well in heavy frost or freezes.

Cool-season vegetables

Artichokes
Asparagus
Belgian endive
Broccoli
Brussels sprouts
Cabbage
Carrots
Cauliflower
Celery
Chinese spinach (amaranth)
Endive
Fava beans
Kohlrabi
Leek
Lettuce
Parsnip
Pea
Potato
Radish
Rutabaga
Shallot
Spinach
Swiss chard
Turnip

Cool-season crops like turnips (above right) need time to mature before warm weather. Okra (below right) is a warm-season crop.

climate research bodies including the Intergovernmental Panel on Climate Change (IPCC), the Hadley Group based in the United Kingdom, and the CSIRO in Australia have indicated an average rise in temperature of around 3.6°F by 2030 with a rise of up to 11°F by 2070. The Hadley Group have forecast a possible rise of 14.5°F by 2100. These higher temperatures also predispose the world to much more extreme weather patterns, changed flows of important climate which moderates ocean currents such as the Gulf Stream, and also brings for the gardener the possibility of many damaging insects previously restricted to hotter areas. Even a one degree rise can have considerable effects on climate, and historic records cannot be expected to apply as the century progresses. Planning for rather more severe conditions than those experienced in the past will allow your garden to continue to thrive.

Warm-season vegetables

Beans, green
Chayote
Corn
Cucumber
Eggplant
Fennel
Lettuce
Okra
Pepper
Spinach
Squash
Sweet potato
Tomato

Small, round, and juicy, peas are seeds encased in a green pod.

Children's gardens

Growing vegetables from childhood fosters a love of nature, a respect for food, and, hopefully, a life-long interest in gardening. The key to children's gardening is to keep tasks simple and fun, fast and fresh.

For example, a tray garden of vegetable tops, such as carrots and turnips, made from leftovers when preparing your night's meal, will easily strike, and potato peelings have eyes that will also sprout if kept moist with peat or leaf mould. This 'magic' sparks an interest that can be developed with the next level of projects. These could be an empty egg shell containing absorbant cotton and germinating alfalfa sprouts or wheatgrass, sweet potatoes grown as indoor vines from chopped up segments of tuber, or hanging baskets dripping with sugar snap or snow peas.

From here, a small plot in the garden or a collection of fruit boxes could be handed over to children from about the age of six to grow simple vegetables such as Swiss chard, root crops like carrots and radishes from seed tapes, and tiny Tim tomatoes which are sweet and bite size. Edible flowers such as nasturtiums, or sunflowers for their tasty seeds will delight children of all ages.

If these experiments are successful, invest in some child-sized tools, a children's gardening book, some packets of seeds and a seed-raising kit, a bug catcher or butterfly net, some fun stakes with decorative tops of spiral forms, and you could even try making a scarecrow. Remember to feed using organic fertilizers, never spray with chemicals, wear gloves, don't touch spiders, and have fun!

Cress are tiny bright green sprouts with small, peppery leaves and are great in salads, sandwiches, or as a garnish. **Cress or mustard seeds** will germinate easily on moistened paper or absorbant cotton.

RADISH
(*Raphanus sativus*)

BABY BEANS
(*Phaseolus vulgaris*)

children's vegetables

Children love to sort things and classifying the food we eat is an invaluable education. Vegetables also grow in many different ways, whether vines, bushes, or roots.

SNOW PEAS
(*Pisum sativum* var. *macrocarpon*)

CHERRY TOMATOES
(*Lycopersicon esculentum*)

SUNFLOWER
(*Helianthus annuus*)

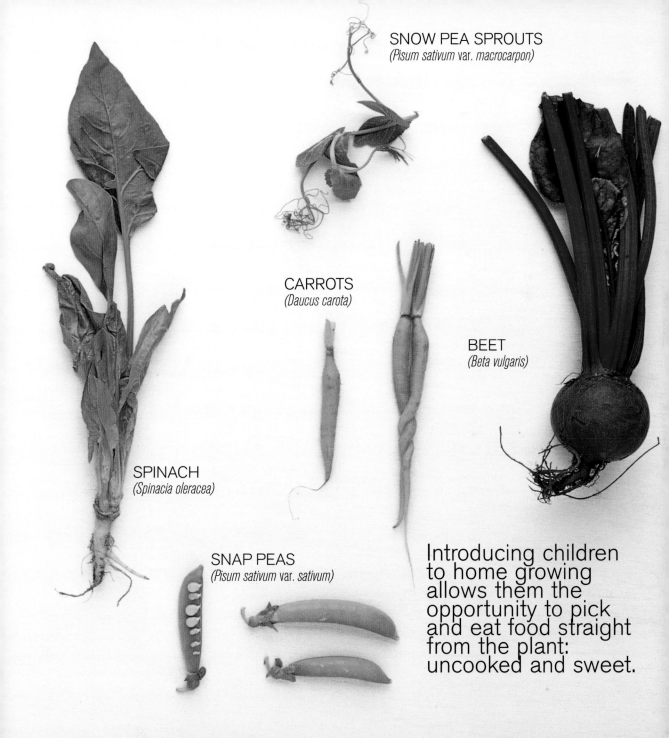

SNOW PEA SPROUTS
(*Pisum sativum* var. *macrocarpon*)

CARROTS
(*Daucus carota*)

BEET
(*Beta vulgaris*)

SPINACH
(*Spinacia oleracea*)

SNAP PEAS
(*Pisum sativum* var. *sativum*)

Introducing children to home growing allows them the opportunity to pick and eat food straight from the plant: uncooked and sweet.

Topography and drainage

Gardens located on flat, or nearly flat, land should be inspected after heavy rain so that drainage patterns in the garden can be checked. Rather than attempt the expensive business of draining areas that remain wet for some time after rain, it is better to consider these as a microenvironment to be exploited with moisture-loving plants.

Land that is too steep to be easily managed is best terraced. This will slow the flow of water off the land and allow it to percolate downwards. Steep slopes drain away rapidly and the dry soil grows many vegetables poorly. Steep slopes are also difficult to tend. The banks of terraces can either be formed into gentle slopes and grassed (a cheaper option but one that reduces the possible width of terraces), or more steeply cut and held with slightly backward-sloping retaining walls. In high rainfall areas, a drain may be used in front of a retaining wall to divert excess water.

Installing a drainage system

1 Using a garden line and canes, mark out the route of the drain where the drainage pipes are to be used.
2 Dig a trench about 2–2½ feet deep, and about 1 foot wide. Keep the topsoil and the subsoil separate.
3 Place a 2 inch layer of gravel, ash, and sand in the bottom of the trench, and lay or 'bed' the drainage pipes on top of this layer. Place the pipes so that they are touching one another end to end.
4 Refill the trench with a layer of gravel, ash, or sand over the pipes to within about 10–12 inches of the surface. Fill the trench with topsoil to leave a slight mound over the trench (this will settle down in 4 weeks). Do not press the soil into the trench, especially if it is wet. Spread any remaining soil over the site, where it will be incorporated into the topsoil over a few months. The drain should feed into a natural outlet, such as a ditch or stream.

Easy digging

If possible, lay a drainage system when the soil is dry, to produce easier working conditions. If working in wet weather, use broad wooden planks to prevent the soil becoming even more wet and sticky from being walked on. Dig the trench on a sloping site, starting from the lowest point and working upwards, so that any water is draining away from you as you work.

Clay-loving water chestnuts.

Drainage systems are often arranged with drains in a herringbone pattern of trenches. The trenches slope toward the lowest point of the garden, and the branch drains all link to a main drain.

Drainage systems in clay soil

Heavy clay soils can hold large amounts of water, making digging and other cultivation impossible at certain times of the year. Some form of drainage system will be necessary to lower the water level, so that the upper layers of soil, at least, are drier. The siting and layering of drains in the garden is normally a fairly straightforward procedure.

Moisture-loving celery requires plenty of water during the growing season, especially during hot, dry weather. If it doesn't get enough water celery stalks will be small and dry.

Vegetable gardens can be delightful places and, like flower gardens, they can be designed in many styles. If the vegetable patch is to be a feature of a garden, rather than just a practical production unit, many possibilities exist.

garden design

Edible landscaping

Even the smallest of gardens can be beautiful, eccentric, fun—and amazingly productive. Vegetables and fruits were once considered to be plants with fascinating textures, colors, and interesting architectural shapes. Then for a long period they were relegated out of sight.

But in the 1980s a revolution began. Edible landscaping was pioneered, and gardeners looked with fresh eyes at familiar food plants. They could have a dual purpose—they could be ornamental before they were eaten.

Cardoons, like artichokes, are a type of thistle, grown for their stalks. The plant, which can grow to 8 feet, makes a stunning backdrop to a perennial garden bed.

Designing with vegetables

All sorts of vegetables can be used in place of more conventional, non-edible choices in garden planting designs.

Low-growing plants for the front of a border could include a mixed planting of different-colored lettuces and endive—frilled and plain leaf, in greens of every shade, spotted and splashed, or brightly colored in crimson or bronze. Curly kale and edible-flowered clove pinks and violets are other possibilities.

Middle height can come from celery, chard (which comes in a rainbow of stem colors), spinach, beets, carrots, potatoes, curly kale, and ornamental pink-tinged or red cabbage.

Zucchini form a rosette of sculptural leaves and boast large golden-yellow flowers, which are also edible. Bush squash are equally handsome. Try planting them in tubs in sunny positions. Cantaloupes such as "Sugar Bush" also do well in large containers.

In this attractive combination, a bed of **fava bean** plants is bordered with a row of low-growing, pale green **oak leaf lettuces.**

Dramatic height can come from corn, sunflowers, purple-flowered cardoons and artichokes, and tall, staked tomatoes. A bold planting of huge, golden-headed sunflowers and lush tall green corn all tangled with purple-flowered, purple-podded beans makes a real garden showstopper—bold and exciting, as well as edible.

Accent vegetables

Edible landscaping is a style of gardening that sees beauty in the textures, shapes, and colors of vegetables and incorporates them fully into the ornamental garden. The architectural qualities and beauty of plants such as artichokes, cardoons, corn, and sunflowers are stunning in the flower garden. Rosette-style lettuce and endive are delightful at the front of the flower garden. Ruby chard is a dramatic introduction, together with beautiful lavender-and-white-striped or rose-colored Italian eggplant, tomatoes laden with glowing red fruits, golden-fruited zucchini, and fountains of fresh celery.

Interplant vegetables among other **flowering plants** for design and color. Here, low-growing cabbages are planted with tall poppies.

Endive.

A large **bean teepee** can make a wonderful summer cubby house for a small child.

Window gardens

Window boxes can be filled with dwarf tomatoes and herbs like basil, which also repel flies from windows. Lattice work and the sides of garden sheds and summer houses can be covered with climbing beans and peas, annual nasturtiums in flaming reds and golds, and climbing squash.

Teepees

Teepees constructed of bamboo canes stuck into the ground in a circle, tied together firmly at the top, and planted with a mass of tall "Telephone: peas, or stunning flowering beans like "Scarlet Runner" and "Purple King" make a spectacular feature in any garden.

Interplanting

Interplant the garden with herbs, companion plants, and masses of flowers, then add flowering fruit and nut trees and hedges of berries, and you have a true paradise. Whatever style chosen, separate perennial and annual crops. Perennial vegetables such as asparagus need a space devoted exclusively to their culture.

Old-fashioned vegetables

While modern vegetables are largely standardized in form and color, heirloom vegetables offer not only wonderful old-fashioned flavor and vigor, but come in amazing variations in color and form. They lend themselves to creating beautiful vegetable gardens. Organizations like the Seed Savers Exchange in Iowa, the HDRA in the United Kingdom, and the Seed Savers Network in Australia, offer wonderful opportunities to access the rarest of material and also help to preserve it for the future.

Beautiful vegetable gardens

Simple palette gardens consisting of a series of raised and edged rectangular beds are serviceable, easily tended, and have a simple charm when filled with vegetables and herbs. Ideally beds should be no wider than 4–5 feet wide as this allows for easy reach when weeding and harvesting. Old-fashioned country vegetable gardens are often set in grass, with raised rows of many vegetables and soft fruits, becoming a humming jungle of neatly tended abundance as the season progresses. The paradise vegetable garden tumbles abundance across paths, using the vertical space of walls, trellises, sheds, and summerhouses to create a tapestry of rioting flowers, herbs, and vegetables worthy of Eden. The formal potager garden is like a Persian carpet edged with herbs and embroidered with salad leaves and vegetables, every color and texture chosen with care. The designs for such potagers were common in medieval and Tudor gardens, and can feature standard honeysuckles and roses, pots of topiary, and a sundial to mark the alignments of axes. They have become very fashionable once more.

Beds are raised, and rambling vines are confined to the outer fence boundaries in this well-planned, cottage-style, flower and vegetable garden. Careful consideration has been given to the color palette, which uses a variety of pink and white-blooming plants. Using leaves that are tinged with pink, such as ornamental cabbage, adds further beauty.

Raised beds

Using raised beds for growing vegetables and herbs is an ideal way of incorporating a vegetable patch or 'edible garden' where space is limited. There are various benefits associated with growing plants in this way.

A raised bed encourages plants to root deeper into the soil, which means less watering. The plants can also be planted closer together and often in 'square' planting arrangements rather than in rows. This will aid the production of slightly smaller vegetables that are ideal for people living alone or couples. Planting at such a higher density cuts out the total amount of light that reaches the soil and thus reduces the development of weeds. This particular type of bed system will allow the growing season to be extended if necessary, as it is easy to cover part or all of the bed with either clear polyethylene sheeting or fleece suspended on wire hoops that are fastened to the retaining wall of the bed. The beds can be any length or height required, but the width of each bed is very important. The ideal width of each bed is about 5–6 feet, so it is possible to reach the center of the bed from each side, rather than having to walk on the soil in the bed.

CONSTRUCTING A RAISED BED

1 Mark out the area and dimensions of the raised bed, and remove any surface vegetation. Level the soil along the lines where the timber sections are to be positioned. Lay out the first layer of timber to create a low wooden 'wall' for the planting bed, and use a builder's square to check the right angles of the structure. Also, use a level to check the timber sections are level. Repeat the process, working around the wall, stacking timber sections to raise the height of the wall. Drive 6 inches into the corner joints on each layer of timber in order to keep them stable.

2 When the wall has reached the required height, fix the top row by driving 6 inch nails at an angle through the vertical joints.

3 Dig over the soil inside the bed area. Add some extra soil and organic matter and mix with the existing soil to aid drainage and water movement. Firm the soil well enough to reduce uneven settling later when the plants are in place.

4 Finally, plant the vegetables and herbs into the new bed. These are usually planted slightly closer together than when growing plants in rows in the garden.

Improving fertility

When clearing areas to make raised beds, use the removed topsoil to fill the raised beds, or mix it with some new topsoil, incorporating plenty of bulky organic matter such as compost or well-rotted manure to encourage bacterial and worm activity. These bulky materials also retain more moisture, which reduces the need to water the plants so frequently during dry weather.

Adding soil to the bed

When adding soil to the bed, always mix it with some of the original soil as this helps water to be drawn up from the surrounding soil outside the bed.

A potager provides a formal and practical, yet stunning, garden design.

A potager

Luscious leafy vegetables such as cabbage, lettuce, and spinach can be handsome plants, coming in a vast range of colors and textures. Blue-green, red, or rich green cabbages, glossy green or reddish brown lettuces, ruby chard, and purple kohlrabi are just a few that are perfect for dotting about flowers or for adding structure to formal displays. Even parsley looks great as a border.

Many herbs and vegetables have beautiful flowers in their own right. Runner beans have scarlet flowers in profusion and climbing peas have pretty white flowers that are edible. Nasturtiums have vibrant red, orange, and yellow flowers, while lavender, chamomile, chives, and borage will pretty up any boring vegetable patch.

Winter is the right time to be planting ornamental kale (*Brassica oleracea* Acephala Group) for a spring display. Its bright pink and frilly green foliage makes it an interesting potted plant but it also brightens up a vegetable garden when it is used to make decorative patterns. Grow kale in full sun, in a free-draining position, although you may need to occasionally dust with derris or diatomaceous earth to keep away the snails and cabbage moth caterpillars.

Growing vegetables in containers

Vegetables grow easily in containers, many of which are ornamental as well as edible and can be used to lovely effect on a deck, verandah, or in a courtyard. Frilly-leaved lettuces, scarlet-flowered beans, purple or cranberry beans, purple mustard, and red cabbage are just a few of the beautiful vegetables that can be used with other flowers, or to lift the greens of your vegetables.

The key factor with any container is the root zone. If you nurture down at this level, plants will repay you with healthy, delicious growth. Choose a premium grade potting mix that contains fully composted organic material for water-holding ability and nutrient supply, double washed river sand for drainage and texture, slow-release fertilizer for sustained supply of nutrients, and water crystals to stop the medium from drying out. This should be available from a garden center or nursery.

Choosing containers

Next, ensure that the container you choose suits the crop you're trying to grow. Obviously root crops will need a deep container suitable for the length of underground tubers. Old tyres stacked on top of each other are perfect, especially for potatoes as the height

Zucchini will grow well in a medium-sized container, showing off its striking flowers and soft, attractive leaves.

can be added to, which encourages further production of tubers. Top heavy crops such as tomatoes need weighty pots that don't blow over in the wind and can secure a stake, so large cement troughs that hold a trellis are perfect. Other climbers, like snow peas, will trail equally as well as they climb, so large hanging baskets are a space-efficient way of growing them.

Containers don't have to be limited to the stock standard plastic pot, however. Think outside the square and imagine what's possible. Rustic-style trugs and wooden crates look great filled with leaf crops and flowering nasturtiums oozing color. Wicker baskets (lined with perforated plastic and treated with marine-strength varnish) come in all shapes and sizes, and match cane teepees or tripods perfect for growing peas, beans, tomato, and cucumbers. Even modern items such as plastic organizers and shoe pockets can have drainage holes punctured and make super spots for small vegetables like lettuces and other perennial cut-and-come-agains, and are easily transported and light which makes them ideal for mobile gardeners.

Of course, there are also many units for growing hydroponics, so even the indoor gardener can have pots of produce, provided an investment in the right equipment (grow lights, water recirculators, and so on) is made.

Chilies and other fruiting vegetables, such as cherry tomatoes, peppers, or eggplant can be easily grown in containers. Rooting vegetables such as radishes, baby carrots, or scallions are great choices, too.

SALVIA
(*Salvia* spp.)

SUNFLOWER
(*Helianthus annuus*)

GERANIUM
(*Pelargonium* spp.)

AMARANTH
(*Amaranthus hypochondriacus*)

FIG
(*Ficus carica*)

edible flowers

Many flowers are not only attractive but edible, too. Roses and jasmine are made into teas. Blooms, such as dandelion, sunflower, and nasturtium, are eaten fresh in salads. Others, like violets, lavender, or rosemary, may be used in desserts or candied as decorations.

AMARANTH
(*Amaranthus hypochondriacus*)

GARLIC CHIVES
(*Allium tuberosum*)

WHEAT
(*Triticum aestivum*)

SOCIETY GARLIC
(*Tulbaghia violacea*)

ROSEMARY
(*Rosmarinus officinalis*)

ROSE
(*Rosa* spp.)

JASMINE
(*Jasminum* spp.)

LAVENDER
(*Lavandula* spp.)

NASTURTIUM
(*Tropaeolum majus*)

DAY LILY
(*Hemerocallis lilioasphodelus*)

The hydroponic vegetable garden

Although hydroponics is thought of as a modern invention, it has been used in simple forms for many centuries. The floating gardens of the Incas, for instance, consisted of rafts of rushes covered with soil and planted with crops, then tethered in the shallow waters of lakes. The roots grew through the raft to obtain a continuous supply of water and nutrients.

The advantages of hydroponics

The ideal garden for most vegetable growers is a plot of rich earth in a sunny place. But for apartment dwellers who hope to raise at least some fresh vegetables, hydroponics, the art of cultivating plants without soil, can offer a solution. It is also a helpful technique in growing crops in the home greenhouse where space is limited, and for gardeners in arid areas where water is scarce.

In hydroponic systems, plants are supported by an inert growing medium such as scoria, perlite, or

You can add **organic fertilizer** to your hydroponic reservoir by making a **"tea bag"** out of an old pair of pantyhose. Place the fertilizer in the toe of the **pantyhose** and tie to seal. Then suspend the tea bag in the reservoir.

Tomatoes and peppers can be grown hydroponically.

pea gravel, or by an artificially created medium such as Rockwool. The open nature of these types of media allow for good aeration of the plant roots, which are continuously flushed with a nutrient-rich solution. Unlike soil-grown plants, everything required for growth must be supplied by the growing system. Very precisely formulated commercial nutrient supplies are injected into the water that is pumped to the plants, and any excess is usually recycled via a reserve tank.

As the root systems of plants grown hydroponically do not need to explore widely for nutients as do soil-raised plants, the root systems are smaller, and a higher density of planting can be made. Hydroponic plants grow rapidly as they suffer no setbacks in terms of water and nutrient supply. The inert medium in which the plants are grown ensures that there are minimal weeds and few diseases. Plants grown indoors require additional light which should be supplied by full spectrum fluorescent

lights. An additional benefit is that the system can be automated allowing the gardener to be safely away from the crops for short periods.

On the other hand, some gardeners express the opinion that hydroponically raised vegetables lack flavor and question their nutritional value in comparison to plants raised in rich, well-composted gardens. Due to rapid growth, plants may also lack stem strength. Salad leaf vegetables are ideal crops for raising by hydroponics. Tomatoes, cucumbers, and peppers are also good subjects, and the vines should be supported in their growth.

A number of different commercial hydroponic systems are available for home gardeners, and range from single pot systems to growing bags and domestic greenhouse units. These are usually powered by external pumps.

Hydroponics, also called aquaculture, nutriculture, or soilless culture, is the cultivation of plants in nutrient-enriched water, sometimes also using the support of an inert medium such as sand or gravel. Not all vegetables are suited to this system, but leafy salad greens are one of the ideal candidates.

Vegetable timbales

Steam 3 medium carrots until soft. Steam 11 cups watercress until wilted, then squeeze out any liquid. Purée each vegetable, adding ⅓ cup cream and 3 egg yolks to each; season. Divide the carrot purée among 4 greased timbale moulds. Spoon the watercress purée on top. Put in a bain-marie and bake at 300°F for 1¼ hours. Turn out to serve. Serves 4.

No-dig gardening

Australian Esther Dean first became famous in the late 1970s for a specialized form of sheet composting which became known as the 'no-dig' garden. This technique can be used anywhere, even on the worst and most compacted soils, or directly onto lawn, to yield excellent crops.

First provide an edging for the future garden. Then give the soil a good soak. As a first step, overlapping, thick layers of newspaper are laid on the ground (cardboard or even old carpet can also be used), followed by a layer of alfalfa hay, a layer of organic fertilizer, a layer of loose straw, and another thin layer of organic fertilizer. After watering well, depressions can be made in the surface and filled with compost. Well-established seedlings, large seeds, tubers, and bulbs can then be immediately planted. If there is sufficient compost available, a layer of compost can be placed on top of the garden, rather than creating compost pockets. The contents reduce in height quite rapidly, and will grow excellent crops. Smaller seeded plants and seedlings can be planted in the following season.

No matter how heart-breaking the original soil is, if the mulch is turned aside a few months after the garden was constructed, a great improvement in texture will be found as well as pleasing numbers of earthworms.

Use strips of **pantyhose** or stockings to tie tomatoes and other plants to **stakes.** The ties are flexible, soft, and do not weather easily.

Climbing vegetables

The value of vertical gardening is often overlooked, but the space gained by going up is invaluable. Traditionally, wire supports, wooden stakes, trelliswork, and cane tripods carry the weight of plants such as climbing beans and peas, cucumbers, and tomatoes. Even old tools, ladders, and pot stands, however, can be used to add character—pretty scarlet runner beans on an arbor make a beautiful feature.

Some plants climb by themselves, given a support, such as beans and peas, due to their tendrils. Others, such as tomatoes and cucumbers, will need securing using budding tape or other flexible ties. Others happily trail on the ground, but are less likely to succumb to rot if lifted up with a support, such as zucchini.

Other edible climbers to include in your vertical garden include:

- Chayote vines on the fence, which are simple to grow.
- Sweet potatoes or yams, which can grow on 13 foot wide trellis in frost-free positions.
- Malabar spinach, also known as Indian spinach (*Basella rubra*), which has green and red forms, is a vigorous climber with leaves resembling spinach perfect for tropical areas.
- Soybeans can also be grown on tripods.

Buy a spineless chayote at the greengrocer early in spring, keep it on the kitchen window sill until it begins to sprout, and then plant it at the base of the fence or shed that you want it to cover. You should have a crop of chayotes by around midsummer.

Even low-growing forms of pea cultivars benefit from some support.

Supporting beans

In order to encourage runner beans to grow upwards, you will need to provide some sort of support structure. Canes are ideal for this.

1 Insert the canes at least 6 inches into the ground at appropriate planting distances, and plant about 2 inches to the side of each supporting cane.

2 The plant will twine itself around the cane until it reaches the top. You can then pinch out the leading shoot to prevent further growth.

Support and protection

Plants that have weak stems or a climbing habit will require some kind of support. Among these are cucumbers, tomatoes (tall varieties), peas, and beans. The form of support will be determined by the plant's habit. Beans, which are vigorous growers, will need 6 foot canes, tied together in a teepee shape or in a row. The canes must be anchored firmly, as the weight with the full crop is considerable. Tomatoes are best supported with a single, stout bamboo cane. Tie in the stem as it grows. Cucumbers can be trained flat to a trellis panel. With any fast-growing climbing vegetables, you will need to pinch out the growing point once enough fruiting trusses have formed, and you may need to remove some of the leaves from the sideshoots so that the fruit can ripen.

Plants that are vulnerable to attacks from flying pests will benefit from being grown in a polytunnel, or covered with netting. This will also help to protect against cold. However, those plants that are insect-pollinated must have the covers removed once they flower in order to set fruit.

Making a tomato support system

In recent years, there has been a dramatic rise in growing food crops in all kinds of containers. These range from long-term plants, such as apple trees with a life-span of 15 to 20 years, down to plants as fast growing as radishes, which grow from seed to maturity in a number of weeks.

If you have a small patio, you could buy or make your own growing bag (a strong plastic bag filled with growing medium in which you simply have to cut holes). Growing bags make convenient containers for short-term plants, such as low-growing vegetables, which will usually only be in residence for one growing season.

Although seen as short-term containers, there can be a fair amount of fertilizer residue left in the growing bags at the end of the season, especially when plants such as cucumbers, peppers, and tomatoes have been grown in them. Therefore, they can be used twice, to grow salad crops such as lettuces and radishes without the need for any extra fertilizer.

Unfortunately, it is common to encounter problems when growing taller plants, such as eggplants, cucumbers, and peppers, because the growing bags do not have the depth to allow for canes to be used as supports. This can be overcome by making a frame around the bag and fastening the support structure to the frame, so that the plants grow up toward the support.

Grow bags are a great solution for balcony gardeners as they can be persuaded to fit into awkward corners and spaces.

Supporting tomatoes

1 To make the base, measure and cut two lengths of timber to the same width as the growing bag. Drill and screw the long and short lengths together in order to form a rectangle. Cut a section of wire mesh to cover the top of the wooden rectangle and staple the wire mesh to the edges.

2 Turn the rectangle over and drill one ⅝ inch hole (about 3 inches deep) at each corner. Place the growing bag inside the frame and insert a stout cane into each of the drilled holes.

3 Draw the two canes at each end together and tie them at the top to form an arch. Tie a cane horizontally from one cane arch to another (just above the point where the arching canes are joined.) Next, tie long strings to the horizontal cane and lower them to the growing bag.

4 Place the tomato plants into the growing bag and water them well. Tie the strings around the base of each plant, so that, as the plants grow, they can be twisted around the string and it will provide support. After 3 weeks of growth, the tomatoes will start to flower.

Digging and cultivating techniques will help you get the most from your soil. Gardening practices such as crop rotation and companion planting will also benefit and increase your vegetable garden crops.

cultivating

Deep cultivation

Any soil cultivation deeper than 8–10 inches can be regarded as a form of deep cultivation. Deep digging is a practice that can be beneficial to heavy and compacted soils, as it can aid drainage as well as improve conditions in the root zone. The top 6 inches of the soil is the most biologically active, containing a thriving, organically rich community of beneficial organisms such as bacteria, fungi, insects, and worms. These organisms will feed on the organic matter and plant debris in the soil, breaking them down into forms that are available as food for the resident plants. Incorporating organic matter, such as garden mix or rotted manure, into this zone, or just below it, will improve natural soil fertility, as well as putting nutrients close to the roots and improving the texture of the soil. An additional benefit is that the decomposing organic matter is

However you lay out your vegetable beds, you should make a plan—maybe numbering the beds—to show what you are planting where.

Stinging nettles
are a sign of fertile soil. For an organic liquid **fertilizer**, fill a bucket with water and a bunch of nettles. Allow the nettles to rot down for about 3 weeks. Use the resulting liquid as a nutrient-rich **foliar spray** that is also useful against aphids, black fly, and mildew.

very good at retaining moisture close to the plants' roots, a factor that can be hugely advantageous during dry summer conditions. Burying the manure or potting mix in the bottom of the trench during digging (providing it is not too deep) will encourage deeper-rooting plants.

The deep bed system

Organic growing systems aim to reduce the amount of soil cultivation in order to preserve natural fertility and soil structure. Materials such as manure and other organic fertilizers are crucial to organic growing practices, since they help to build and maintain a good soil structure.

When using the deep bed system, the soil structure is improved to the required depth with one cultivation, combined with the incorporation of large quantities of organic matter. From this point on, deep cultivations are kept to a bare minimum so that a natural soil structure develops and remains largely intact, and walking on the soil beds is avoided in order to prevent disturbance or compaction.

Very often the only cultivation that takes place once the bed has been established will either be digging shallow planting holes to transport seedlings of the next crop or digging up root vegetables when they are harvested. With further organic matter being added only as mulches and top dressings, it is quickly incorporated by the high worm population, allowing a natural soil structure to develop.

To achieve optimum results with a deep bed system, the soil must be loose and deeply dug, so the roots can penetrate to the required depth rather than spreading sideways.

The soil must also be enriched with plenty of organic matter such as compost or manure. To reduce pest and disease problems, crop residue should be removed and composted in a separate area before being returned to the deep bed area later.

Garden structures

A garden shed is useful for storing equipment and can be placed in an unproductive area of the garden. The siting of any other structures such as compost bins, garden seats, a summerhouse, or a greenhouse should be considered in creating the overall design. All-weather access to the garden is essential for easy harvesting under bad weather conditions. Raised paths paved with stone or bricks, or constructed from gravel, are attractive as well as practical.

Deep bed system

1 Mark one edge of the bed with a planting line. Measure 4 feet across with a planting board and set up another planting line parallel to the first. Using canes, mark a trench 2 feet wide; dig it out one spade deep and keep the soil to cover the last trench. Break up the exposed subsoil in the bottom of the trench with a fork, so the roots can penetrate deeply.

2 Put a 2–3 inch layer of well-rotted manure into the bottom of the trench.

3 Leaving a cane in the corner of the first trench, measure another 2 foot section with the other cane, so it contains the same amount of soil. Dig the soil and transfer it to the first trench, spreading it to cover the manure.

4 Add another 2–3 inch layer of manure to the first trench. The bulk of the manure and the loosened soil will raise the bed height. Continue to dig out soil from the second trench and cover the new layer of manure, leaving a deep bed of loose, organically enriched soil in the first trench. Scrape the soil from the bottom of the second trench. Break up the exposed soil. Repeat steps until the whole plot is cultivated. Use saved soil to cover the manure in the final trench.

Double digging

With double digging the soil is cultivated to a depth of two spade blades. This technique is most frequently used on land that is being cultivated for the first time or where a hard subsurface layer (called a pan) of soil has formed, impeding drainage and the penetration of plant roots.

This method of digging improves the friability of the subsoil without bringing it nearer to the surface, so the most biologically active layer of topsoil is always closest to the roots of cultivated plants. It is very important to avoid mixing the subsoil with the topsoil. If the two are mixed together, the fertility of the topsoil is diluted, rather than improving the fertility of the subsoil. Although this type of digging is hard work and can be very laborious, the benefits of double digging a plot can last up to 15 years, provided the soil is managed correctly. To double dig an area so that deeper-rooted plants such as roses, shrubs, trees, or fruit bushes and trees can be grown, a number of gardeners favor adding a layer of

Double digging method

1 Starting at one end of the plot, mark out an area 2 feet wide using a garden line and canes. Dig a trench of the full width, and the depth of one spade. If it is very large, the plot may be divided in two for convenience.

2 Remove the soil from this first trench and take it to the far end of the plot, laying it quite close to the area where the final trench is to be dug. When the soil is removed from the first trench, fork over the base of the trench to the full depth of the fork's tines. If required, compost or manure may be forked into the lower layer of soil or scattered on top of it after cultivation.

3 When the base of the trench is cultivated and the compacted layer broken through, mark out the next area 2 foot wide with a garden line. Using a spade start to dig the soil from this second area, throwing it into the first trench, while making sure that the soil is turned over as it is moved. This process will create the second trench and the base is forked over.

4 The process is repeated until the entire plot has been dug to a depth of about 1¾ feet.

well-rotted manure or compost into the bottom of the trench before the topsoil is reincorporated. In the vegetable garden, however, this organic matter may be laid over the surface of the soil after double digging as it will then be drawn into the topsoil by worms and insects. This way, the soil-borne bacteria and fungi break it down. On heavier soils a layer of ash, sand, or gravel may be mixed into the bottom of the trench before the topsoil is reincorporated, to help improve the damage.

Beans prefer well-drained, fertilized soil with plenty of added organic matter.

Making straw compost

Old straw makes excellent bulky organic matter to incorporate into soil to help improve drainage, moisture retention, and fertility. Alternatively, it can be used as an organic mulch, spread over the soil surface to preserve moisture and suppress weeds. This layer will be gradually incorporated into the soil by the activity of worms, bacteria, and other soil-borne organisms.

1 Cover the base of the area with 12 inches of loose straw. Soak the straw with water.

2 Sprinkle a light covering of nitrogenous fertilizer over the straw to speed up decomposition.

3 Add another 12 inch layer of loose straw to the stack, water it, then add more fertilizer.

4 As the straw decomposes, it becomes covered in white mold and resembles well-rotted manure.

Wild rice
Wild rice is not actually a species of rice but an annual large seeded water grass *Zizania palustris* that is native to the Great Lakes Area of North America. Wild rice can only be collected today with a licence, and gathering must be carried out using traditional techniques. Cultivated wild rice is also available.

Aquatic and moisture-loving vegetables
While good drainage is essential to growing most vegetables, some require quite wet soils or flourish beside or in streams, lakes, and the sea.

Seaweeds
Not all seaweeds are edible, but among those eaten are species of kelp or kombu (both known as wakame when dried); papery *Porphyra,* which is sold dried as nori or laver; green-leaved sea lettuce (*Ulva lactuca*); and the popular salty flavored dulse (*Palmaria palmata*). These are used to flavor soups and stews, in salads, in stir-fry dishes, and as sushi wraps. Seaweeds should only be harvested from waters known to be unpolluted.

Salicornia
The marsh samphire (*Salicornia*) is a succulent subshrub that colonizes tidal marshes. Its bright green, thin stems led to one of its common names sea asparagus. It is used raw and crisp in salads, as a bed for fresh seafood dishes, briefly boiled and served as a vegetable with butter, or Italian-style with olive oil and a squeeze of lemon.

Sea beet
The sea beet (*Beta maritiima*) grows wild along the coasts of Europe and North Africa, as well as eastward to India. The coarse white flesh of the

Kombu.

root has little to recommend it. The leaves, on the other hand, are well worth harvesting. They have a flavor comparable to their modern incarnation as chard. The leaves can be steamed and served with butter or used in any dish as a substitute for spinach.

Sea kale

Sea kale (*Crambe maritima*) grows naturally just above the tideline, and resembles a loose head of broccoli. At this stage it is bitter, but if the emerging shoots are "blanched" by covering them from the light with pebbles or sand on the beach, or garden pots in the garden or glasshouse, for a week or more, the shoots become creamy white, tender, and delicious. They are cooked and eaten like asparagus with melted butter.

Watercress

Watercress can easily be grown in well-composted soil that is kept moist and located in a lightly shaded area. It is easily propagated from tip cuttings rooted in a container of water, then transplanted into the soil.

Lotus

The beautiful perennial water lotus (*Nelumbo nucifera*) has long been grown in ponds and slow moving streams in Asia not only for its long-stemmed pink or white waterlily-like flowers sacred to Buddha, but for its edible rhizomes that are perforated in cross section, and for the nut-like seed shaken from huge pepperpot-like ripe receptacles.

The sliced rhizome is cooked as a vegetable or candied.

Water chestnuts

Water chestnuts are the underwater corms of *Eleocharis dulcis*, native to Asia. They are quite easily raised in warm climates in a water container such as a wading pool with a plug, or baby bath or, for balcony gardeners, in an aquarium. They require a long growing season of 180–220 days, but the corms can be presprouted for earlier planting. Their sweet, finely textured flesh is crisp and crunchy and is sliced to add texture to Chinese dishes or eaten fresh.

Lotus root

When sliced horizontally, lotus root displays a floral-like pattern of holes. This decorativeness along with its crisp, delicately flavored flesh is much appreciated in Chinese and Japanese cuisine. First peel the root, then slice it before eating it raw or cooked. Add it to salads or stir-fries, or cut into chunks, or stuff. Store in water with a squeeze of lemon juice to prevent it from turning brown. The seeds are also edible, eaten out of the hand, or used in Chinese desserts and soups. The leaves are used to wrap food such as whole fish for cooking. Lotus root can be bought fresh, dried, frozen, and canned.

moisture-loving vegetables

As space suitable for farming becomes more and more limited, crops that can be grown in poorly drained sites and even in the ocean will become increasingly popular and necessary. Of course, many edible plants have traditionally been grown in these environs.

TARO
(*Alocasia macrorrhiza*)

WATER
SPINACH
(*Ipomoea aquatica*)

MARSH
SAMPHIRE
(*Salicornia* spp.)

WILD RICE
(*Zizania palustris*)

WATER MINT
(*Mentha aquatica*)

MEMORY PLANT
(*Bacopa monieri*)

DRIED SEAWEED

WATER CHESTNUT
(*Eleocharis dulcis*)

MEMORY PLANT
(*Bacopa monieri*)

Crop rotation

Long before science and technology began taking an interest in gardening after World War II, farmers and home gardeners practiced a very complex rotation of vegetable crops each season. Phases of the moon were taken into account and the whole method took on almost mystical qualities.

In the garden vegetable patch it is very wise to break the crop relationship cycle. Plant a root crop such as turnip or carrots where you've just had a leaf crop such as lettuce. Plant onions prior to a crop of tomatoes, and peas and beans after cabbages and Swiss chard. And avoid planting anything in the same family season after season in the same bed—for example, do not plant tomatoes after potatoes, or cabbage after broccoli.

It was Charles "Turnip" Townsend who introduced the turnip, a root crop, to England from Europe in the early 1700s and advocated its use in crop rotation. The turnip is from a different family from the potato, the most popular root vegetable, so farmers could alternate their root vegetable crops and still practice crop rotation successfully. This basic rotation of crops stops any soil-borne insects and diseases from remaining in the same garden bed year after year, and avoids the depletion of certain soil nutrients that results from planting similar vegetables in the same plot.

Cabbages are heavy feeders while beans and peas are less needy.

Perennial vegetables, such as artichokes and asparagus, don't need to take part in crop rotation. They can be given permanent beds in the garden.

How crop rotation works

Different crops use nutrients in different ways, so that soil can be depleted of these nutrients despite your best preparation. The lists below will help you identify the groups to which your vegetables belong. To make crop rotation easier, keep records of what you plant and where.

- Cabbage, Chinese spinach (amaranth), cauliflower, broccoli, Brussels sprouts, kohlrabi, radish, rutabaga, turnip, mustard greens
- Tomato, pepper, chilies, eggplant, potato
- Pea, fava bean, dwarf bean, climbing bean
- Winter squash, squash, cantaloupe, cucumber, zucchini, marrow
- Carrot, parsnip, celery, parsley
- Swiss chard, beet, spinach
- Lettuce, globe artichoke, Jerusalem artichoke
- Onion, garlic, shallot, leek, chive

In the home garden crops may need to be grown in the same area more frequently than they should be, but try to rotate crops as the reduction in disease (especially soil-borne disease) is considerable. Grow your vegetables according to the appropriate season. If you try to grow them out of season the results will be very poor.

Crop rotation is simple in principle: don't plant the same crop in the same bed 2 years running. First, it avoids the build-up of any crop's particular pests and diseases. Second, it helps get the best value from your compost. The need to grow vegetables quickly means they must have rich soil, and that means the vegetable garden will take most of your compost. But not all need their soil equally enriched. Leafy things such as lettuces and cabbages need it richest; fruit crops such as tomatoes, peas, and peppers are not so greedy; root crops are less greedy still.

Onions.

Unripened tomatoes.

Companion planting

Companion planting is an effective way to protect plants from the unwanted attentions of pests and diseases. A number of plants give off strong odors that can confuse the olfactory (smell) senses of pests. Many herbs are useful for this purpose, including basil, lavender, rosemary, rue, thyme, chives, and garlic. For them to be effective, you should plant them throughout the garden.

However, companion planting is much wider in scope than just confusing an insect's sense of smell. In its broadest sense, it includes any plant that is beneficial in some way to another plant. Think of companion plants as "good neighbors."

It may be a simple matter of a plant shading another or modifying the humidity. One plant's roots might aerate the soil, or help drain excess water. And some plants can protect others as much as themselves by virtue of defence mechanisms such as thorns and stinging hairs, or by producing compounds that are poisonous to insect pests.

Other plants offer benefits to their neighbors by attracting or housing desirable insect predators, or by exuding odors that attract insect pollinators.

Still other plants are able to supply neighbors with nutrients. Nitrogen-fixing plants, such as lupins, peas, sweetpeas, beans, and alfalfa can convert gaseous nitrogen in the atmosphere to nitrogen compounds with the assistance of specialized bacteria located in nodules on their roots.

Some plants, like alfalfa, have very deep root systems that bring buried mineral nutrients to the surface soil where other plants can benefit, or may be a specific nutrient accumulator. Dandelions, for example, accumulate copper while buckwheat accumulates calcium.

Here tomatoes are underplanted with French marigolds (*Tagetes patula*) for protection against pests such as the destructive nematode, or eelworm.

Fabulous basil

Of all the olfactory confusers basil is perhaps the best. And it is impossible to have enough basil in the summer garden—as a companion plant, for the sheer sensuous delight of its fragrance, and for the kitchen. There are more than thirty different basils available. Many are decorative with ruffles, purple, red, or striped foliage, and lilac or white flowers. Some have delicious scents of lemon, sweet licorice, cool sweet camphor, or spice mixed with traditional sweet basil scent. Basil makes a wonderful insect-repelling centerpiece during summer.

The blessing of marigolds

Nematodes, or eelworms, can be hugely destructive to a variety of vegetable crops. Some species of nematode are responsible for severe crop damage, resulting in reduced growth, low yields and wilting. When infected plant roots are dug up, they appear to have tiny gall-like growths over the surface. Gardeners often mistakenly attribute these effects to drought or poor soil fertility.

However, nature has also produced a powerful nematicide, a biomolecule produced to some degree by all species of marigolds (*Tagetes* spp.). The substance is exuded by the roots. Marigolds can be used as barrier plantings around gardens, and the dwarf French marigold (*Tagetes patula*) is particularly useful for this purpose. If the brilliant golden or orange flowers upset your garden color scheme, it is an easy matter to shear the heads off.

Good companions

These plants have long been regarded as good companions:

- Basil with tomatoes, asparagus, beans, grapes, apricots, and fuchsias
- Beans with potatoes and corn
- Cantaloupes with corn
  Chives with carrots, cucumbers, and tomatoes
- Cucumbers with potatoes
- French marigolds (*Tagetes* spp.) with tomatoes, roses, potatoes, and beans
  Hyssop with cabbages and grape
- Leeks with celery
- Lettuce with carrots, onions, and strawberries
- Mint with cabbages and other brassicas and peas
- Nasturtiums with cucumbers, zucchini, squash, and apple trees
- Onions with carrots, kohlrabi, and turnip
- Peas with carrots

Bad companions

Some bad combinations to watch out for include:

- Apples with potatoes
- Beans with garlic
- Cabbages with strawberries
- Gladioli with strawberries, beans, and peas
- Sunflowers with any vegetable but squash
- Wormwood with almost everything

Some examples of traditional good companion planting combinations

Plant	Companian plants	Activity
Asparagus	Tomatoes	Repel asparagus beetle
Beans	Carrots Cauliflower Cabbage Parsley Peas	All considered to promote healthy growth in beans
Beet	Onions	Considered to promote healthy growth
Cabbages, cauliflower, broccoli, and Brussels sprouts	Beets Celery Beans Potatoes Onions Sage Thyme Mint Dill Hyssop Potatoes Nasturtiums Tansy	Considered to promote growth Repels cut worms from seedling and caterpillar stage of white butterfly
Carrots	Peas Sage Parsley Onions Leeks Chives Radish Lettuce	Most of these act to deter carrot fly (N.B. Around four times as many onions should be planted as carrots)

Plant	Companian plants	Activity
Celery	Dill	Promotes growth
	Beans	
	Leeks	
	Tomatoes	
	Cabbage	Repels cabbage white butterfly from
	Broccoli	the whole cabbage clan
	Cauliflower	
	Brussels sprouts	
Corn	Potatoes	
	Fava beans	
Lettuce	Strawberries	Promote healthy growth
	Carrots	
	Onions	
	Beets	
Onions	Carrots	Protect against onion aphid
	Lettuce	Promotes healthy growth
	Chard	
	Beets	
Parsnip	Peas	Promote healthy growth
	Beans	
	Potatoes	
Potatoes	Marigolds	Repel nematodes (eelworms)
	Beans	Lure away Colorado beetle
	Horseradish	Acts as an insect deterrent
	Eggplant	Will act as a trap plant for Colorado beetle
	Nasturtium	Repels insects
Squash	Corn	Offers physical protection
Tomatoes	Basil	Acts as an insect repellent
Zucchini	Nasturtium	

Mushrooms

Mushrooms can be grown and harvested from kits all year round. Many types of mushrooms are highly poisonous, so only experts should forage in the wild. A much safer bet is to plant your own. Fungal spore can be purchased for a whole range of varieties, with more of the exotic Asian types, such as shiitake and oyster, coming onto the market daily. All they need is a cool, dark place, such as a garden shed or cellar, in which to grow.

Shimeji mushroom.

Store mushrooms in the fridge in a paper bag to allow them to breathe.

Cultivated **mushrooms** don't need to be washed before use—simply wipe over them with a paper towel or damp cloth to remove the soil and grit.

Culivated mushrooms

Cultivated mushrooms are available in varying stages of development. The smallest, button mushrooms, have a mild flavor and keep their pale color when cooked. Use raw in salads or cook in white sauces. Closed-cup mushrooms are good for slicing and adding to stir-fries. The larger open-cup mushrooms are more flavorsome and are ideal for adding to stews and casseroles. Flat (open or field) mushrooms have a good earthy flavor and a meaty texture. Chestnut (crimini) and portobello mushrooms are relatives of the button mushroom. They have a creamy brown cap, buff-colored stalks and a more pronounced flavor than button mushrooms.

Wild mushrooms

There are many unusual forms of wild mushroom available. Porcini mushrooms, with a brown cap and thick white stem, are rich, sweet, and nutty in flavor and are sold fresh and dried. Enoki mushrooms grow and are bought in clumps. They have tiny cream caps on slender stalks and a delicate flavor. Shiitake mushrooms have dark brown caps and are sold fresh or dried. Oyster mushrooms are large flat mushrooms. Shimeji mushrooms are small oyster mushrooms with long stalks.

MUSHROOM KIT

1 To make the mushroom kit you'll need peat, lime, mushroom spore, and a suitable container, such as an old wooden box, lined with plastic. Moisten the peat with a little water until it feels damp all over and releases some water when you squeeze it.

2 Thoroughly blend the peat and lime together.

3 Spread the peat and lime to a depth of about 6 inches over the mushroom spore.

4 The completed mushroom kit is now ready to be stored in a cool, dark place. The fruiting bodies, or mushrooms, appear about 4 weeks later.

Horn of plenty mushroom.

Mixed mushroom stir-fry

Trim and clean 1 pound mixed mushrooms, slicing any larger ones. Melt 1 tablespoon butter in a frying pan and add 1 tablespoon olive oil. Add 1 finely chopped chili, 1 finely chopped shallot, and 1 garlic clove and fry briefly. Add the mushrooms and toss over high heat until cooked through and beginning to brown (if you are using shimeji or enoki mushrooms, put them in at the end). Add 1 tablespoon chopped cilantro, 1 tablespoon soy sauce, season well and drizzle with sesame oil. Serve tossed through noodles or pasta or on bruschetta. Makes enough for 12 bruschetta or 4 appetizer noodle or pasta serves.

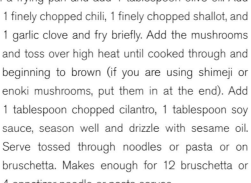

Mixed mushroom stir-fry.

Vegetable seed is easy to grow and you can usually sow it directly where you want the plants to live. However, starting seed indoors lets you begin the season even earlier. Staggering planting times also prolongs the harvesting period.

propagating

Seed-raising basics

We are still dependent on seed crops for survival—all agricultural production starts with seeds; and vegetable, grain, and cereal crops are grown from seed. On another, more personal level, raising plants from seed is a thrill for the home gardener. All gardeners find it very satisfying to see something as small as a pinhead emerge into a lovely flowering plant or something good to eat. Nothing beats the taste of fresh produce from the garden or the delight of seeing a floral display you've grown from seed.

Winter squash seed can be sown all year round in hot climates and throughout spring in warm zones but, in cold regions, plant winter squash only in early summer.

Getting started

Growing plants from seed is interesting and straightforward. Begin by sowing easy-to-handle seeds that are known for their reliable germination. Vegetables that are easy to handle include beans, peppers, cucumber, cantaloupes, peas, winter squash, Swiss chard, corn, tomatoes, and zucchini, but there are others.

The top of the **refrigerator** is just the right temperature to give bottom heat for trays of **germinating** seedlings.

Advantages of using seed

Growing plants from seed is economical. If you are starting a new garden or have large areas to plant, growing from seed will save you money. Plant a few seeds at a time over a period of several weeks to ensure a long cropping period. This makes more sense than having ten lettuces or ten cauliflowers ready for harvest at the same time, which is what will happen if you plant established seedlings.

Growing plants from seed is also often the only way that you can obtain a range of unusual plants for the garden. Seed companies produce a very large range of seeds for plants that are not available as seedlings or ready-grown plants. The seeds often include unusual color ranges or unusual forms of familiar plants. The less common types of vegetables must also be grown from seed. Quite a number of these vegetables are best sown where they are to grow as they will suffer considerable setback to their growth if they are transplanted.

When to sow seed

It is important to check seed packets for the correct sowing times. Most seeds are dependent on temperature and/or day length for their germination and development. For a better chance of success follow the directions on the packet. Bear in mind that there can be some climatic variations from year to year that have a bearing on soil temperature and sowing times, as well as regional differences. If you live in a cool climate, mark on your

To grow some of the more unusual types of eggplant, you'll need to start plants from seed.

calendar the date of the last expected spring frost. Then, working backwards, calculate when you need to sow seed. Check the Vegetable Directory at the back of this book for details about when to sow specific vegetables.

Seed-raising mixes

For seed raising in trays or pots you can make your own mix or purchase a ready-made commercial seed-raising mix. These mixes are ideal for germinating seed and raising seedlings of vegetables, but are not generally suitable for long-term growth.

The simplest seed-raising mix is made up of two parts coarse washed river sand or propagating sand with one part peat moss or coconut fiber peat. You will find these items at nurseries and garden centers. Beach sand is unsuitable for use in seed-raising mixes, as is builder's sand which sets like concrete if wet and dried again. Coconut or coir fiber peat is often sold as cocopeat. Well-aged, crumbly garden compost can be used as a substitute for the peat. Vermiculite is also used in seed-raising mixes as it is able to absorb large quantities of water and can hold nutrients in reserve for developing seedlings. Perlite is another good addition. It is extremely light but can hold 3–4 times its own weight of water. It has no nutrients but aids in the aeration of mixes. Both perlite and vermiculite are used in seed-raising mixes at the ratio of 1 part added to 2 parts of sand.

Sow **fava bean** seeds directly into the bed where they will grow to maturity.

Depth and spacing

Seed packets give useful details of suitable planting depth and spacing for that particular plant. The rule of thumb is that seeds are planted at a depth of roughly twice the diameter of the seed. Fine seed is generally planted no more than $\frac{1}{4}$ inch deep with a very light covering of soil or potting mix. Large seeds are planted deeper, according to their size. However, if you plant seeds too deeply they won't germinate and may rot in the soil. Some seeds need light to germinate and should therefore not be covered at all. Good soil preparation prior to sowing is vitally important. If the soil is heavy and the drainage poor many seeds will fail to germinate.

Garden soil, however good it is in the garden, is generally unsuitable for seed raising. Both drainage and aeration can be poor, leading to very low seed germination rates. Seed-raising media must always drain well and be well aerated. Even the best soil tends to compact to a certain degree when placed in containers. It is also impossible to guarantee that garden soil does not contain pathogens. Soil should only be used if it is pasteurized, which means that it has been kept at a temperature of 120°F for 30 minutes to kill off any pathogens. Soil can be baked in the oven or in a microwave, but you should note that this is a messy business and the soil will still be unsuitable for using on its own for seed raising.

Containers

In the past, seed boxes were always made of timber. Timber boxes are easy to build. They should be 3½–4 inches deep with a width and length that make them convenient for you to lift and move around. The timber pieces that form the base of the box should be spaced slightly apart to allow for drainage.

Plastic trays such as those that are used at nurseries to hold seedling punnets are ideal if you can get hold of some of them. You should line the base of the trays with a single sheet of newspaper to prevent the seed-raising mix from falling through the holes.

Cell trays that hold individual seedlings can be purchased or recycled. These make transplanting very easy and are most suitable when you want to raise only a few plants at one time. You can also sow individual seeds in egg cartons—these can easily be pulled apart so that you can plant the seedlings without disturbing their roots. The cardboard carton will break down in the soil.

Sowing large seed outdoors

1 Rake a fine tilth in the garden bed.

2 Level the bed with a straight piece of timber.

3 Use the edge of the timber to create seed drills.

4 Plant the seeds in the drill. The distance between the seeds will vary according to what you are planting.

5 Backfill and water gently. Keep the soil moist until seedlings appear.

Sowing fine seeds outdoors

1 Create a fine tilth in your vegetable patch. Draw a drill in the soil.
2 This strip is encrusted with carrot seeds. Simply lay the tape in the drill.
3 Backfill lightly.
4 Water in the newly planted seeds.

Turnips are very easy to grow from seed and are delicious to eat at all stages of growth.

Peat pots in which seeds can be sown are available commercially. Once the seedlings are large enough, plant them—still in the peat pot—straight into the garden.

Clean, used margarine or butter tubs are useful containers for seed sowing. Make sure that the tub will drain well by perforating the base with a skewer in several places.

Seed-raising kits are also available, which provide you with everything you need to get started. These are available at garden centers.

Sowing seed outdoors (in containers)

Most seeds should be sown in a seed tray or in punnets initially, then pricked out and planted into larger containers as the seedlings develop.

When sowing fine seeds add fine dry sand to make spreading the seeds easier. Just tamp these seeds down slightly after sowing, rather than covering them over. Add sand to hairy seeds to stop them sticking.

Slightly larger seeds can be sown straight from the packet or container. Draw a line (called a drill) with a pencil or stick, sow the seed, then backfill slightly. Pricking out, or removing seedlings from trays, can be done after the first set of true leaves appears (these develop after the baby pair of leaves, or cotyledons) and before the third set has arrived, to minimize root damage. The more leaves a seedling grows, the more roots it develops; transplanting might disturb these roots.

Using a greenhouse or cold frame to propagate your own plants will give you immense satisfaction.

Cold frames

In colder climates, cold frames are ideal for raising seeds. A cold frame is a raised enclosure, framed in brick or timber, with a glass or plastic cover. The frames are built higher at the back so the cover slopes, allowing rain to run off. If the frame is being used for seed raising, fill it with seed-raising mix. There will be less temperature fluctuation and fewer problems with the growing medium drying out. You could also use a seedbed, which is essentially the same. A seedbed is a raised bed, probably no more than 3 feet square, enclosed by brick or timber. A removable cover of 30 percent shade cloth will provide light shading for seedlings and reduce the impact of heavy rain. The cover can either be attached to a metal or wooden frame with legs or it can be supported on bricks.

Always harden plants off before planting them out. A spell in an open, shaded position toughens them up and is particularly important if you have covered your seedling tray with glass to retain warmth and moisture. Try to gradually acclimatize the seedlings to cooler growing conditions, and watch that your seedlings don't dry out or get eaten by pests at this stage of their growth.

Sowing seed indoors

If you sow seed indoors, it allows you to start the new season earlier than if you have to wait for the weather to plant outdoors. You will also be able to control your environment, so seeds will germinate more strongly.

Vegetable seeds need quite a warm place to germinate (between 75°F and 90°F) so try and find a suitable spot indoors. On top of the fridge or above a water heater are both good positions. At some garden centers, horticultural heating mats are available. Be sure to place these mats on a heatproof surface.

Once the seeds have germinated, keep them by a sunny window, or under special fluorescent plant lights. The seedlings will require between 10 and 16 hours of light a day.

As mentioned above, if the seedlings start to become crowded, transfer them to their own containers.

About 2 weeks before you plan to transplant the seedlings outdoors, start to reduce watering and fertilizing. A week before you move the plants outside, take the seedling containers outdoors and put them in a position protected from full sun or wind. Just start them outdoors for an hour to start with, then bring them indoors again. Over the following week, gradually leave them out for longer and longer. At the end of the week they should be ready for transplanting outdoors.

Sowing seeds outdoors (direct method)

For the maximum number of seeds to germinate successfully, the environment must be right. The soil making up the seedbed must be moist and firm, with a fine, crumbly texture without being too light and fluffy. It should not contain too many stones, as this will make it difficult to draw out a seed drill row to place the seeds into. The smaller the seeds to be sown, the finer the tilth of the seed bed should be.

You can plant large easy-to-handle seeds at the appropriate spacings where they are to grow without any need for you to transplant them.

If you are planting seeds directly into the garden, make a furrow about 6 inches deep, sprinkle a little fertilizer into the base of the furrow, then refill it with soil almost to the original level of the ground. You can then sow your seed and firm down the soil surface. This is the method most often used by vegetable growers, as vegetables must be grown rapidly in order to ensure the very best quality produce.

Different seeds for different climates

There can be a big difference in performance of plants grown from seed, depending on the source of the particular seed. Some plants may grow well in a range of different climates, but this is not always the case.

Seed sourced from plants originating in mild regions with light, free-draining soil may not perform well in areas that have heavy frosts or in areas with heavy clay soils, whereas seeds sourced from warm, low altitudes may not thrive in colder, high-altitude regions. Seed companies aim to supply seed that performs well in a range of climates, and they choose strains of seed with proven superior qualities.

Sowing seed outdoors (broadcast)

Broadcast sowing is a useful technique for salad vegetables such as radishes and scallions, and green manure crops such as comfrey or mustard.

1 Rake the soil to form a seed bed with a fine tilth. Remove any large stones and break down large clods of earth. This will leave the soil with a fine layer on the top surface.
2 Pour a few of the seeds from the packet into the palm of your hand.
3 Sow the seeds by scattering them evenly over the soil surface. Sow from a height of about 1 foot above soil level.
4 Lightly rake over the seed bed in at least two different directions to incorporate the seeds into the soil and to avoid gathering them into clusters. Label the seed bed.

Sowing seed outdoors (drill)

Drill sowing is a good technique for growing most vegetables, allowing you to see immediately when seeds have germinated and to remove weak seedlings from between the drills easily.

1 Rake the soil to form a seed bed with a fine tilth; break up large clods of earth and remove any large stones. Mark out the rows with a garden line (keeping it taut).
2 Using a draw hoe or cane, make a groove in the soil to form the seed drill.
3 Sow the seeds thinly into the drill by hand, aiming for a set distance between the seeds. Never sow them directly from the packet.
4 Using a rake, draw the soil back into the drill, covering the seeds. Gently pat and firm the soil over the seeds using the back of the rake.

Cool climate plants

Seeds of some plants are very sensitive to high temperatures and won't germinate if the weather conditions are too warm. Lettuce, peas, and spinach are in this group.

Some cool climate plants will grow quite well in warm climates but will never flower, often because the lack of chilling prevents the development of flower buds. In nature, chilling stimulates growth and flowering in many species of plants. Seeds that mature in the fall sit in the ground (or in their containers), are dampened by rain, then chilled by frost or snow in winter, and finally burst into life in spring. Some seeds will not germinate unless they have had a sufficient period of chilling followed by a period of rising soil temperature and increasing day length.

Warm climate plants

Plants that will not germinate in low temperatures include beans, eggplant, and tomato. Grow warm climate plants in cool climates with the protection of a glasshouse, at least through the vulnerable stages of germination and establishment. Soil temperature is important for many summer flowering and cropping plants. Seed of these plants will simply not germinate if the soil is too cool. Cold soil can result in the failure of many summer annuals and vegetables if you sow seed too early in spring.

Eggplant seeds require warm soil in which to germinate.

Viability

Seeds vary greatly, too, in their viability or ability to grow. Some have a very short period of viability while others may maintain their ability to grow over many years. Seeds from commercial growers have a use-by date on the packet that indicates how long the unopened packet should last in good condition and still give good germination rates. Fresh seed usually gives the best results, and after opening a packet it is advisable to use the remaining seed within 6 months.

Seeds must be stored in a cool, dry place, even in the refrigerator. Enclose packets of seed in sealable plastic bags before storing them in the fridge. You can also store seed in the freezer for long periods. Commercially packaged seed is contained and sealed in airtight foil envelopes to ensure that the seed remains dry and clean.

High temperatures and damp conditions are the worst enemies of stored seed. In damp conditions seeds absorb moisture, providing ideal conditions for fungal organisms to take hold. If conditions are too wet the seeds may absorb enough moisture to swell and start to germinate; they will then rot, and the whole batch of seed will be lost.

Seed companies grow their own seed or contract special growers to produce their seeds to ensure that the packeted seed is of the highest quality. Their seeds are tested regularly for purity and germination rates.

Many seeds will **germinate** in a short time. In the right conditions many will germinate in as little as 5–10 days. Beans and peas are among this group. Other plants are quite slow, taking 3–4 weeks.

FIDDLEHEAD
(Dicksonia antarctica)

BELGIAN ENDIVE
(Cichorium intybus)

shoots and sprouts

We all enjoy young, fresh produce and juicy shoots and sprouts are the best of all. Sprouts come from all sorts of plants, including broccoli, onion, alfalfa, beans, peas, and wheat. These are literally just germinated from their seed. Shoots refer to the tender new growth on more mature plants, such as the underground spears of the bamboo plant or asparagus, which sends up new spears from a perennial plant each spring.

SNOW PEA
SPROUTS
(Pisum sativum var.
macrocarpon)

LEMONGRASS
(Cymbopogon citratus)

BAMBOO SHOOT
(Phyllostachys spp.*)*

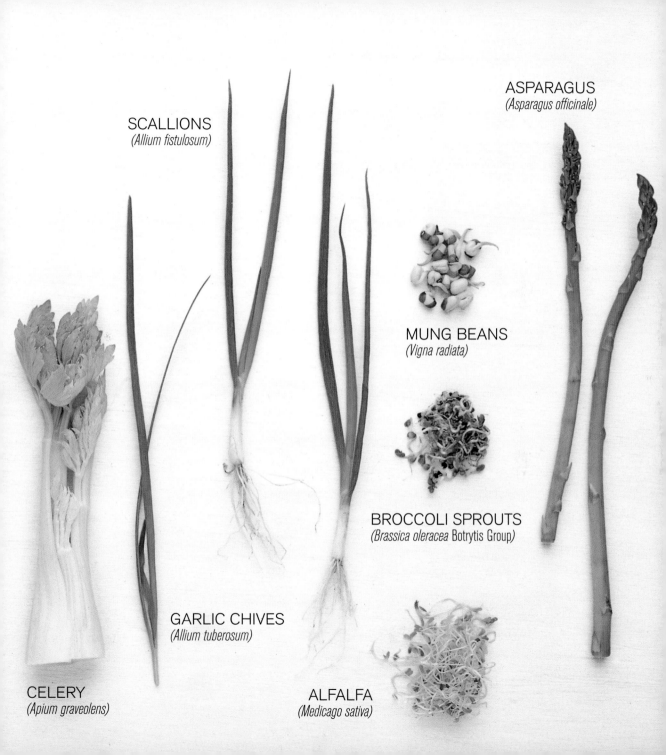

ASPARAGUS
(Asparagus officinale)

SCALLIONS
(Allium fistulosum)

MUNG BEANS
(Vigna radiata)

BROCCOLI SPROUTS
(Brassica oleracea Botrytis Group*)*

GARLIC CHIVES
(Allium tuberosum)

CELERY
(Apium graveolens)

ALFALFA
(Medicago sativa)

Germination tips

Problems with growing media, soil, or mix

May be too wet

Heavy, poorly drained soil or mix holds too much water, causing seeds to rot. You should use good quality seed-raising mix or open up heavy soils by adding organic matter. Water only often enough to keep the seed moist but not wet.

May be too dry

Seeds cannot germinate without moisture. Once seeds swell and start to germinate they will die if they dry out. You should check moisture levels regularly. Cover sown seed with shade cloth, glass, or even paper to conserve moisture.

Soil-borne fungal disease

Sow seed only in fresh seed-raising mix in clean containers or in the garden in well-prepared, well-drained soil. Don't sow seed in areas where disease has been present. You should practice crop rotation to avoid continuing problems. Avoid overwatering and don't sow seed in poorly drained sites.

Growing medium too loose or too compacted

If you haven't firmed down the mix after seed sowing there will be too much air around the seed—this lack of contact with the mix means seed will dry out. If the mix is too compacted drainage will be poor and seeds will be deprived of oxygen.

Planting depth

A good general rule of thumb for seed sowing is to plant at a depth of twice the diameter of the seed. Very fine seed should just be pressed into the surface of the mix. If you sow seed too deeply it may not have enough food reserves to provide the energy needed to reach the surface. Shallow-sown seed is more likely to rot if given constant watering. By the same token, if the sowing depth is too shallow the seed is at risk of drying out, unless you are vigilant about watering. The lower soil temperature at a greater depth may also affect germination.

Other problems

Pests

Animal pests, such as cats and dogs, often dig up freshly tilled soil. It is therefore strongly recommended that you cover your seed beds with wire netting to prevent this kind of damage. You can also place strong smelling mothballs or other animal repellents around the bed to further discourage pets. Contrary to popular belief, the plastic bottle of water method does not work. Snails and slugs can totally demolish young seedlings that are emerging from the soil. You can use physical barriers such as sharp shell grit scattered around the sown area, or you could sprinkle commercial snail baits on the seed bed. It is vital to ensure that neither children nor dogs are able to reach the baits.

Fertilizer

Fresh fertilizer in the soil can burn seeds and emerging roots. To avoid this problem, apply fertilizer in bands on either side of the planting row. You also have the choice of waiting until the seedlings have emerged and are growing strongly before you apply any fertilizer. Do not allow the fertilizer to touch the leaves or stems of the seedlings, as it could scorch them.

Alternatively, you can place the fertilizer in a furrow well below the seed-sowing area. Make the furrow about 3½–4 inches deep, place the fertilizer along the trench, then backfill with soil. Firm the soil down with your hands and sow the seed.

Seed viability

The seeds of many plants lose their viability quite quickly once you have opened the sealed packet. Lettuce and parsnip are two plants that rapidly lose their freshness and ability to germinate. Generally, once you have opened the foil packet of seeds it is a good idea to try to use the seed within 6 months. Store the seeds in a cool dry area to prolong the period of viability—both heat and moisture will cause rapid deterioration of seed.

Raising seedlings in containers in a protected environment will mean they are more sturdy when you come to transplant them to the open garden.

Thinnings of many vegetables are delicious in salads, or lightly wilted. Try endive, turnips, radish, Swiss chard, and beet.

Sow spinach seed directly into the garden bed, ½ inch deep and 1 foot apart in rows 1 foot apart. Lightly cover seeds with compost and keep just moist.

Pricking out

Container-grown seedlings must be thinned out to wider spacings once they are growing strongly. This process, which is known as pricking out, allows for optimum development of the seedling. If the seedlings are very crowded, prick them out as soon as you think they are large enough to handle. At this stage they will probably be about 6–8 inches high and have their first true leaves (that is, the leaves that emerge above the seed leaves). Plant them out in another container to grow on until they are ready for their intended growing positions. Seeds that have been planted at adequate spacings, usually large seeds, can be left to grow on where they are until they are 3½–4 inches high. At that stage they will be ready to be planted out in their permanent positions either in the ground or in containers.

When you are pricking out and replanting these tiny seedlings, work out of the sun and out of the wind. Spread out a sheet of plastic or newspaper so that you have somewhere to place the small bundles of seedlings once they have been removed from the seed pots or trays.

Fill a seed tray or pot with a suitable potting mix and, using a pencil or stick, make holes in the mix ready to receive the little plants. Make the holes around 1½–2½ inches apart. The wider spacing will be needed for plants with large leaves such as lettuce or cabbage.

Use a

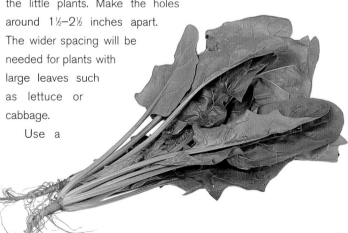

flat blade or a stick to separate and lift out a bunch of seedlings from their original container. Place them on the sheet of paper or plastic that you have previously spread out in readiness and gently separate them. Hold the seedling firmly but gently and lower its roots into the hole, then backfill the hole by pushing the potting mix around the roots with a stick or with your fingers.

Gently water the plants with a fine spray and set the container in a sheltered spot. The container should receive some sun but preferably only early morning sun until the seedlings have recovered from their move.

Once the plants have recovered from transplanting shock, gradually expose them to more sunlight and give them some liquid fertilizer at half strength. When the plants are growing strongly and have reached a height of 3½–4 inches they are ready to be planted out into their permanent positions.

Watering and fertilizing

Watering at this stage is very important, and you should check the soil around plants by scratching away the surface to feel or see whether it is moist. As you want to encourage your plants to put down deep roots it is better to thoroughly soak the area every few days rather than sprinkle it daily. Of course, the frequency of watering will depend on the season and the weather, as well as the conditions of your local climate.

After a few days, when the seedlings have recovered from the move, you should give them a dose of half strength liquid plant food. It is also important to keep the area free of weeds so that the young plants are not competing for water or nutrients.

Carrots need a deep, stone-free soil if they are not to grow forked and misshapen. However, if you have unsuitable soil, you can get around this problem by growing the round or stump-rooted varieties.

Succession planting means planting a second crop after you've harvested a first, in the same position, so you get two crops from the same space in just one season.

Transplanting

When transplanting the seedlings into the ground or into their permanent containers, you should make sure that everything is ready before removing them from their trays or pots. Have the garden soil well prepared, marking out planting holes with a narrow-bladed trowel or your fingers.

Lift the seedlings with a trowel or flat blade, disturbing the roots as little as possible and leaving soil attached to the plant roots. Lower the plant into the hole and firm the soil around the roots, leaving a small depression

around the plant to ensure that water is directed to the root zone. Give the plant a thorough watering. If you have some old compost or manure you can sprinkle this around the plants as a mulch to help conserve moisture—just make sure that you leave a little space around the plant stem. It may also be a good idea for you to sprinkle some snail bait around the newly planted seedlings, especially if the weather is damp or dewy.

In hot weather do your transplanting in the evening as this allows plants some time to recuperate. Plants may well wilt the following day when the full heat of the sun is upon them, but if the soil is moist they should recover once the sun moves off them. If it is extremely hot you could consider providing plants with some form of shading through the middle of the day.

Transplanting young plants

Once plants raised in a seed bed become sufficiently large you will need to transplant them to allow them space to carry on growing steadily.
1 Lift the seedlings to be transplanted carefully, holding the leaves rather then the stem, which is liable to bruise easily.
2 Make a hole in the new position and insert the plant, firming down the soil around it. Water plant in well.

Transplanting plants

Transplanting	Row width	Plant spacing
Cauliflower	1½ feet	2 feet
Celery	1½ feet	1½ feet
Garlic	8 inches	8 inches
Onion sets	8 inches	6 inches
Potatoes	1¾ feet	1 foot

Raising new plants

Seed sowing	Row width	Plant spacing
Beets	1 foot	4 inches
Broccoli	40 seeds per tray sown indoors	
Brussels sprouts	40 seeds per tray sown indoors	
Cabbage (summer/fall)	1½ feet	1 foot
Cabbage (winter)	1½ feet	1½ feet
Carrot	6 inches	4 inches
Cauliflower (summer)	40 seeds per tray sown indoors	
Cauliflower (winter)	1 foot	6 inches
Cauliflower (spring)	1 foot	6 inches
Celeriac	40 seeds per tray sown indoors	
Celery	40 seeds per tray sown indoors	
Corn	1 seed per 3 inches pot sown indoors	
Cucumber (ridge)	1 seed per 3 inches sown indoors	
Eggplant	1 seed per 3 inches sown indoors	

Successive sowing means you plant the same vegetable, successively, at several locations, at 10–14 day intervals for a continuous harvest.

Interplanting is to plant more than one type of plant in the same place, in among each other. Ideally, mix early- and late-maturing types, such as carrots with cucumber.

Raising new plants

Seed sowing	Row width	Plant spacing
Fava bean	1 foot	9 inches
Green bean	1 foot	3 inches
Kale	2 feet	1½ feet
Kidney bean	1 foot	6 inches
Kohlrabi	1 foot	6 inches
Leek	4 inches	1 inch
Lettuce	1 foot	1 foot
Marrow	1 seed per 3 inches sown indoors	
Onion salad	4 inches	2 inches
Onion seed	1 foot	4 inches
Parsnip	1 foot	6 inches
Peas	5 inches	5 inches
Pepper	1 seed per 3 inches sown indoors	
Radish	6 inches	1 inch
Rutabaga	1¼ feet	9 inches
Tomato	1 seed per 3 inches pot sown indoors	
Turnip	1 foot	6 inches

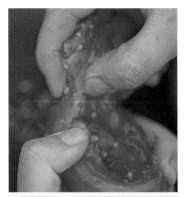

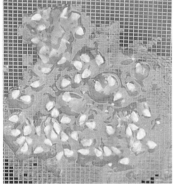

Saving tomato seed

Tomato seed is surrounded by a sac of jelly that contains germination inhibitors. To remove this, squeeze the seed from ripe fruits into a non-metal container. Add an equal amount of water and allow it to ferment for 3–4 days, then pour through a sieve, and completely dry the seed on a plastic or china plate.

Store the seed in an airtight labeled container. Tomato seed will last for 3 or more years if properly stored.

Seed saving

Various techniques are used for seed collection—depending on the growing and seeding habits of the plant.

Plants in the Apiaceae family (previously Umbelliferae) including celery, carrots, celeriac, and parsnips form lacy heads of tiny flowers followed by progressively ripening seed. To prevent much of the seed spilling on the ground, pick the entire head once the most mature seed are fully sized and brown, place in a paper bag, tie with string and suspend upside down in a well ventilated area out of the direct sun. The seed will all fall into the bag.

Clean the seed looking for any insects, place in an airtight container, label (including a date), and store in a dry, cool place.

Apiaceae seed is generally viable for only one year, so plant a crop every year. Seed of the onion family Alliaceae is treated in the same way.

Pepper and chili seed can be removed from the fully ripened fruit and dried for storage (gloves are recommended for the process, as the chili oils are hot).

Peas and beans are left growing in the field until the pods are dry. Pull the bushes from the ground at the end of the season and thresh on a sheet to release the seed.

Brassicas too should be left in the garden. They will explode their seed as soon as fully dried so enclose heads in large paper bags to capture as many seeds as possible.

For stronger crops, let your very best plants **go to seed** each year, and use those seeds for the next planting season.

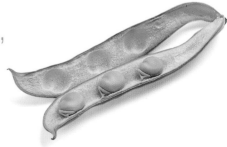

Cross pollination

It is important to prevent cross-pollination between closely related cultivars. Fortunately, three of the most collected groups, tomatoes, peas, and beans, are normally self-pollinating and their seed can safely be saved. Other groups including cultivars of squash, brassicas like cabbage, broccoli, Brussels sprouts, chilies and peppers, beets, corn, and eggplant are likely to cross between cultivars.

There are various ways to prevent this happening. The easiest is to allow only one cultivar of each type to reach flowering in any season. Plants can be isolated by net cages, or newly opened flowers can be hand fertilized and prevented from cross fertilization by covering them with white paper bags or net.

In long season areas, it is often possible to plant two cultivars several weeks apart so that their flowering periods do not coincide. This technique is often used by gardeners for corn. However in corn-growing districts, wind-blown pollen is carried far and wide and only hand pollination of newly emerged cornsilks protected beneath paper bags or paper cones will ensure that seed is not accidentally contaminated.

Hand-pollinate corn by taking pollen from the tassels and sprinkling it on the silks.

Heirloom crops

One of the rewards of growing your own organic crops is being able to indulge in the incredible richness and diversity of our inheritance of traditional and heirloom vegetables and fruit. The beauty and flavor of heirloom produce is almost beyond dreams. Imagine translucent apricot-striped green "Zebra" tomatoes; huge clusters of tiny "Red Currant" tomatoes glowing like jewels; big pink "Brandywine", an Amish heirloom considered to have the finest and most intense flavor in the world; emerald green "Evergreen" with strong, fresh, sweet flavor for salads and the equally delicious "Aunt Ruby's German Green"; huge pleated fruits the size of plates like rich crimson "Zapotec Ribbed" and "Ruffled Yellow"; tiger gold and red striped "Tigerella"; mahogany red richest-flavored "Black from Tula"; and delicious black tomatoes like "Black Russian" and "Black Krim"

There are hundreds of heirloom tomato cultivars being rescued from extinction around the planet, along with thousands of ancient and heirloom forms of every other vegetable, grain, herb, and fruit.

Edible tubers

Beet	Kohlrabi
Burdock	Parsnip
Carrot	Peanut
Cassava	Potato
Celeriac	Radish
Dandelion	Rutabaga
Galangal	Salisify
Ginger	Scorzonera
Ginseng	Sweet potatoes
Hamburg parsley	Taro
Horseradish	Turnip
Jerusalem artichoke	Yam
Jicama	

Both the leaves and the swollen stem of **kohlrabi** are edible.

Beet.

Planting edible tubers

Tubers can either be swollen roots or swollen stems for storage. The humble potato is the most commonly grown tuberous plant in the world, and the most consumed vegetable in the western world.

Tubers themselves are a starch-based storage system for the plant to adapt to extremes of climate such as cold and drought and help the plant vegetatively propagate itself. They should be grown quickly to produce sweet-tasting crops and need large amounts of potassium and phosphorus in the fertilizer used to help promote root development.

Like other vegetables, root crops need a full sun position. The soil needs to be well worked over prior to sowing seed and most crops enjoy liberal quantities of organic matter dug through. Even small clods of earth can misshape crops such as carrots, radishes, rutabagas, and turnips, so make sure a fine tilth is created before sowing seeds in shallow drills. Potatoes and Jerusalem artichokes are less fussy with soil, and any well-drained area will suffice.

Tuberous vegetables have long been of use as food, especially as winter vegetables as they keep so well once dug and in cold areas form the basis of many staple dishes.

Despite their popularity as winter fodder, there are root vegetables for all seasons. From spring to fall beets, carrots, potatoes, sweet potatoes, Jerusalem artichokes, kohlrabi, radish, and parsnip make great eating, and as the season progresses, rutabagas and turnips come to the fore. Don't overlook the more unusual root crops either. Salsify, scorzonera, horseradish, and dandelions make pleasant accompaniments and yams, cassava, taro root, and jicama are exotic root crops worth sourcing in hot or tropical climates.

Planting edible bulbs

Bulbs are swollen underground stems and each leaf is a fleshy scale, folded one on top of another and encasing a flower. These are full of plant foods such as starch, protein, and sugar, which not only provide nutrients for new plants, but also in the case of the *Allium* genus, make a delicious ingredient in cooking.

Historically, records show that onions have been eaten for thousands of years, with references to them in the Bible and an inscription on the Great Pyramid. Their volatile acids give them their strong flavor and antiseptic qualities.

Alliums are all extremely adaptable to climate and soil types, providing the correct variety for the time and place is chosen. They also make an excellent winter crop and many varieties store well. To grow alliums, prepare the bed well, removing clods and scattering a preplanting

Potatoes

Potatoes are the most widely eaten vegetable in the western world. Potatoes are tubers, a root modified as a starch storage vessel. They can be propagated from the "eyes" of seed potatoes, normally purchased in your local nursery as certified disease-free. For a similar flavor, try Jerusalem artichokes.

Although readily available in shops, home-grown spuds can be harvested early, to eat as "chats", which are sweet baby potatoes. Other interesting potatoes include "Desiree", which has pink skin; "Purple Congo" which has purple or bluish skin; and sweet potatoes.

Planting seed potatoes

1 Keep some seed potatoes until they sprout. This is called "chitting" potato tubers and will give your plants a head start.

2 Using a spade or hoe, double dig a trench. Create a wide, flat-bottomed or V-shaped 6 inch trench with a trowel.

3 Cut the seed potatoes into pieces so that each piece contains an eye.

4 Plant the pieces of seed potato in the trench. Backfill the trench with soil and water in thoroughly.

Water chestnuts.

Edible bulbs

Chives

Garlic

Leeks

Onions

Ramp (Canadian wild onion)

Scallions

Shallots

Water chestnuts (corm)

Earthing up

Other vegetables are covered with earth, but it's the stems and leaves that are eaten, not the roots. With asparagus, celery, and Belgian endive, you can really surpass shop-bought specimens if you take a little time with the growing process. The taste of these vegetables can be improved enormously by a technique called "earthing up"—mound the soil around the plants as the shoots emerge and the stalks will become elongated, white, and tender. Asparagus, however, won't be ready for full harvesting for 5 years.

fertilizer high in potassium. The soil needs to be around neutral, so liming may be necessary for acid soils. Sow the seed in drills very lightly on the surface onto dark, damp soil and after 2 weeks young seedlings will have emerged. Thin seedlings out as they develop so that each plant has about 4 inches to grow into. Leeks are ready to harvest from about 3 months, while onions take up to 8 to fully mature. Don't be tempted to hill plants or mound earth around them, as bulbs like to sit on the surface.

Corms are similar to bulbs but do not have the fleshy scale leaves, instead they are a swollen stem. Water chestnuts are a type of corm, and not related to the chestnut family at all. The dark brown "nut" grows at the base of a water plant with reed-like leaves and has sweet white flesh that can be eaten raw or cooked once the skin is peeled. They grow best in warm to hot areas in a container or pond that stays moist.

Shallots.

Asparagus.

Garlic bulbs, fresh garlic, garlic oil, and peeled cloves.

The onion family

The members of the *Allium* genus—onions, scallions, leeks, shallots, garlic, and chives, among others—belong to the lily or Liliaceae family. Some of the most stunning ornamental plants are to be found in this family, such as hyacinths, tulips, and lilies. Like their family members, many edible plants in the *Allium* genus sport exquisite, showy flowerheads.

Garlic

For centuries garlic has been renowned as a remedy and preventative of infections. Its sulphur content acts as a strong disinfectant. In the Middle Ages it was hung outside the door to stop the plague and the juice has been used to heal gunshot wounds: sphagnum moss soaked in garlic juice was used in World War I as a wound dressing. Roman soldiers ate garlic to keep their strength up. Garlic is also said to prevent leaf curl in peaches and ward off black spot on roses. The longer garlic is cooked, the milder the flavor. Reduce "garlic breath" by eating parsley, basil, mint, or thyme, or do as the Chinese do and chew cardamom pods.

Onions need the richest soil of all root crops, so give the bed a dressing of manure before planting. Sow seeds in spring, thinly along the rows, and mulch well. Onions are **shallow-rooted** and are easily damaged when you are weeding.

To cater for your whole plant, it is important to understand soil, compost, mulching, fertilizing, and the organisms that make it all happen, as well as the organisms that cause trouble. There are three main factors in improving the soil in your garden: fertilizers, compost, and mulch.

maintenance

Once all the planning and planting is over, it's time to think about maintaining the garden's state of good health with regular care.

Watering

Watering seems to be the aspect of cultivation that causes the gardener the most problems. The best advice is to use your common sense. Consider the time of year, temperature, humidity, time of day, weather, soil conditions, and the stage of development of the plant.

Seeds cannot germinate without moisture. Keep the seed-raising mix evenly moist, but not wet, until seedlings emerge. Once seedlings emerge, water them regularly and gently with a fine spray. You should be aware that overwatering will cause the collapse and death of seedlings. Once seedlings have been planted out they will need regular watering until they are well established.

Fertilizing and watering are essential activities to ensure a healthy vegetable garden.

The age and type of plant will also affect the amount of water required. Baby seedlings with very few shallow roots will need more frequent watering than established plants that have their roots deeper into the ground. Plants with large leaves generally need more water than those with fine feathery leaves. Annual vegetables may need watering twice a week, weekly, or every 2 or 3 days depending on weather and soil conditions. You should note that sandy soils dry out much more rapidly than clay soils.

It is more effective to water early in the morning or in the evening, as there will be less moisture lost through evaporation. In winter, water in the morning so that the foliage does not remain wet overnight. This also applies to plants that are prone to fungal disease; avoid overhead watering for these plants. In summer, water in the evening so the water has a chance to soak into the ground. Don't water in the middle of the day in summer or when it is very windy, as a lot of water will be lost to the atmosphere straight away.

Fertilizing

Keep your seedlings growing rapidly by fertilizing. Vegetables must be grown quickly for maximum flavor and tenderness. There are several methods of maintaining a steady supply of nutrients.

Granular fertilizer can be used prior to seed sowing by banding it along the sides of rows or by placing it in a furrow or trench well below the sowing depth. Soluble powders or liquid concentrates, which you dilute and apply in solution, can be used to boost plant growth once seedlings are growing strongly. Slow-release fertilizers can be mixed with the soil or potting mix prior to sowing or applied once seedlings have started to grow. Never apply fertilizer to dry soil as there is a good chance this will burn the plant roots.

While it is preferable to feed plants through their roots, some growers like to use foliar feeding (feeding plants through their leaves). When using fertilizer in solution to spray directly onto leaves, there should be plenty of moisture around the plant roots.

Composting is not the complete solution for a healthy garden. Vegetables will generally require fertilizer at one time or another.

Types of fertilizer

Fertilizers can be separated into "natural" fertilizers, such as seaweed extract and animal manures, and artificial combinations or chemical fertilizers. Organic fertilizers can encourage soil organisms and lead to better structured soils. Chemical fertilizers can be fast acting and balanced, and many are designed to cater for the specific needs of certain plants. Fertilizers are classified according to their component ratio of nitrogen, potassium, and phosphorus (known as the NPK ratio). These are particularly important elements, as they are needed for basic plant growth and function and are used in relatively large quantities. The "big three" are all highly soluble, so if you apply excess fertilizer it washes straight into waterways and eventually causes algal growth. It is particularly important to remember this when you are feeding your lawn.

Handy feeding hints

- Always fertilize when the soil is moist and water thoroughly after you have completed the application.
- If in doubt, apply fertilizer at half-strength, twice as often.
- Plants don't use much food in winter, so don't bother feeding then. Spring, summer, and fall feeds are generally better value.
- Nitrogen is responsible for leaf growth, but too much nitrogen can cause floppy growth and poor flowers.
- Phosphorus is vital for strong roots and stems.
- Potassium maintains the rigidity of plants and is important in promoting flowering.

Blood and bone.

Chicken manure.

Slow release fertilizer.

Mineral fertilizers

Even though you feed your soil with good quality compost, it may still lack mineral nutrients if the original soil is poor. A soil test will show major deficiencies, which then can be remedied by the use of rock dusts and other adjuncts.

Calcium is best supplied by dolomite derived from dolomitic limestone and this form also supplies magnesium to the soil. Ground limestone can be used as an alternative. Phosphate is usually supplied by the dust of natural rock phosphate. Potassium can be added to the compost heap in the form of wood ashes. Sulphur comes in the powdered form "flowers of sulphur", which is mined from volcanic deposits.

Many soils, particularly in old geological areas, lack one or more trace elements. Rock dusts of the individual trace element can be added but dispersal is difficult. Thankfully, liquid seaweed fertilizers are an excellent means of supplying them, together with seaweed meal. But such additions should never take the place of regular doses of compost.

Base dressing

Above left: Base dressings of fertilizer are applied to the soil before the plants or seeds occupy the site. This helps to maximize the nutrients in the soil that will be available to the young plants.

1 First sprinkle a measure of the appropriate fertilizer onto prepared soil in the area you intend to plant or sow.

2 Incorporate the fertilizer into the top few inches of soil using a garden or wooden rake.

Top dressing

Below left: Most vegetables grow relatively quickly and will almost certainly need an extra feed during the growing season. A top dressing of fertilizer applied around the plants will help to increase both bulk and yield.

1 First, carefully sprinkle the fertilizer onto the soil around the plants. Make sure the fertilizer does not land on the foliage as it will burn it.

2 Use a hoe or tined cultivator to incorporate the fertilizer into the soil. Do not cultivate too deeply or some plant roots may be damaged.

Liquid fertilizers

Liquid fertilizers give a rapid growth boost to plants that have been stressed or are under insect attack. Perhaps the finest organic liquid fertilizer is seaweed fertilizer, which is readily available commercially. Some products incorporate fermented fish and other seafood wastes and, though the smell is memorable for the first hour or two, many of these are quite excellent, stimulating not only plant growth but also desirable microbial activity. Plants suffering from black spot and other fungal diseases respond rapidly with a clean flush of new growth after a spray of these substances, diluted as recommended.

You can brew your own seaweed fertilizer. A visit to the beach can often turn up a sack of seaweed washed up onto the tideline. Tie the sack, immerse it in a large container of water, then leave for 7–14 days. It will make an invaluable, although strong smelling, liquid garden feed.

A similar process can be used with a bag of manure. The resultant "manure soup", needless to say, also can have a somewhat evil odor initially. But it's an absolute treat for organically grown produce.

Making blackjack

Blackjack is an excellent, nutritious plant "pick-me-up", which is very useful during flowering or fruiting periods. Although it is not sweet-smelling, your plants will be very grateful for the application.

1 To create blackjack, you will first need a quantity of animal manure that has been well rotted down.
2 Add some soot (which provides nitrogen) and wood ash (good for potassium) to the manure. Put the mixture into a plastic-net bag.
3 Seal the bag carefully and suspend it in a barrel of rainwater. Leave it in position for several weeks.
4 Once the solution is ready, decant it as required into a watering can, diluting it to the color of weak tea, and apply it to your plants.

There are a variety of ways to produce good compost, but all techniques fall into one of two baskets depending on whether they rely on bacteria that are aerobic (oxygen users) or anaerobic (non-oxygen users) to break down the raw materials.

Aerobic composting is very efficient. It generates sweet, nutty-smelling compost rapidly, and with none of the feared evil smells that accompany some backyard disasters. The compost can reach temperatures of 138°F, hot enough to sterilize weed seeds and kill many disease organisms.

Anaerobic composting is much slower and takes place at cooler temperatures. This method is prone to undesirable odors, and depends on very ancient and less efficient species of bacteria.

Worm farms

Worm farming can be an excellent way of dealing with modest amounts of household scraps, and producing quantities of an excellent natural fertilizer. Commercial worm farms are available and it's quite a simple matter of following the instructions in order to assemble it. But a worm farm can be made from a simple bin or box, vented with air holes around the side and about 2 inches below the rim. You should also make a row of drainage holes. Keep in mind that the worms are active only between the temperature range of 50–77°F. Make sure the bin is moved into a warm area and insulated throughout winter in colder regions, and placed out of the sun and in a cool area during hot summers.

The magic of compost

Nature constantly makes compost, that almost magical, soil-like material which results from the decomposition of organic material and forms the basis of the organic garden.

However, the natural composting process is fairly slow. Relying on the backyard "rubbish heap" is rarely satisfactory. It can take 12 months or more to complete the recycling process and produce usable compost—and most of us want results a little quicker than that.

Clockwise from top left: mushroom compost, prunings, liquid fertilizer, kitchen scraps.

Only species of worm adapted to living in decomposing organic matter are suited to worm farming, such as *Lumbricus rubellus* and the red wiggler worm or Brandling worm *Eisenia foetida*. These are available at some garden centers and can also be mail-ordered.

What goes in the compost heap?

Some people say that anything that has lived before can be put into a compost heap, and it is a good general guideline.

So what does go in the compost heap? For a start, if you eat plenty of fresh fruit and vegetables in your diet, every night will produce a bowl full of vegetable and fruit peelings. Other kitchen waste—like crushed eggshells, tea leaves, and coffee grounds—is also ideal.

Time spent working in the garden will yield weeds, soft and hardwood prunings, as well as the remains from harvested vegetable crops. Mowing the lawn will contribute a pile of fresh, moist grass high in nitrogen. In the fall, add piles of leaves high in carbon from deciduous trees.

When you start composting it is inevitable that you will become expert at scavenging. Garden materials bagged and waiting to be sent by neighbors to waste disposal sites will develop a magnetic attraction. Before long even the shyest gardeners will find themselves knocking on doors to ask for those unwanted bagfuls.

A day fossicking beside the beach will provide seaweed, torn off by wave action and stranded along the tideline.

Waste paper and cardboard can also be composted, and sheets should be individually crumpled before use so that they increase the aeration of the heap. Color printed material was once considered undesirable as it might contain toxins, but modern processes have reduced that likelihood. But you must avoid including in your compost heap any materials that may have been sprayed with chemicals.

Sawdust and wood shavings are still relatively easy to acquire. Timber mills have found that these are a saleable commodity, so that free clean sawdust is often difficult to acquire. But large bales of dried sawdust are still quite cheap and make an excellent addition to the compost heap.

Spoiled hay and straw are often available at a reduced price after a period of rain. These are bales that have become wet and already started to break down, so that they are no longer of any value as animal feed. Spoiled alfalfa hay is particularly valuable for the home gardener since it is high in nitrogen and minerals.

If space permits, particularly in cooler areas, it can work well to have three compost bins adjacent to each other for maximum efficiency and ease of use. The first two bins alternate to hold the compost heap when it is inverted. The third bin is used to build a new heap.

Mushroom growers often advertise spent mushroom compost but some care should be exercised in choosing your supplier. Mushrooms are often grown with surprisingly high levels of insecticidal chemicals, the compost is often almost exhausted of nutrients having grown successive flushes of mushrooms, and the pH of spent mushroom compost can be stongly alkaline making it unsuitable for acid-loving plants. If you choose to use mushroom compost, it is a good idea to recompost it and leave the pile for a few months before using it.

Animal manure

One of the most vital ingredients, animal manure is a must for making good compost. There was a time when, even in large cities, extraordinary amounts of unwanted manure were yours for the asking, as long as you were willing to gather it and take it away yourself. Now that so many gardeners are learning the benefits of compost for their garden, there is increased competition for such raw materials. Obliging stables, dairies, poultry farms, and other once easily accessible sources now often have an agreement to supply professional compost companies. But keep an eye out for farms on the outskirts of cities and large towns that still advertise sacks of horse, sheep, and cattle manures at their gates. Just a couple of sackfuls can go a long way toward building excellent compost. Pigeon fanciers and poultry farmers may also be willing to allow you access to droppings, to take away for your garden.

A mixture of manures works best. Poultry manures are particularly high in nitrogen and will allow the compost heap to reach high temperatures. Horse and cow manures are a more even mixture of nitrogen and carbon, and while of good quality will not create such high temperatures.

Keeping the compost moist

Well made compost heaps are moist and hold water like a squeezed sponge. If the pile has been made off the ground, any excess water which would displace air from the pile cannot accumulate. If your compost heap gets excessively wet, it will not heat. As a result, it will become anaerobic, start to smell unpleasant and both you and your heap will end up rather unpopular with your neighbors.

Speeding up the process

The greater the surface area of material exposed to the activities of composting micro-organisms, the more rapidly will they be able to convert a compost heap to usable compost.

A shredder can be invaluable to help reduce woody materials to chips, which have an infinitely greater surface area than the original stems and branches. Alternatively, chop larger pieces of prunings and clippings with a spade.

And get the hammer out to break up the tough stems of corn stalks and cobs, broccoli, and Brussels sprouts stems, and other tough vegetable remains. Eggshells can be crushed in your hands before adding to the compost container in your kitchen.

Maintaining the right temperature

Compost heaps are often hidden in dank corners, commonly behind shrubberies and in the dripline of branches. It's far better to place them in a warm, wind protected, but not overly hot situation that would dry the heap unnecessarily.

And size does matter if a compost heap is to heat effectively. Little compost heaps never reach the desired temperature, so save up materials to make a larger heap. Ideally the heap should be at least 3 feet wide, long, and high.

Larger heaps are even better. To prevent a big heap falling over as it decomposes, and to make it less vulnerable to family pets and small children, you can enclose the pile within a compost bin.

Aerobic composting is much faster in warm weather. The time taken in hot, humid summer areas may be as short as 14–20 days, and in somewhat cooler areas around 2 months.

Building a compost heap

A good compost heap is like a well laid fire in a fireplace, allowing oxygen to be drawn up and vented though the heap.

The easiest way to achieve this is to build the compost pile on top of an open "mattress" of thick, branched sticks. Larger tree and woody shrub prunings are ideal for this purpose. Alternatively, you can use a section of heavy gauge wire lattice balanced over bricks placed at each corner.

To provide venting inside the heap, stick four or more stakes, depending on the intended size of the heap, vertically into the pile after the first layers have been established. Continue to build the pile around the stakes, and when it is complete, wriggle the stakes loose and carefully pull them out. This creates "chimneys" through the pile that will draw air upwards. Material like freshly mown grass that is moist and tends to compact in the pile, should be mixed with drier materials like sawdust or straw.

Some gardeners dismantle the heap when it begins to cool down, and invert the pile by forking the outside to the inside and vice versa. This fluffs up the pile and makes air readily available. Material turned into the center is also exposed to the warmer, moister heart of the pile where the greatest

No go!

There are exceptions to what materials can be composted— at least in backyard compost heaps, which do not always reach high enough temperatures to break down all manner of organic refuse. Fish and chicken bones, meat scraps, cheese, and other protein-containing material will almost inevitably attract unwanted attention from hungry animals (including rats) and should be excluded from the pile. And never place severely infected prunings or plants in the compost heap. The infective organisms need to be burned to prevent the spread of the disease.

"Zoo poo"

Not so long back, many zoos around the world were having trouble disposing of the vast amounts of manure accumulated on a daily basis. Now many enterprising major zoos are recycling their animal wastes through composting destined to supply public gardens. But they also sell bagged, mixed manures of the most exotic kinds, from elephant and zebra droppings to those of peacocks, marketed under labels such as "Zoo Poo"—and it is brilliant for the compost heap.

A plastic compost bin here blends into a cottage-style garden, flanked by pink society garlic (*Tulbaghia violacea*) to soften its appearance.

microbial activity is taking place. The pile will heat up for a second time. But if such physical work is difficult for you, the pile can be left as is, although complete composting will happen more slowly.

Commercial compost bins

Commercial bins are popular with some organic gardeners. They don't take up much space and they effectively exclude animals—both household pets and vermin. Resembling garbage bins, they do provide some insulation and allow microbes to remain active longer in the season. And they can look very neat and tidy, if that is a priority for you.

Compost tumblers

Compost tumbling systems are usually fairly low volume but will still handle all the household scraps generated by a small family. Under ideal conditions they will convert organic material to compost in as short a period of time as 3 weeks—approximately the time of a well constructed aerobic compost heap.

The bin is rotated on a daily basis, remixing the contents and maintaining high microbial activity. Pack the bin loosely to ensure that adequate turning of the contents will take place. A mixture of about half dry and half green material is needed. You can store material for future batches in bags until required—or set up a two-bin system.

Woody material such as prunings or cabbage stems will decay quicker if they are shredded before being added to the heap.

The far end of the heap is ready to use; the fall leaves, still fresh, will be composted by spring.

Constructing a compost bin

There are a number of methods for "binningæ compost, but in many ways, simple wire netting compost bins are ideal. They are very easy to make and to dismantle, allow excellent access for air, and are not themselves composted. What's more they are cheap to build and the materials can be readily recycled for other purposes. Tall, vertical, metal star posts or wooden posts are embedded into the soil to make the corners. Wire netting is used to form the sides, and wire ties can be used for the construction.

Compost boxes can also be made by constructing the sides with open fence palings but in time these will rot.

Some gardeners construct the walls of the heap with bales of straw arranged with small gaps between. Less air is accessible but the walls themselves contribute to the compost and are easily dismantled when composting is completed. The partly composted hay bale walls can become the foundation of the next compost heap. In cool climate areas, hay bale walls have the added advantage of helping to insulate the pile from heat loss.

Never construct a compost bin around a tree. The bark will compost, allowing in unwanted disease organisms.

When is the compost ready?

You know the composting process is completed when the pile has completely cooled and the content has the appearance and texture of rich brown, crumbly earth. It is not unusual to find the remains of a few tough, fibrous ingredients like corn cobs. If you want, you can sift the compost by tossing it in forkfuls through a panel of wire netting. Then just add any uncomposted remains to a new pile.

Protect the top of the finished pile of compost with a plastic sheet or tarpaulin. Otherwise, if the pile is left exposed to the rain, the nutrients will be leached out.

Leaf mold

Leaf mold is one of the most valued sources of organic matter a gardener can get. It makes an excellent soil conditioner, but also has low levels of nutrients (0.4 percent nitrogen, 0.2 percent phosphate, and 0.3 percent potassium), and is usually slightly acidic.

Leaf mold is a material that would slowly form naturally beneath trees in a woodland setting over many years, and making your own is quite a long-term project, as the leaves take time (up to 2 years) in order to decay into a dark, coarse and crumbly compost-like material.

1 Rake up the fallen leaves into heaps. The best time to do this is just after it has rained, when the leaves are moist; but they can also be collected dry and wet later. Make sure to remove any foreign material, such as plastic wrappers from the heaps. Collect up the leaves and place them in either plastic bags or black bags. The latter are better as they block out most of the light and encourage fungal activity.

2 To every 1 foot layer of leaves add a small amount of organic fertilizer, such as dried, pelleted chicken manure or a measure of organic nitrogenous fertilizer, such as sulphate of ammonia (which contains 16–21 percent nitrogen).

3 When the bag is almost full, place it in the position where it is to be left while its contents decompose, and water it thoroughly so that the contents are soaking wet.

4 Over a period of about 2 years, the leaves will decompose and settle in the bag. These leaves will be pressed tightly together, with some remaining almost whole and others disintegrating completely. When the leaves are ready for use, the bag can be split open and the leaves used as mulch or soil conditioner.

To collect leaves from the lawn quickly and easily, run the lawnmower over them with the grass collecting box on. This will not only gather up most of the leaves, but it will also chop them up, accelerating their decay.

Trench composting

Trench composting can be an ideal answer for those who have larger gardens and for the more patient among us who are willing to wait for results. Trench composting is an anaerobic technique, so keep in mind that the compost materials will not reach the temperatures needed to kill weed seed and pathogens.

Dig a trench about 8 inches deep. Fill the trench with vegetable wastes from the kitchen and garden, before covering with a layer of soil. In a few months, the materials will be fully incorporated.

As this is a cool process, earthworms will actively contribute to turning the organic matter through the soil. You could add commercially obtained earthworms to the trench, but populations of native worms will be attracted to the organic waste and multiply rapidly of their own accord.

1 In the late summer or early fall, mark out the area that is to be dug over in a series of trenches and mark the lines of the parallel trenches.

2 Dig out a single trench about 1 foot deep, and move the soil from the trench to the end of the plot, which will be the very last section to be trenched.

3 As they become available, gradually fill the trench with plant debris, vegetable scraps, and kitchen waste.

4 Dig out a second trench in a similar way to the first one. Cover each additional layer of material in the first trench with the soil which has just been dug from the second parallel trench. After the first trench is full and the second trench has been dug, start filling the second trench by creating a third trench. Each completed trench will gradually settle over a month or two as the plant material decomposes. Woody material such as prunings will decay quicker if they are shredded before being buried, and a small nitrogenous fertilizer may also need to be incorporated to speed up the whole process.

Green manures

Green manure crops are planted to improve the quality of the soil—and enhance plant growth. They are usually nitrogen-fixing plants, often with strong, deep rooting systems that help to break up compacted soil and draw nutrients up to the soil surface where they are available to future plantings. Good choices for green manure crops are dense plants that will also out-compete weeds.

Green manure crops

Type	Length of growing period	Soil	When to plant	Benefit
Alfalfa	Perennial	Neutral to alkaline, well-drained	Spring to midsummer	Nitrogen-fixing, exceptionally deep-rooted
Buckwheat	Annual (2–4 months)	Good on poor soils	Spring to midsummer	Improves soil structure and attracts pollinating bees
Lupin (Lupinus angustifolia)	3–5 months	Acid, sandy to sandy loam	Spring to midsummer	Nitrogen-fixing
Phacelia tanecetifolia	2–4 months; can overwinter	Wide tolerance	Spring to summer	Attracts beneficial insects, soil structure improved
Red clover	2–5 months; will overwinter	Sandy loam preferred	Spring to late summer	Nitrogen-fixing, attracts pollinating bees
Rye	Overwinter	Wide tolerance	Early to late fall	Fibrous root system improves soil structure
White radish (Daikon)	3–5 months	Tolerant	Spring	Flowers attract beneficial insects. Huge roots break up soil for water penetration

The **seed sprouts of alfalfa** have another use, as they are very tasty and are delicious in salads or sandwiches.

How mulch works

Mulch provides a blanket layer over your soil. Normally about 4 inches thick, it:

- regulates soil temperature, by keeping the roots cool in summer and warm in winter;
- conserves moisture and cuts down on watering requirements by reducing evaporation from the soil surface and increasing water penetration; and
- controls weeds by preventing weed seeds from germinating.

Always wet the soil down well before applying mulch, and also wet the mulch down when the job is completed. Dry mulches can be water repellent.

Mulch—and more mulch

It is impossible to overestimate the value of mulches in the garden. Mulches can be divided into organic mulches such as leaf litter, hay, straw, composted sawdust, and wood chips, and inorganic mulches such as rocks and river pebbles.

Both kinds of mulches are invaluable in conserving soil moisture so that plants are less prone to water stress, and thus do not suffer reduced productivity and susceptibility to pest and disease attack.

Mulches also minimize erosion, help maintain an even soil temperature, and reduce soil splash on plants, which can spread soil-borne diseases.

Organic mulches have some additional benefits. As they break down they provide organic matter to the soil, protect and improve soil structure, encourage beneficial micro-organism activity, and are also invaluable in suppressing weeds.

Types of mulch

Mulches are available in many forms, both organic and inorganic. Organic mulches include leaf mulch, pine bark, red gum chips, alfalfa, straw, newspaper, compost, rice husks, and sugar cane. An effective mulch should not be dislodged by wind and rain and should have a loose enough structure to allow water to soak through easily.

Some mulches—for example, alfalfa, compost, and sugar cane—have a high nitrogen content. These mulches improve the soil fertility, but they rot down quickly and so need to be replaced every few months. Never use peat moss as a mulch as it repels water once it is dry; rather, blend it into the soil and use it as a soil conditioner.

Inorganic mulches—such as black plastic, weed control mat, scoria, and decorative gravels and pebbles—are not really "garden friendly." They add nothing to the soil structure and, once these mulches are in place, soil additives are difficult to incorporate. They tend to raise the soil temperature and some can even stop your soil from breathing, which can lead to serious problems.

Depending on the time of year at which you mulch, you can influence soil temperatures. For example, if you mulch at the end of fall, you will keep the soil warmer for longer, while mulching in early spring will keep the soil cooler and prevent heat being trapped in summer.

Applying mulch

You should apply organic mulches at least 4 inches deep. To assist in excluding light from the soil surface and aid with weed suppression, lay down overlapping layers of newspapers before applying the mulch.

Mulches should not be laid until the soil has warmed up after winter. And be careful not to place mulch too close to the trunks of shrubs and trees—it can cause collar rot.

Fruit trees benefit greatly from a mulch of nitrogen-rich alfalfa hay that can be weighted down with stones. Make sure you rake up any fallen fruit and leaves at the beginning of winter and compost them. If you leave them as a mulch they will act as a reservoir of disease for the following season.

Sawdust and wood chips are commonly used as mulch. However, when either raw sawdust or wood chips begin to break down, the responsible soil bacteria require nitrogen for the process. They will rob the soil, and plants that have been mulched with raw sawdust or wood chips will exhibit yellowing due to this temporary withdrawal of nitrogen.

Mulching not only keeps the soil healthy, but also makes less work for the gardener by reducing weed infestation.

Living mulch

Many low-growing plants make ideal living mulches. Groundcovers such as *Ajuga* planted into mulched soil are excellent for excluding weeds in ornamental gardens. Blue-flowered periwinkle is ideal for dry shade areas and is easily controlled at a suitable height with a string trimmer used twice a year. Other "cover crops" such as any of the prostrate-growing plants are effective in reducing weeds.

Actually, weeds may not always be a nuisance but in fact can be helpful. A carpet of weeds can be a protective blanket, another "living mulch" of sorts.

Pennyroyal.

Once the process has been completed, the nitrogen is made available to the soil. You can either add a sprinkling of blood and bone to provide the required nitrogen, or partially compost the sawdust or chips in a pile for a month before use. Sprinkle the pile well with liquid seaweed fertilizer to boost the partial composting process. Sawdust and woodchips often contain levels of tannins high enough to inhibit plant growth and these are also partially leached during composting.

While mulch is invaluable, it is better not to simply throw masses of garden refuse on the soil. Compost it first. Piles of rubbish will often decompose anaerobically into a slimy mess that will encourage disease. Of all mulches, none is better than compost (which can be applied when quite roughly textured) and alfalfa hay.

Dandelion.

The virtues of weeds

Many gardeners make their lives a misery worrying about weeds. They see them as the gardener's curse, and throw their hands up in despair. Or they decide the occasion calls for a military-style attack.

Organic gardeners tend to be a bit more relaxed about "invasion" by "unwanted" plants. They know that weeds are essential to the health of the soil. Bare earth is easily eroded by wind, compacted by heavy rain or foot traffic. It is more easily leached of soluble nutrients and can also lose important gases.

If an area is to remain bare for a while, allowing it to become covered in weeds may not be the neatest solution, but it is sound ecologically. The weeds can be slashed just before they begin to flower and left on top of the soil as a green mulch, or dug through to add valuable organic matter.

There are numerous types of **caterpillars** that can totally defoliate whole vegetable plants.

Repelling invaders

Organic growers long suspected that the more healthy a plant is the more resistant it will be to pest and disease attack. Recent research backs this up. Insect pests are attracted to the weakest, most stressed plants in a crop, apparently detecting them by subtle differences. Improving soil structure and fertility with organic matter makes for healthier soil and this in turn makes for strong, healthy crops—and minimal crop damage. It might sound utopian but it truly works.

Organic gardening techniques also produce plants that grow steadily rather than rapidly, as they do with chemical fertilizers. The plants do not become soft and sappy and prone to attack.

Compost and mulches retain soil moisture so that plants are not water-stressed on hot days. It is also important to water in response to the needs of the plant. Plants that are regularly wilted and stressed, as well as ones which are overwatered, are much more susceptible to attack by insects.

A plant in the wrong position is also liable to be attacked. We all succumb to the temptation to buy and plant things that are marginal for our climate, do poorly in our type of soil, or need conditions we cannot offer like wind protection, or an open sunny site. But plants that survive these impulsive gardener moments remain marginal in the garden and will always be more vulnerable to pests and diseases.

And it pays to plant crops at the optimal time. Plants well may survive being planted too early or too late, but they will never thrive as they should.

You can also choose cultivars that have been selected for resistance. Many strains of vegetables are able to resist attack to some degree. If you garden in an area regularly affected by a particular pest or disease, some research and careful selection will reward you with stronger, less susceptible plants. Neighborhood plant nurseries can be invaluable sources of good advice.

Good garden housekeeping

Many diseases and plant pests can be eliminated from the garden simply by good housekeeping practices.

All garden wastes, including spent crops, should be composted. If material is infected, it should be placed into the center of the compost heap where the high temperatures reached will kill all spores. Infected woody prunings, however, are unlikely to break down fully in the compost and should be burned.

Viral diseases are passed on mainly by sap-sucking insects. As soon as a virus-infected plant is detected, it should be removed and added to an activated compost heap. Or better yet, burn any diseased plant material.

There is an old saying that "The finest fertilizer is the farmer's footprints." In other words, the farmer who regularly walks his or her land, observing carefully and monitoring his crops, is the most important factor in producing a good crop.

Seasonal tasks

Dealing with garden problems as they arise will ensure fewer pests and diseases to be dealt with as the seasons progress.

Fall is an especially valuable time for the gardener. A thorough clean-up at the end of summer or early in fall can do much to prevent pests and diseases in the next growing season. Digging the garden over at this stage not only aerates the soil but can expose overwintering larvae of various pests.

After pruning deciduous trees, check for the presence of borer and destroy any you find by poking a wire into any holes. Use a wire brush to remove any loose bark, which often shelters overwintering pests. Make sure that no vegetables are left on the ground. Any mummified vegetables should be burned if possible.

Don't get mad, get clever

Organic farmers and gardeners have found a myriad of ingenius ways to circumvent crop damage without putting themselves, their families, and the environment at risk. There was a time when organic growers were likely to be challenged constantly on pest management issues. No more. Modern organic pest management means gardens are living larders from which luscious fresh vegetables can be eaten from the hand—and places where children play without fear of toxic sprays.

Biologically friendly pest control

If excessive pest damage does occur in your garden, usually the result of unusual seasonal conditions, there are many additional measures that you can adopt, none of them dangerous to the environment or your family. The more we have come to know of the life cycles and behavior of insect and animal pests, the more we have been able to develop environmentally friendly ways of minimizing the damage they can cause.

Dill.

Barriers and traps

Among the most useful advances in recent times has been the development of finely woven, transparent cloths to protect vegetables and fruit trees. These are woven to allow water and maximum light and air through while excluding insect pests. Floating row covers are ideal for the vegetable garden.

Other relatively newly developed barriers are sticky, non-drying glues that trap insects migrating up the stem or trunk. The glue is placed on a paper collar around the base of the plant. A simple non-sticky collar can be made from a cardboard cup with the base cut out. Placed around the base of a seedling this is sufficient to protect it from cutworm damage.

In some areas, carrot fly is a real problem. But the female fly hovers low over the crop in order to detect the odor of carrots. Erecting a simple, temporary barrier fence of hessian around the row will force the female fly to hover too high to detect the scent.

Trap plants

Some plants are very attractive to pests—either because of their color, smell, or taste—so that they preferentially attract them, thereby protecting other plants. Bright yellow nasturtiums, for instance, attract aphids away from cabbages. Zinnias have long been used as trap plants to lure Japanese beetle. Dill is traditionally used to lure green tomato caterpillar. In themselves, trap plants are not sufficient protection for your garden—but they do contribute toward maintaining healthy crops.

Yellow objects attract many flying insects, and sticky yellow paper ("fly paper") makes an effective trap. These traps can be bought from garden centers.

Insect-repelling "teas"

"Teas" can be made with plant material known to be insect repellent. The leaves are chopped roughly and covered with water in an enamel saucepan. They are simmered for 15 minutes, then strained and the resulting tea cooled for use as a spray. Eucalyptus, wormwood, southernwood, black sage (*Salvia mellifera*), and *Equisetum* are all used in this way.

Quassia tea is prepared from wood chips of the species *Picrasma quassioides*. The tea is made with 3½ ounces of chips very gently simmered with 14 cups water for 2 hours. After straining and cooling, the tea is diluted 1 in 5 with water for spraying against pests. It has the advantage of being non-toxic to bees and ladybugs.

Warning! Take care that no-one is tempted to drink these teas, and they are kept well-labeled.

To spray or not to spray?

If you are planning to have an organic garden with the minimum of problems, never spray with chemical sprays. They will upset the ecological balance in your garden and you will end up with a cascade of further problems. Beneficial predators will also be wiped out so that pests previously under control may take over.

Instead, try one of the organically acceptable sprays. These include garlic spray, wormwood spray, pepper spray, pyrethrum spray, and the fungicides lime sulphur and Bordeaux mixture. The latter contains copper and hydrated lime and is used on potato blight and other fungal problems. Bordeaux spray should be restricted in use as it builds up levels of copper in the soil. And lime sulphur should only be applied when a plant is dormant.

Pyrethrum is derived from the white flower heads of an African daisy species and is useful against aphids including greenfly and whitefly. But note that pyrethrum can also kill useful insects.

Another useful item in the organic gardener's arsenal is insecticidal soap derived from plant fatty acids and used against red spider mite, greenfly, whitefly, black fly, and soft scale. More delicately textured plants can be susceptible to damage from insecticidal soap.

Another spray, derived from rapeseed oil, is used against whitefly, black fly, greenfly, red spider mite, and scale. Soapy water spray made from soft soap (not detergent) is useful against aphids.

Home-made organic sprays

A number of old-fashioned home-made sprays are remarkably effective in helping to restore balance in the garden when a pest reaches the nuisance level. A sensible adage is not to spray the garden with anything that wouldn't be safe to spray on yourself!

Some of these sprays are likely to temporarily clear the kitchen with their odor—and spilled on your clothes they are unlikely to do anything for your social life! But at the same time they certainly won't endanger you or your family.

Garlic spray

1 bulb of garlic, broken into cloves

1 cup of water

1 dessertspoon soft soap or grated soap flakes

3 chilies

Place all ingredients except the soft soap in a blender. Filter through a double layer of cloth or coffee filter paper. Dilute the liquid with 15 cups of water and add the soft soap. This makes a good all-purpose spray. The garlic works on sucking insects such as aphid on roses, while the chili works on chewing insects such as caterpillars. Apply with a clean spray gun.

Onion spray

1 cup roughly chopped hot-tasting onions

1 cup water

5 feverfew leaves (if feeling particularly vicious!)

Prepare, dilute, and use as above.

A sticky end!

Sticky solutions are useful in trapping a myriad of garden pests. Dissolve molasses 1 part in 50 by volume for a sticky sweet end.

Chili and soap spray

You'll need 8 chilies, soap, grater, a sharp knife, and a chopping board. You'll also need a spray bottle and some water. (It's best to use gloves when chopping chilies.)

1 Grate the soap (or you can use soap flakes). Add the soap flakes to a spray bottle that is nearly full of water.

2 Chop the chilies. Add them to the bottle and screw the lid on. Shake the contents vigorously and spray your home-made insecticide onto any plant.

Controlling pests

Pest	Description	Controls
Aphids	Small sap-sucking insects about 1/16–1/8 inches long; may be green, black, yellow, pink, or gray. May appear in small numbers but rapidly increase to form large colonies. They cause curling and distortion of leaves. New shoots can be thickly coated with aphids.	Encourage natural predators like ladybugs, mantises, or lacewings. Remove with a strong jet of water from hose, or squash with fingers. Use an insecticidal soap or spray containing pyrethrum, imidacloprid, or rotenone (Derris dust). These kill the pests on contact.
Cabbage whites	Cabbage whites are frequently seen in gardens. They have creamy white wings with a black spot on the wing tips. Its wingspan is 1¾–2 inches. The caterpillars are green with a pale yellow marking down the side. The caterpillars chew the leaves, especially of cabbages and other brassicas. The caterpillars are often well camouflaged. Look for tell-tale droppings.	Keep gardens as weed-free as possible, as many weeds will act as host plants for the pest. Pick individual caterpillars off plants by hand and destroy. You can also spray with the bio-insecticide *Bacillus thuringiensis* (BT). This is not a knock-down spray but the caterpillars will stop feeding almost at once. Carbaryl in the form of a dust or spray is an effective method of killing all types of caterpillars.
Cutworms and army worms	The larvae of nocturnal moths, which are about 1 inch long. The moths are grayish-brown with dark and light markings. The caterpillars are smooth-bodied, 1½–2 inches long and may be olive green to brown or black. The worms chew the stem at the soil surface.	Try to catch the caterpillars at night. Protect seedlings wiith barriers around them (small milk cartons or plastic drinking cups with bottoms cut out) and pushed into ground over plant. Or spray or dust plants with carbaryl late in the afternoon before the caterpillars come out to feed at night.
Root-knot nematodes (eelworms)	These pests are root feeders. Feeding nematodes inject saliva into plant roots, causing the development of abnormal cells. The lumps, or galls, should not be confused with the nodules of legumes such as peas or beans. Plants become stunted and wilt even when there is ample water in the soil. The nematodes are tiny, thin transparent creatures that are not visible to the naked eye.	Rotate vegetable crops and do not repeatedly plant susceptible varieties in the same area. Onions, cauliflowers, cabbages, and corn are tolerant of root-knot nematodes. If there is no alternative food source, nematodes will feed on marigold roots (*Tagetes* spp.), which exude a substance that is toxic to them. For chemical solutions, you could apply fenamiphos granules to the soil.

Controlling pests

Pest	Description	Controls
Snails	Snails chew holes in leaves and may also completely destroy seedlings. They also move up plant stems to feed on foliage. Wherever they move, they leave behind them a silvery, slimy trail of mucus. The soft body of the snail is enclosed by a broad, spiral shell, inside which they are able to seal themselves through very long periods of dry weather. Snails feed mostly at night when conditions are moist. They are most active when there are heavy dews or showery weather. Snails can live for several years.	Go into the garden at night with a torch to look for snails, particularly after a shower of rain. Squash them or drop them into a bucket of heavily salted water. A short piece of terracotta pipe with a little canned pet food inside will attract snails, which can be cleaned out with a stick. Bury a jar or margarine tub in the soil and pour in $\frac{1}{2}$ a cup of beer. Check the jar daily for snails and top up the beer. You can also use snail pellets containing metadehyde or methiocarb sparingly around plants. Make sure pellets are not accessible to children or pets by placing them inside a length of plastic pipe no more than 2 inches in diameter.
White grubs	These are the larvae of the scarab or cockchafer beetle. They are whitish-gray grubs with an orange-brown head and three pairs of jointed legs. They grow to about 1 inch long, and are usually seen in a curled or semicircular position. They chew the roots of plants.	Dig over the soil and pick out the grubs. Where the grubs are found in potted plants, remove all the potting mix and replant in a clean pot with fresh potting mix. Chemical controls for this pest for the home garden are hard to find.
Whiteflies	Whitefly nymphs sap suck, causing leaves to become mottled and slightly papery. They suck sap from plant leaves, secreting honeydew on which sooty mold feeds. The tiny, white flying insects have a wingspan of about $\frac{1}{8}$ inch. When disturbed, they rise in a cloud from the plant. They can cause problems in greenhouses. Tomatoes and beans are frequently attacked.	Parasitic wasps are available that prey on whiteflies but these are better for controlled environments like greenhouses. Use yellow sticky traps. Or spray affected plants with cyfluthrin or dimethoate to control whitefly infestations.

Controlling diseases

Disease	Description	Control
Anthracnose (*Colletotrichum* spp. and related genera)	This fungus manifests itself as dark patches or spots on both foliage and fruit. Often the spots will enlarge until they run together, forming black patches. On some plants, as the spots enlarge the center becomes dry and papery, eventually falling out. Ripening avocados first show small brown spots that rapidly enlarge and blacken, becoming slightly sunken. Beans may show dark spots or patches on leaves, stems, and pods until leaf veins turn black.	Prune off any dead leaves that may harbor fungal spores. Rake up and destroy any fallen leaves or fruit that may be carrying spores. Water plants with a soaker hose or by drip irrigation. Sprays of copper oxychloride or mancozeb can be effective. Spray approximately once a month or more often during wet weather.
Gray mold (*Botrytis cinerea*)	The symptoms of this fungal disease vary to an extent depending on the host plant, but gray mold is generally characterized by gray, furry growth. Gray mold affects a wide range of vegetables. This fungus can survive on both living and dead plant material.	Practice good housekeeping and rake up dead leaves from the ground beneath plants. Affected leaves should be cut off and destroyed. Allow good spacing between plants to ensure good air circulation. Don't water from overhead or late in the day as the increased humidity will remain around the plants overnight, maintaining the conditions that are favorable for the spread and growth of this fungal disease.
Leaf spot (*Septoria* spp., *Mycosphaerella* spp. and *Cercospora* spp.)	Fungal leaf spots on plants have many and varied forms. The spots are brown to black in color, but several types then produce a secondary ring or halo around the original spot. Sometimes these haloes are pale yellow but they may also be black, brown, or gray. In severe cases the spots coalesce so that large areas of the leaf are affected. On some plants the dead tissue at the center of the spot falls out, making holes in the leaf. These diseases do well in warm and cool humid conditions.	Prune off and destroy any affected leaves. Avoid overhead watering or watering late in the day. Thin out the foliage of dense plants to allow better air circulation and allow adequate spacing between plants. Where vegetable crops have been affected, practice crop rotation. If a chemical control program is selected, thorough spraying with mancozeb or copper oxychloride should prevent this fungal disease from spreading.

Controlling diseases

Disease	Description	Control
Mosaic disease (many strains)	The symptoms of viral diseases are variable and these viruses may manifest themselves as yellow streaks, rings, wavy lines, or sometimes a mottling of pale and dark green. Some of the discolored leaf areas turn brown or black as they age. The leaves of cucurbits (such as winter squash, cucumber, and zucchini) show some mottling. Viral diseases are spread through plant sap. Aphids provide a means of transmission for many viruses as they move from plant to plant, but infected sap can also be transmitted on hands, secateurs, or any garden cutting tool. Many weeds act as hosts.	Remove or isolate infected plants. Wash your hands and disinfect any garden tools that have been in contact with diseased plants. Keep the garden free of weeds. For chemical controls, since aphids are the main means of infection, the best treatment is to spray to control aphids with pyrethrum, imidacloprid, or dimethoate. However, when aphids are the means of transmission they have normally infected a plant by the time they are noticed.
Powdery mildew *Oidium* spp., *Sphaerotheca* and related genera	This is a fungus. Gray-white powdery spots appear on leaves. If humidity is high, these spread until large patches or whole leaves are covered. Young leaves can become curled and misshapen, sometimes folding in on themselves. Buds, stems, and fruit may also be affected, becoming covered in a powdery coating. It occurs in high humidity. Strains may attack cucurbits (cucumber, zucchini, winter squash, and marrow).	Where possible, plant varieties that are resistant to this disease. Plant breeders continue to work to develop resistant strains of plants. There are cucurbits with good resistance. Wettable sulphur provides good control of powdery mildew but it cannot be used in temperatures over 77°F or it will burn the plants. Choose cool weather if using this method of control. There are some sprays containing triforine that are registered for the control of this fungal problem.
Rust *Puccinia* spp., *Uromyces* spp. and related genera	Rust is a fungal disease and is generally first noticed when pale, often yellow, spots appear on the upper surface of a leaf. On the underside of the leaf there will be a reddish brown, powdery pustule. This reddish brown powder is made up of the fungal spores that will be rapidly spread by the wind. Leaves on some plants eventually wither and may die.	Plant resistant varieties where possible. Remove and destroy infected leaves or whole plants as soon as the problem is noticed. Avoid overhead watering and improve air circulation around plants. For chemical solutions, spray affected plants with mancozeb or copper oxychloride, following the manufacturer's directions on the product labels.

The vegetable garden calendar

One of the most difficult aspects of running an edible garden is remembering what to do when. All too often, you only recollect that you should have sown the seeds of a particular vegetable well into the season, and if you leave it too late you will miss the best time of year for growth.

The times of greatest activity in the vegetable garden are spring and summer. You need to plan carefully to ensure that you find the time to sow, transplant, weed, and harvest during these busy periods. You may find that mulching the surface of the soil will help you to cut down on your weeding chores, thereby reducing the workload,

The chart here provides you with an outline of what will be needed when, but the detailed planning depends very much on the particular plants you want to grow and also your local climatic conditions. It is a good idea to keep a notebook in which you record the performance of plants and when certain tasks must be carried out.

Early spring

- Chit seed potatoes indoors.
- Sow vegetables such as fava beans, runner beans, kohlrabi, beets, carrots, and scallions outdoors.
- Start sowing seed outdoors for eggplants, peppers, outdoor tomatoes, and lettuce.
- Force rhubarb by covering with an upturned bucket.
- Harvest the last of your wintered vegetables, such as corn salad, Brussels sprouts, winter cabbage, leeks, and parsnips.
- Plant onion sets.
- Prepare any beds that you failed to dig over in the fall.
- Add straw or bulky manure to give soil good texture.
- Check over any stored vegetables for signs of rotting.

Mid-spring

- Carry on sowing seed successively for vegetables already mentioned.
- Plant rhubarb, shallots, onions and garlic.
- Plant potatoes.
  Harden off the transplants of indoor-sown seeds of beans, tomatoes, cucumbers, peppers, and eggplants, and cloche the more tender plants such as corn, peppers, eggplants, and tomatoes

Late spring

- Carry on sowing seed indoors for eggplants, corn, green and runner beans, cucumbers, zucchinis, and tomatoes.
- Sow all hardier vegetables, including Brussels sprouts, cabbages, kale, carrots, leeks, parsnip, peas, Swiss chard, and turnips.
- Plant lettuces.
- Start to hoe and weed between rows of crops.
- Earth up the earliest potatoes.
- Harvest spring cabbages, leeks, scallions, parsley, overwintered salad plants, and spinach.

Early summer

- Direct-sow outdoor crops such as carrots, beets, peas, zucchini, lettuce, and radishes.
- Plant Jerusalem artichokes.
- Carry on weeding regularly.
- Earth up potatoes.
- Stake peas and beans.
- Watch out for pests, such as black fly on fava beans.
- Make small successive sowings of salad plants.
- Harvest rhubarb, fava beans, fall-sown onions, radishes, spinach, and turnips.

Midsummer

- Harvest vegetables such as peas, fava beans, lettuces, radishes, zucchinis, beets, and scallions.
- Tie in shoots of outdoor tomatoes and cucumbers. Stake peppers and eggplants.
- Water, mulch, and feed all crops as necessary.
- Pinch out growing points of beans.
- Top-dress vegetables with fertilizer.
- Remove excess foliage from tomato plants.
- Watch out for flying pests, and use netting for susceptible crops.
- Hoe regularly to keep the weeds under control.
- Cover with black plastic any areas of soil that have not been planted, to keep weeds at bay.

Late summer

- Feed tomatoes regularly.
- Harvest beans, peas, potatoes, beets, cabbages, carrots, outdoor cucumbers, tomatoes, corn, lettuces, garlic, and zucchinis.

Early fall

- Lift onions and shallots when the tops have died down.
- Dig up any vegetables that have finished cropping, and put the leaves and stalks in your potting mix.
- Harvest tomatoes, peppers, eggplants, zucchinis, beans, lettuces, and salad greens.
- Store maincrop potatoes.
- Harvest peas.
- Cloche any tomatoes, peppers, and eggplants that have not yet ripened.
- Plant onion sets for an early-season crop.
- Order farmyard manure.
- Burn all garden material that cannot be added to the compost heap and use the resulting ash for potassium fertilizer.

Mid-fall

- Start to dig over the plot, incorporating well-rotted manure and compost.
- Earth up leeks.
- Plant cabbages for spring.
- Clean, sort, and store stakes that are no longer needed.
- Compost tomato and bean plants.

Late fall

- Continue digging over the ground.
- Sow fava beans for over-wintering.
- Plant onion sets.
- Cloche salad vegetables for winter use.
- Lift and store root crops for winter use.
- String onions and garlic.

Winter

- Continue to dig if the weather is warm enough.
- Check the acidity of the soil using a kit. Add lime if necessary for any brassicas.
- Lift leeks and parsnips.
- Harvest spinach.
- Check vegetable stores for signs of rotting and remove any specimens that have been affected.
- Order seed catalogs, then prepare your seed order.
- Protect any overwintering vegetables with cloches.
- Tidy the garden shed and sharpen all blades.
- Oil mowers and other equipment with moving parts.
- Check the structure of the garden shed and carry out any repairs as required.
- Plant garlic.

legumes

Legumes are the edible seeds and pods of plants such as beans and peas.

CRANBERRY BEAN
(*Phaseolus vulgaris*)

SHELLING PEA
(*Pisum sativum*
'Earlicrop Massey')

FAVA BEAN SEEDS
(*Vicia faba* 'Aquadulce')

BUSH BEAN
(*Phaseolus vulgaris*
'Blue Lake')

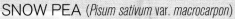

SNOW PEA (*Pisum sativum* var. *macrocarpon*)

BEAN SEEDS
(*Phaseolus vulgaris*
'Redland Pioneer')

PEA SEEDS
(*Pisum sativum* 'Greenfeast')

Left to right:
DWARF SNOW
PEA SEEDS,
YARD-LONG
BEAN SEEDS,
FAVA BEAN
SEEDS

LIMA BEAN (*Phaseolus lunatus*)

BEANETTES

LIMA BEAN SEEDS
(*Phaseolus limensis*)

RED KIDNEY
BEAN SEEDS
(*Phaseolus vulgaris*)

SUGAR SNAP PEAS
(*Pisum sativum* var. *sativum*)

BEAN SEEDS
(*Phaseolus vulgaris* 'Scarlett Runner')

Keen gardeners like to squeeze a little bit more time from the growing season. With protective structures like greenhouses and cold frames you can get a head start in spring, and stretch the season end in the fall.

extend the season

Protecting plants

Although many vegetables and fruits can be preserved for winter by techniques like drying, salting, fermenting, canning, and deep freezing, extending the growing season to provide fresh food all year round is the ideal. Not only is this the healthiest of all options, but it reduces the fall chores involved in preserving the harvest, and saves valuable indoor storage space. With the help of a wide variety of quite simple protective structures, other than in areas with the very coldest of winters it is possible to achieve a flow of fresh vegetables into the kitchen for most of the year. These range from modest devices like cold frames and cloches, to larger structures such as polytunnels and greenhouses.

Tomatoes are a favorite greenhouse crop and there are specific varieties available that are suited to greenhouse growing.

Rather than harvesting a matured crop in late fall, many vegetables can be left in the soil during the winter months if they are provided with the protection of cloches and portable frames. These crops can be supplemented with vegetables such as kale and winter cabbage, which are exceptionally cold-hardy and grow outdoors without the benefit of frost protection, together with various crops from warmed greenhouses.

Protective structures such as greenhouses, conservatories, cold frames, and cloches are truly multifunctional. Seedlings of spring crops can be raised well in advance of open sown seedlings, extending the growing season by a month or more. Vegetables requiring a warm growing season or long summer growing period can be matured satisfactorily, and winter crops of leafy vegetables raised.

Greenhouses

Greenhouses can be either freestanding, or a lean-to construction built against a sunny brick wall to take advantage of the solar heat absorbed by the bricks during the day and re-radiated at night. Re-radiation from brick walls can raise nearby temperatures by 41°F at night. Choose a position that is open to the sun all year when siting a greenhouse.

Greenhouse design

Home greenhouses can often be quite small, around 6 x 8 feet, but as they are multipurpose you are unlikely to regret not building one at least double this size. The frame is built either with rot-resistant timber like cedar, or with galvanized steel or aluminum. Glass is still the preferred

A **greenhouse** is the hallmark of the serious gardener. Greenhouses may be simple structures, or have sophisticated heating and ventilation apparatus.

glazing although polycarbonate is also used. The latter transmits lower light levels but has useful insulating properties. Unless greenhouses are well ventilated, the internal temperatures can rise too high and cause damage or death of plants. Ventilation is essential not only to lower heat but also to moderate high humidity, which encourages fungal infections. Ventilation can be achieved via louvres, but temperature-regulated, automated roof vents may be installed. The floor should be easy to clean to prevent build-up of fungi and alage.

Greenhouses can be quite elaborately designed. Waist-high benching makes work more easy. Benching may be made of treated wood with slatted tops. Steel benches are virtually indestructible. Wooden pallets raised on bricks can be a useful temporary solution but may need replacing.

Greenhouse irrigation equipment

Gently hosing plants is a pleasant chore, but other methods of delivery can be more reliable. Drip irrigation is particularly useful for larger pots and growing bags. Capillary matting is ideal for delivering water to punnets of seedlings and smaller pots on benches. Misting units on timers can also be attached along benches. Plants will require less water in winter than summer, and a simple sensor that monitors soil moisture can be used to activate watering according to the needs of the plants.

Greenhouse insulation and heating

In cold areas, additional insulation during winter months is advisable. Cheap, temporary solutions in use at the moment are polystyrene blocks or sheets used to line the lower walls, and sheets of clear

A magic environment

While smaller structures have the advantage of mobility and low cost, and are most commonly used to protect in-ground crops, greenhouses and polytunnels allow the gardener to share the protective environment with their plants. In cold weather, few places are more pleasant. Inside, all is a miracle of warmth, humidity, and rushing growth. There is the smell of rich humus and the green fragrance of young plants mingling with that of potted flowering plants. It is the perfect retreat from the cold of a winter world.

In cold climates, **conservatory** extensions of the kitchen or the sunny side of the house provide a place to enjoy warmth and light, as well as fresh, juicy **vegetables,** even in the coldest months.

polycarbonate or bubble plastic used to insulate the inside of the roof. In addition, lengths of fleece can be draped over any plants at risk during a cold snap. Even a small heater can allow many quite exotic plants to be grown, and reduces the possibility of cold damage or death of plants.

Summer heat can be regulated with a cover of shade cloth, in combination with good ventilation. Shade cloth comes in a variety of densities from 10 to 90 percent. Many gardeners still use the older but effective method of painting the glass roof with shading paint in summer. In some areas, low light intensities or short day lengths in the middle of winter can make supplementary lighting necessary to maintain healthy growth and germinate seedlings. Full spectrum fluorescent lamps are ideal to supplement existing daylight. They should be arranged well above the level of foliage.

A heated bench is a small luxury well worth building or buying. It consists of a strongly built, usually galvanized, tray on a bench, containing soil-warming cables buried in approximately 6 inches of sand or fine quartz gravel. The bottom heat provided by a heated bench speeds up both the germination of seed and the rate at which cuttings form roots. Some seeds, such as those of peppers, are difficult to germinate without considerable warmth and benefit from bottom heating. Heat mats are also available to place under pots.

Polytunnels

Polytunnels are cheaper to construct than greenhouses, consisting of a covering of heavy grade, ultraviolet-resistant, plastic sheet stretched over a frame of galvanized iron or steel hoops. The skin is anchored around the outside by embedding it in a trench and backfilling with soil. Doors are provided at both ends for ventilation as polytunnels maintain higher humidity than glasshouses. It is for this reason that wider, shorter polytunnels structures are preferred for home use. Depending on the quality used and the conditions, the skin should be replaced about every 3 to 7 years. Reinforced PVC covers are also available.

To improve accessibility in the polytunnel, straight-sided rather than curved polytunnels are preferred by some vegetable growers, although they are more expensive. As polytunnels are more temporary in nature than larger structures like greenhouses, their fittings should be easily moved. With this in mind, they can be equipped and modified for seasonal changes in much the same manner as greenhouses. Some growers treat full-sized polytunnels as the equivalent of a giant tunnel cloche. The soil under cover is dug, enriched with organic matter, and crops planted in rows. Every few years the polytunnel can dismantled and moved to another site to prevent the build-up of soil-borne diseases.

Growing plants in greenhouses and polytunnels

The moisture and warmth in polytunnels and greenhouses encourages the growth not only of plants, but also of pests and diseases. For this reason extra care should be taken not to introduce infested plants into these structures. If plants are being introduced from elsewhere, check them carefully. A good additional precaution is to isolate new introductions for a fortnight to ensure no infections develop before placing them in the greenhouse. Very regular inspections of the greenhouse for potential pests and diseases are advisable. Sticky insect trapping strips can be suspended to provide a sample of any flying pests such as whitefly. Biological control agents are particularly effective in the closed system of a greenhouse or polytunnel.

Try to keep the greenhouse or polytunnel very clean and weed-free, and wash down all surfaces with hot soapy water at least four times a year. Make sure there is nowhere for snails and slugs to hide by day. They can devastate the plants at night.

Summer heat often encourages spider mites. Water well under the leaves of affected crops. A foliar spray with seaweed solution, drenching both sides of the leaves, in the cooler hours, is also helpful.

Regular watering in greenhouses and polytunnels readily leaches nutrients from pots, and higher temperatures rapidly reduce organic matter levels. Applications of foliar sprays such as commercial seaweed solution will help to maintain good nutrition. If crops are grown in beds, strict attention needs to be paid to crop rotation to prevent the build-up of pests and diseases in the soil.

Tomatoes.

Crops for greenhouses and polytunnels

Many crops that fail or are unreliable under conditions where the summer is too short or cool can be successfully grown under greenhouse or polytunnel conditions. Tomatoes are a prized greenhouse crop, along with peppers and eggplants, saladings like lettuce and endive, cucumbers, Asian greens for stir-fry dishes, and even corn.

Many modern **cold frames** are made from polycarbonate materials, which are much more durable than glass. These materials make the frames less of a safety hazard for children, as there is far less chance of them being injured than if glass was used and accidentally broken.

Cold frames

Cold frames have long been popular with gardeners. They can be easily made in a range of sizes, and are a cheap alternative to large structures like greenhouses. Traditionally, they consist of a low, rectangular bottomless structure with wood or brick sides, and topped with one or more wood-framed windows, which are usually hinged so that they can be easily propped open in balmy weather. Lightweight, rigid plastic sheets are sometimes used now in place of glass windows. Timber-constructed cold frames can be placed on a brick or pebble base to ensure they do not rot. Lightweight commercial versions are available but home-made frames are quite often sturdier and offer better insulation. They are easily constructed from recycled materials. A finish with white paint ensures that the maximum light is reflected onto seedlings. Movable wooden frames can also be placed onto garden beds to protect crops.

While frames are most commonly used for seed and cutting propagation, larger ones can be used as they were in the past to raise cantaloupes in areas where they would not mature fruit in the open, and to produce extra early and late season salad greens. Frames should be located where there is good light in both spring and winter. When supplied with bottom heat, cold frames are known as hot frames.

Growing plants in cold frames

Seeds and cuttings can be started into growth 3–4 weeks earlier than if they were growing outside in the open. The frame will also keep the air humid around the tops of cuttings and prevent them from drying out. Some gardeners prefer to construct their own cold frame, either from the timber with a soil base or a brick-built frame with a concrete base and wooden lid with glass panels. These structures are excellent for protecting plants, but they are usually fixtures, and unless the frame is correctly sited, they can have limitations, such as lack of light at certain times of the year.

An alternative is to get a self-assembly "kit frame" available from many DIY centers. Most are made with materials that have good insulation properties while still allowing good light transmission, and are quite light and easy to move about the garden, giving the gardener greater flexibility.

Radicchio.

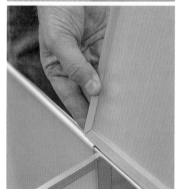

Constructing a cold frame from a kit

1 Remove the contents from the package and check that all the items listed on the assembly instructions sheet are present.

2 Using the corner clips provided, fit the grooved aluminium edges to the two lid sections (with the hinged bars at one end of each panel). Following the assembly instructions, fit the grooved aluminium edges to the top and bottom of each of the base panels (with the hinge bar on the top of the rear panel).

3 Using screws, fasten the corner brackets onto the side base panels. Make sure that they are fixed firmly into position before sliding the front and rear base panels into the corner brackets and fastening them into position using screws. Attach the lid to the frame's base by sliding the two hinge grooves together on the frame's rear panel. Repeat with the second section of the lid so that the frame is complete.

4 Fasten a spacing bar on to the lid of the frame (this is to allow the frame to be ventilated in gradual stages). Place the frame in its allotted position and add plants that need protection or shelter.

Cloches

Cloches are small, mobile greenhouses and they are only limited in form by ingenuity. Some are designed to cover single plants while others may enclose an entire row. Bell cloches, used popularly in Victorian times, were originally made of glass and shaped like large bottomless bottles.

Cloches are now quite often made of heavy clear plastic but can still be purchased in glass. A low-cost version is made from recycled plastic drink containers by cutting off the bases. The bottle's screw top is removed to allow heat to escape.

Tunnel cloches are popular, usually now made of corrugated clear plastic strengthened by supporting hoops, and wide enough to cover a row of vegetables or a garden bed. In general, traditional glass cloches offer better cold protection and allow better access to light, but plastic forms are cheaper and lighter.

Growing plants in a cloche

Cloches can be easily constructed on any sheltered area of the vegetable garden and are ideal for giving plants an early start in the spring. They can often promote growth up to 3 weeks ahead of unprotected plants. This type of temporary shelter can be important for protecting early vegetables from late spring frosts.

Some gardeners are put off using a cloche as they can look quite forbidding and difficult to use. However, if the cloche is well constructed and positioned, it should be quite easy to maintain your plants within it. When you need to tend your plants, simply lift up the plastic covering and remove the wire mesh.

As a precaution on sites that are particularly windy, it is best to position the cloche tunnel so that one end faces squarely into the prevailing wind. This will present a much smaller surface area to the wind than if the cloche is positioned side-on, making it less vulnerable. It is also much easier to reinforce the smaller ends of the tunnel than the sides.

In Victorian times, perfectly **miniaturized greenhouses** were devised and can still be purchased. Modern **cloches** are more simple A-frame structures or tunnels made from plastic.

Row or crop covers

Row covers or crop covers are the simplest of all forms of frost protection. They consist of lightweight fabrics that can be laid over the top of crops to provide protection against frost. They have the advantage of being easily applied and as easily removed in response to changing weather conditions, and can serve a secondary purpose in protecting crops from insect attack. Row covers can consist of long life, fine mesh plastic that will also exclude larger insect pests, or very fine gauge mist netting that will exclude small insect pests. Both allow good air flow. Fleece covers are also available and are the best option for frost protection. On the other hand, they are more opaque, cause excessive humidity and need to be replaced quite frequently. Row covers can be pegged down, or the edges weighted down with bricks or wooden boards. Row covers should be removed as soon as all danger of frost has passed unless being used as an insect barrier.

Make your own cloche

1 Place the prepared wire mesh sections over the plants to be protected, with the plants occupying the central position within the cloche. Position the sections together with their ends touching, adding as many sections as required to cover the row of plants.

2 Take a sheet of clear plastic, unfold it and draw it out over the wire mesh carefully, so that it does not tear. Allow at least 2 feet of surplus plastic at each end of the cloche.

3 At the sides of the cloche, lay down a section of 1 x 2 inch wooden batten drilled with holes at 1 foot intervals. Position these at the edges of the plastic. Anchor the plastic along one side of the cloche by pushing 6 inch nails or plastic pins through the holes and plastic into the soil below.

4 Stretch the plastic taut on the remaining side of the cloche and pin it down with battens, before cutting off any excess plastic. Gather up the surplus plastic at the ends of the cloche. Bury it in the soil or peg it down with pins and battens using the same method as on the sides of the cloche.

RADICCHIO
(*Cichorium intybus*)

PURPLE KALE
(*Brassica oleracea*)

ONION CHIVES
(*Allium schoenoprasum*)

cut and come again vegetables

The "cut and come again" method of growing vegetables will provide a continuous supply of certain perennial leafy greens. As the plants grow, harvest just the outside leaves of the plants, or cut off the tops of the leaves with scissors, leaving the rest of the plant to continue on growing in the ground, to be harvested again later.

PLAIN CHARD
(*Beta vulgaris* var. *cicla*)

WATER
SPINACH
(*Ipomoea aquatica*)

CHERVIL
(*Anthriscus cerefolium*)

WHITE
FRILLED KALE
(*Brassica oleracea*)

MIZUNA
(*Brassica juncea*)

ARUGULA
(Eruca vesicaria subsp. *sativa)*

WHITE CHARD
(Beta vulgaris var. *cicla)*

BABY ARUGULA
(Eruca vesicaria subsp. *sativa)*

RED CHARD
(Beta vulgaris
var. *cicla)*

**YELLOW
CHARD**
(Beta vulgaris
var. *cicla)*

**PURPLE
MUSTARD**
(Chorispora tenella)

**GARLIC
CHIVES**
(Allium tuberosum)

**CHICORY
FLOWER**
(Cichorium intybus)

CURLY ENDIVE
(Cichorium endivia)

ITALIAN PARSLEY
(Petroselinum crispum var.
neapolitanum)

**BELGIAN ENDIVE
"PANE DE SUCRE"**
(Cichorium endivia)

Vegetable gardens for dry areas

Gardeners in hot, dry climates have an abundance of sunshine although arid inland areas do have cool to cold nights. The greatest limiting factor for successfully raising vegetables is lack of water, and a three-pronged approach to drought-wise or xeriphytic gardening will ensure success.

Choosing vegetables

First, the right choice of vegetables is important. Becoming known as "xeric vegetables", these are cultivars that are promoted as drought-tolerant or drought-resistant. Water delivery systems that minimize water usage or, alternatively, watering regimes that encourage deep rooting into moister soil layers form the second approach to consider, and increasing the water-holding capacity of the soil provides the third.

Species that originate from areas with hot dry summers such as the Mediterranean Basin, the Middle East, and Mexico are likely to thrive in any part of the world with a comparable climate. They include vegetables such as artichokes, cardoons, many Mexican beans, peppers, chilies, eggplants, tomatoes, and corn.

Drought-tolerant cultivars

Search among old cultivars recommended by experienced farmers and gardeners in your district to find reliable performers. Joining organizations preserving and exchanging heirloom seeds is very worthwhile as it will give access to cultivars that have been reselected by many generations of farmers and gardeners to meet the most extreme demands of a particular climate. Often doing no more than changing over to these cultivars known to perform well in drought will ensure success.

Mulches are critical to success in dry climates. They can greatly reduce moisture loss from the soil.

Artichokes are considered the vegetable of the gods, especially beloved by the ancient Greek god, Zeus.

Growing tips

In arid areas or during prolonged droughts, encourage plants to explore deeply into the soil to reach cooler, moister soil levels. This can be done by reducing the intervals between watering once plants are well established, but watering deeply. Plants that are watered lightly and frequently have their root mass near the surface. This is the ideal for perennial vegetable crops. Annual vegetable crops rarely penetrate deeply into the soil, and drip irrigation is preferable. Recycled gray water can be critically useful in extreme drought, along with the collection of all rainwater via guttering and downpipes to holding tanks.

Drought-prone soils usually lack organic matter that acts in the soil like a sponge to hold moisture. Soil that is well enriched with compost will greatly reduce the water needs of the garden. If pumice stone is available, it makes an excellent natural addition to the soil as it is able to absorb any extra water and release it back to plants as the soil dries.

Mulches reduce the loss of moisture from the soil and suppress weeds, which steal water from crops. At the same time, they reduce daytime soil temperatures and hold in warmth absorbed from the sun, releasing it in the cool to cold night hours. Plants grow better when the root systems are exposed to less extreme daily fluctuations. Organic mulches such as hay or compost are ideal for garden beds. Keep mulches away from tree trunks to prevent collar rot and insect damage under the bark.

Disturb the soil as little as possible. Cultivation increases the rate of loss of moisture. Wind can also be a major factor in drying garden soil, and well placed windbreaks can counteract much of this problem.

Drought-tolerant vegetables

Artichoke
Cardoon
Chilies
Corn
Eggplant
Peppers
Tomato
Zucchini

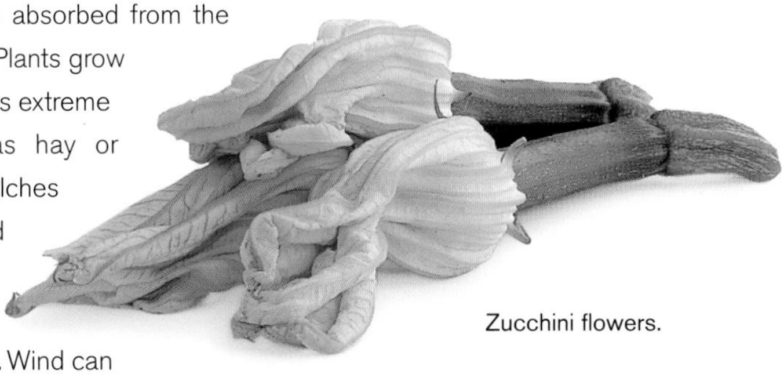

Zucchini flowers.

Taro plant and tubers.

Vegetables for tropical areas

Bush okra

Cassava

Collards

Ethiopian mustard

Jicama

Katuk

Malabar spinach

Tampala spinach

Taro

Tomato, wild and currant

Warrigal greens (New Zealand spinach)

Yam

Vegetable gardening in the tropics

Gardening at lower altitudes in the tropics is both a blessing and a curse. High humidity and summer temperatures combine with torrential seasonal rain. In the wet season, growth rates can be

Taro shoots.

astonishing but so too is the growth of weeds and pests. Other problems can include damage to soil structure, erosion of garden beds, severe storm damage, leaching of nutrients from the soil, and rapid decomposition of soil organic matter. In many tropical areas there is also a marked dry season. The illusion of gardening in paradise is short-lived for many gardeners.

A major problem for vegetable growers in the tropics lies in plant selection. Few of the vegetables originating from outside the tropics will thrive. But the tropical pantry is so rich in exciting flavors, with a tropical vegetable equivalent for all those used in milder regions, that the key is to grow only tropical species, or cultivars proven to succeed under tropical conditions. Many tropical food species have been selected over thousands of years and excellent cultivars exist.

Leafy vegetables substitutes

A variety of leafy vegetables is available to replace cabbages, spinach, and iceberg lettuce. Suitable substitutes include Malabar spinach (*Basella alba* and *B. rubra*), collards, Ethiopian kale, tampala spinach (*Amaranthus giganteus*), bush okra or jute mallow (*Corchorus olitorius*), and katuk (*Sauropus androgynous*), a staple vegetable in Borneo where it is grown as an edible hedge and the leaves, tips, and flowers used cooked or raw. Katuk tastes of green peas and is now being commercially grown in Hawaii, while Borneo is exporting it to Japan as "tropical asparagus". It has an astonishing growth rate, tolerates full sun to shade conditions, and seems to be virtually disease- and pest-free. Warrigal greens or New Zealand spinach (*Tetragonia tetragonioides*) is an excellent hot-climate spinach substitute that will continue to thrive in the dry season.

Some cultivars of true lettuce succeed well in the tropics. Almost all are open-hearted in form and include "Anuenue" (from Hawaii) and "Mairoba" from Brazil. "Montello" is an excellent hearting lettuce cultivar that has done well in many tropical areas including southern Florida and the Caribbean. Brazilian spinach (*Alternanthera sissoo*) is often preferred in Brazil to lettuce and is eaten in similar ways.

Other vegetables

Most modern tomatoes are exceedingly difficult to grow in the tropics, but the "wild tomato", a large vining type producing sweet, cherry-sized fruit in great abundance never fails and is remarkably pest and disease resistant. The currant tomato, a closely related species, is also highly productive.

Onions are more difficult to raise in the tropics as their growth pattern is day-length dependent. Short-day cultivars will form bulbs but long-day cultivars will only form small bulbs. In some tropical areas, gardeners raise onions as sets (baby onions) replanting them at the beginning of the rainy season to complete their growth.

Biennial vegetables, which normally complete their lifecycle over two growing seasons, often fail to develop or set seed in the tropics. Some tropical carrot cultivars have been identified that complete their seed to seed cycle in one season. Jicama, cassava (*Manihot esculenta*), taro (*Alocasia macrorrhiza*), yam (*Dioscorea* spp.), and sweet potatoes (*Ipomoea batatas*) are admirable substitutes for the cooler climate potato. Tropical corn cultivars are also readily available.

Cassava is a tropical vegetable and an admirable substitute for the cooler climate potato.

Growing tips for the tropics

Mounded beds are necessary for good drainage during the wet season, but tend to be flattened by heavy rain. Beds edged to a height of around 10 inches will hold soil in place. Tropical soils are easily denuded of organic material, becoming leached of vital nutrients and structureless after pounding rains. The regular addition of quantities of organic matter is essential to growing vegetables in the tropics, replacing both lost nutrients and humus in the soil. Inorganic fertilizers will do nothing to save the soil's structure, or its moisture and nutrient retentive properties. Mulches are also vital. Not only do they reduce soil temperatures and retain soil moisture in the dry season, but they reduce the impact of heavy rains on soil. Partially composted chopped palm and banana leaves are useful for this purpose. Weeds are also effectively suppressed by the use of mulches, a necessity as they can overwhelm a crop in a short period of time and incur much hard labor.

HARVESTING

AND USING

A bountiful harvest is the reward you reap for all your hard work. You can either feast on the freshly harvested vegetables or freeze, dry, bottle, or preserve them for later use, until your cupboards are bursting.

harvest time

Timing is everything

Naturally, you harvest each vegetable just when it is at its peak of maturity and flavor. Often this only lasts for quite a short period, and you may well have made successive small plantings so you have a series of harvests. This is a sensible practice, but with vegetables that freeze well, such as peas, beans, cauliflower, or Brussels sprouts, you may prefer to make one big planting, gather your harvest in all at once, and freeze what you don't need for the kitchen immediately.

How you choose to harvest and store your vegetables will make a difference to their quality and flavor.

Harvesting and storing

It is important that only the best of the crop are selected for storage, although produce with some marking or slight damage can still be used immediately. Any parts of the plant that are brown, wilted (when they are not supposed to be), damaged, or showing any signs of pest and disease damage should not be stored, as these problems may be transferred to the healthy plants in the store.

The harvesting and storage of vegetables will depend on a number of factors, particularly the climate and the type of vegetable. In cooler climates, where crops mature fairly slowly, it is possible to leave them growing and harvest them only when required, especially as many are not eaten until they reach maturity. Others, such as the salad types of vegetable that are harvested while semi-mature, are cut while they are still quite young.

The biggest problem, espeically with leafy vegetables or those that are harvested when quite young, is one of short-term storage; that is keeping the soft, edible tissue fresh and palatable until it is eaten.

Some vegetables, such as beans, cabbage, chilies, garlic, marrows, onions, peas, and tomaotes will keep quite well if they are stored in a dry condition and allowed to dry slowly in a cool, dry, frost-free place, but others will need to be kept in airtight containers.

Harvesting leafy vegetables

1 Start in the morning while the weather is still cool and, with a sharp knife, cut through the stem just above ground level and trim off any damaged or dirty leaves.
2 Wash the vegetables in cold water, and leave them in there for 30 minutes after they have been harvested. This will lower their temperature dramatically and prolong their keeping qualities.
3 Remove from the water, and allow to drain.
4 Store the vegetables in clear, open plastic bags and leave them in a cool, damp place, until required.

Gai choy.

Drying vegetables

1 Start by carefully removing the bean pods from the plant, using both your hands.

2 Place the bean pods in a tray or in a container of your choice. Leave them to dry in a dry, cool room. When the pods split, remove the seeds for storage.

Vegetables can be dried
outdoors in warm, dry, windy weather conditions for a period of 24–36 hours. Some vegetables suitable for drying include beans, beets, carrots, chilies, corn, mushrooms, okra, onions, peas, peppers, and winter squash.

Storing root vegetables

Many root vegetables are stored in boxes over winter to protect them from frost and, for convenience, these boxes are usually placed in sheds or cellars. It is often much easier to go and collect vegetables stored in this way than to go outdoors in winter weather to collect "field-stored" vegetables that have been stored in a clamp.

Boxes or barrels of slightly moist sand are used to keep produce fresh and to extend its storage life. Ideally, these containers should be kept in a frost-free place to protect their contents as much as possible. Vegetables stored in this way must be handled carefully to reduce the risk of bruising and any soil must be cleaned off the produce before it's stored. Soil left on the roots may contain fungal or bacterial spores, which can attack the produce and cause it to rot while it is in storage. Never store any vegetables that are showing signs of rotting or severe damage. These "suspect" vegetables will be a source of primary infection, causing rotting among the healthy plants, and should be discarded straight away. Use any lightly damaged vegetables as they will also rot quickly.

Beet

This colorful root vegetable, once highly valued by the ancient Greeks and Romans, is considered a caretaker of the immune system. Both the leaves and root are edible and packed with goodness. Beets should be harvested when they are about 1 inch in diameter. When removing the tops from the root, leave about 1 inch of stem attached to the root to prevent "bleeding".

Storing root vegetables in sand

1 Harvest the vegetables that are to be stored. Handling them carefully, brush off any loose soil. For vegetables such as beets, carrots, parsnips, and turnips, trim off leaves and stalks and remove any long, thin roots. Discard all vegetables that show any signs of rot or damage. Wash the vegetables to remove any remaining soil and leave them until the water has drained away, but the surface of the vegetable is still moist.

2 Place a sturdy container, such as a barrel or box, in a frost-free site, where the temperature is just above freezing. Cover the bottom of the container with a 4 inch layer of damp sand. Remove any stones or gravel to avoid them damaging the vegetables.

3 Place a layer of vegetables on the sand, with the root tips facing the corner of the container. Cover with a layer of sand, and another layer of vegetables. Make sure the vegetables are not touching one another, as this will help prevent the spread of fungal or bacterial rots. Place the largest vegetables at the bottom and smallest at the top (the smallest ones are prone to drying out and should be used first). Repeat this process until the container is filled to within 6 inches of the upper rim. Place at least 2 inches of sand between each layer of vegetables and the sides of the container.

4 Cover the topmost layer of vegetables with a 6 inch layer of damp sand. Gently pack the sand down to remove as much air as possible and lightly water it to form a surface crust or "seal" to reduce moisture loss. Check frequently to see if it is drying out. If it becomes too dry, gently moisten it with a fine spray from a watering can.

Keep the sand moist at all times. If it dries out it will draw the moisture out of the vegetables, causing them to desiccate and spoil. Plastic containers do not lose moisture as readily as wooden crates or boxes.

WHITE RADISH
(DAIKON)
(Raphanus sativus var. longipinnatus)

GALANGAL
(Alpinia galanga)

RADISH
(Raphanus sativus)

MINI ROUND
CARROT
(Daucus carota)

BEET
(Beta vulgaris)

PARSNIP
(Pastinaca sativa)

RED ONION
*(Allium cepa
Cepa Group)*

PURPLE CARROT
(Daucus carota)

NICOLA POTATO
(Solanum tuberosum)

GARLIC
(Allium sativum)

KOHLRABI
*(Brassica oleracea
Gongylodes Group)*

SWEET
POTATO
(Ipomoea batatas)

SCALLION
(*Allium fistulosum*)

SHALLOT
(*Allium cepa*)

BABY GARLIC
(*Allium sativum*)

RUTABAGA
(*Brassica napus*
Napobrassica Group)

FINGERLING
POTATO
(*Solanum tuberosum*)

YAM
(*Dioscorea* spp.)

tubers, roots, and bulbs

The underground part of a plant is easily overlooked, but can often be the most important component. In the world of vegetables, roots really come into their own, whether they are potato tubers, onion bulbs, or roots, such as carrots.

BEET
(*Beta vulgaris*)

GOLDEN
BEET
(*Beta vulgaris*)

BEET
(*Beta vulgaris*)

Vegetable storage clamp

The traditional method for storing root vegetables in cold areas is in a clamp or "pie". These are low mounds of vegetables, laid on a bed of loose straw for insulation, and encased in a layer of soil or sand to hold the straw in place and provide extra protection.

Parsnips.

These clamps can be made either outside on a well-drained site or under cover in a shed or outhouse. Although the storage conditions are very similar to those in the ground, a clamp is often more convenient. It is easier to remove vegetables from the storage clamp in severe cold weather when the ground is frozen than it is to dig them out of the soil in the vegetable plot.

Unfortunately, the amount of waste from rodents and rotting can be high. For extra protection, a clamp may be formed against a wall or hedge, and if long-term storage is your objective, choose a north-facing site if possible, as this will receive much less sunlight in the winter months.

Storing vegetables in a clamp

1 Clear and level the area of ground where the vegetables are to be stored (it is important to select a site with a free-draining soil).
2 Spread out a layer of dry, loose straw to cover the area to a depth of approximately 8 inches.
3 Build up a mound of vegetables on the straw to form a cone shape to the required height (carrots should not be stacked more than 2½ feet high). Once the mound of vegetables has reached the required height, cover the whole mound with a 6 inch layer of dry straw.
4 Cover the mound with a layer of soil about 4 inches deep. The soil is provided by digging a trench around the base of the clamp for drainage, and throwing the resulting soil up over the straw-covered mound.
5 Finally, firm the soil over the mound by patting it down with the back of a spade. This helps keep the straw dry and reduces the chances of rain washing the soil down from the top of the mound. Leave a small area of straw exposed at the top of the clamp, keeping the vegetables cooler.

Storing vegetables

Vegetable	Storage method
Artichoke, globe	Harvested buds will keep in a cool place for several weeks or in the refrigerator for no more than 2 weeks. Keep them dry in an airtight container or plastic bag.
Asparagus	Fresh asparagus will keep in the refrigerator for 7–10 days after being harvested. Break off the rough ends and stand upright in 1½ inches water.
Bean, fava	Freshly harvested pods will keep in the refrigerator for up to 2 weeks. Shelled beans can be dried, or preserved by bottling.
Bean, green climbing, dwarf	Do not wash the vegetable after harvest. Freshly picked beans will keep in the refrigerator for up to a week or they can be successfully bottled or pickled when mature.
Beet	Swollen roots of the beet will keep for up to 3 weeks in the refrigerator and the leaves for up to a week if stored in an airtight plastic bag. Roots can be pickled or bottled.
Belgian endive	Belgian endive does not store well and becomes limp soon after exposure to light. It may be kept in the refrigerator for a few days but a greening of the leaves from exposure to light indicates a developing bitter taste.
Broccoli	Heads will keep in the refrigerator for up to a week, after which broccoli gradually turns yellow and becomes tasteless.
Brussels sprouts	Early winter sprouts left on the stem and hung in a cool dry place will keep for up to a month. Singly harvested, they will keep for 7–10 days in the refrigerator. In both cases, first remove all the loose and discolored leaves from the plant and only wash the vegetables just before you are ready to use them.
Cabbage	Cabbage will keep for several weeks in the crisper compartment of the refrigerator. Pickled as sauerkraut, cabbage makes a delicious preserve.
Carrot	Like potatoes, carrots can be stored in the ground in cool winter areas. The soils must be kept well drained and not waterlogged. Leave the leafy tops attached. Once cropped, the top can be removed and the carrots stored in containers packed with dry sand. Keep stored in a cool position. Carrots will also keep crisp in the refrigerator for 4 weeks or so if protected in plastic bags. They are delicious if pickled or bottled.
Cauliflower	Heads will keep for up to a week in the refrigerator.
Celery	Celery stalks will keep crisp for up to 10 days in the refrigerator. Leaves can be dried and chopped and used as a dried herb for flavoring purposes. Seeds are also dried and used in soups and pickles.
Chayote	Freshly picked chayote will keep in the vegetable crisper of the refrigerator for 1–2 weeks.

Vegetable	Storage method
Chilies	Keep in a cool, dark place for up to a week or in a sealed container in the refrigerator for 3 weeks. Chilies are also excellent when dried.
Chinese cabbage (wong bok)	Keeps fresh in the refrigerator for several weeks, even months, in cool, dry places such as a cellar. When ready to use, discard outer discolored and battered leaves to reveal firm, central head. Never store in plastic bags.
Chinese kale (gai larn)	Keeps in crisper compartment of the refrigerator for up to a week.
Chinese spinach (amaranth)	Leaves go limp soon after harvesting. Young shoot thinnings are best eaten straight away and are good in salads. Older leaves can be stored in refrigerator crisper but will not keep for more than a few days. Steam or cook in the same way that you would cook other leafy vegetables.
Corn	Corn contains lots of sugar when it is harvested. The sugar soon turns to starch and the vegetable loses a great deal of its flavor, so freshly picked corn should be eaten as soon as possible. Storing in the refrigerator for a couple of days will slow down the sugar loss. Alternatively, kernels can be stripped from the cob and then snap frozen.
Cucumber	Will keep in refrigerator for 7–10 days but at very cold temperatures the flesh will turn soft and translucent, rendering the cucumber inedible. It is ideal for pickling, especially if fruit is picked when young, at the "gherkin" stage and 2–2¾ inches in length.
Eggplant	Recently cropped fruit will keep for 7–10 days in a cool spot. It is ideal for pickling.
Endive	Will keep for up to 2 weeks in the crisper compartment of the refrigerator, the inner leaves being best for salads.
Fennel	Fennel leaves do not keep for more than a couple of days in the refrigerator.
Garlic	Leaves are left attached to the bulb then left to dry in clumps in full sun for a few days. On no account let bulbs get wet. Move inside if rain threatens. Hang in an open mesh bag in a dry, airy position.
Ginger	Mature rhizomes store well in cool dry places. If stored in the natural state for too long, however, the flesh will become dry and the flavor turns toward bitterness. Dried ginger can be ground into powder.
Jerusalem artichoke	As with other root crops, the simplest method of storing is to leave the tuber in the ground, digging up only when necessary and thus having a ready supply out of season. Harvested vegetables will keep for a month in dark, cool places away from intense cold. Pack into boxes and surround tubers with peat moss.
Kohlrabi	Bulbs can be stored in the refrigerator for 7–10 days.

Vegetable	Storage method
Leek	Will keep 7–10 days in the refrigerator.
Lettuce	Will keep 7–10 days in the crisper section of the refrigerator.
Marrow	Handle carefully and do not wash or brush skin of the fruit before usage to prevent skin damage. Marrow will keep for up to a week in the refrigerator.
Mushroom	Mushrooms can be stored in the refrigerator (not in plastic bags or they will sweat) for around 5–7 days. They can also be dried or pickled and stored in bottles.
Okra	Pods may be used fresh or dried. They are widely used as a flavoring in soups and in meat cooking, or can be fried or boiled and eaten as a vegetable.
Onion	Store bulbs in a cool, dry place in an open-weave mesh basket to allow free air circulation around them. Do not store close to other vegetables.
Parsnip	Parsnips can be kept in the ground 2–3 months after reaching maturity in cool to cold climates, but see that beds are kept reasonably dry during this storage period. Low temperatures convert starches to sugars giving a sweet root. Freshly cropped vegetables will keep in refrigerator 2–3 weeks, slightly less in cool dry cupboards where they tend to lose their firmness.
Pea	Pods keep for a short time in the refrigerator. The seeds will lose a great deal of their sugar content within a few days, converting it to starch.
Pepper	Peppers will keep for up to a week in the refrigerator. They can also be broiled or baked and, with the skins and seeds removed, preserved in spicy vinegars. Hot peppers can be dried successfully.
Potato	Keep crop in a cool, dark airy place and exclude sunlight to prevent skin becoming tinged with green. Young or "new" potatoes will not store for long periods.
Radish	Radish will keep for a week to 10 days in the crisper section of the refrigerator.
Rutabaga	These have a long storage time and can be kept in or out of the refrigerator.
Shallot	Bulbs will keep in a cold, dry place for several months or the flesh may be chopped and frozen similarly to onions.
Snow pea	Pods keep for a short time in the refrigerator
Spinach	Spinach leaves keep in the refrigerator for up to a week but are better eaten immediately.
Squash	Handle carefully and do not wash or brush skin of fruit before usage to prevent skin damage. They will keep for up to a week in the refrigerator.
Sugar snap pea	Pods keep for a short time in the refrigerator. The seeds will lose a great deal of their sugar content within a few days, converting it to starch.

Vegetable	Storage method
Sweet potato	Very easy vegetable to store but do not wash before putting away. Will keep for at least 4 months in this condition. Do not store in refrigerated conditions below 50°F.
Swiss chard	Swiss chard will keep for up to 2 weeks in the crisper drawer of the refrigerator but it is best eaten when freshly picked before the leaves become limp.
Tomato	Tomatoes will keep between 2–4 weeks in the refrigerator although they tend to lose their flavor over long periods. They can be pulped then bottled or processed into soups and sauces and frozen. Tomatoes are best left at room temperature.
Turnip	Turnips do not store as long as rutabagas but, like them, can be kept in or out of the refrigerator.
Water chestnut	Examine the vegetable for rotten spots and remove damaged corms. The unpeeled crop will keep in bags in the refrigerator for up to 2 weeks. If peeled in advance of use, store in cold water in the refrigerator to prevent browning, again for up to 2 weeks, but water must be changed daily. Chestnuts can be dried and ground to a flour. Commercial crops are cooked and preserved by canning—flavor and texture being lost in the process.
White radish (daikon)	If the root has developed a hollowness inside, it will not store long, but generally will keep in the refrigerator at very low temperatures for several weeks. White radishes can be eaten raw, cooked, dried, pickled, fermented, or preserved in brine.
Winter squash	Handle carefully and do not wash or brush skin of fruit before storing. It will keep for several months in a cool, airy place or in boxes. Check occasionally for rotting or damage to skin and flesh by vermin.
Zucchini	Handle carefully and do not wash or brush the skin of fruit before usage. They will keep for up to a week in the refrigerator.

Freezing vegetables

Vegetable	Freezing method
Artichoke, globe	Remove outer leaves. Wash, trim stalks and remove "chokes" and blanch them, a few at a time, for 7 minutes. Cool in iced water for 7 minutes; drain. Pack in freezer bags, remove air from bags, then seal and label. Freeze for up to 6 months.
Asparagus	Wash and remove woody portions and scales of spears, then cut into 6 inch lengths and blanch in boiling water for 3 minutes. Cool in iced water for 3 minutes; drain. Place on a tray in a single layer and freeze for 30 minutes. Pack into suitable containers, then seal and label. Freeze for up to 6 months.
Bean, fava	Shell beans and after washing blanch in boiling water for 1½ minutes. Cool in iced water for 1–2 minutes. Place on a tray in a single layer and freeze for 30 minutes. Pack into freezer bags, remove air, then seal and label. Freeze for up to 6 months.
Bean, green climbing, dwarf	Remove any strings and top and tail. Blanch for 2 minutes and cool in iced water for 2 minutes. Drain, spread on tray in a single layer, then freeze for 30 minutes. Pack into freezer bags, remove air from bags, then seal and label. Freeze for up to 6 months.
Beet	Only freeze young tender beets, not more than 2–3 inches across. Cook until tender and slice, chop, or leave whole. Cool and transfer to plastic containers, cover with lids, then label. Freeze for up to 6 months.
Belgian endive	Wash well. Blanch for 3 minutes. Drain, place on a tray in a single layer, then freeze for 30 minutes. Pack into plastic bags, remove air, then seal and label, or pack in containers leaving some space at top. Freeze for 2–3 months.
Broccoli	Choose tender young heads with no flowers and tender stalks. Wash well and divide into sprigs. Blanch for 3 minutes in boiling water. Cool in iced water for 3 minutes. Drain and spread on a tray in a single layer. Cover with plastic wrap to stop the strong smell of broccoli penetrating the freezer, and freeze for 30 minutes. Pack in freezer bags, remove air from bags, then seal and label. Freeze for up to 6 months.
Brussels sprouts	Remove outer leaves and cut a cross at the stem end of sprout. Wash thoroughly and then blanch for 3 minutes. Cool in iced water for 3 minutes, then drain and spread on tray in a single layer. Cover with plastic wrap to prevent strong odor of sprouts penetrating the freezer. Freeze for 30 minutes, then remove from tray and pack into plastic bags. Remove air from bags, then seal and label. Freeze for up to 6 months.

Vegetable	Freezing method
Cabbage	Remove outer leaves and wash the remainder. Cut into thin wedges or shred. Blanch for 1½ minutes if shredded, or 2 minutes if cut into wedges. Chill in iced water for 1–2 minutes. Drain and pack in freezer bags, then seal and label. Freeze for up to 6 months.
Carrot	Wash and scrub carrots and cut large carrots into pieces. Blanch for 3 minutes in boiling water. Chill in iced water for 3 minutes; drain well. Spread on a tray in a single layer and freeze for 30 minutes. Pack in freezer bags, remove air from bags, then seal and label. Freeze for up to 6 months.
Cauliflower	Divide into florets and wash. Blanch for 3 minutes in boiling water. Chill in iced water for 3 minutes. Drain and place on a tray in a single layer. Cover with plastic wrap to prevent strong odor of cauliflower penetrating the freezer. Freeze for 30 minutes. Transfer to freezer bags, remove air from bags, then seal and label. Freeze for up to 6 months.
Celery	Use young tender stalks. Remove any string, then wash and cut into 1 inch pieces. Blanch for 2 minutes in boiling water. Chill in iced water for 2 minutes. Drain and place on a tray in a single layer. Freeze for 30 minutes. Pack freezer bags, remove air, then label and seal. Freeze for up to 6 months.
Chayote	Cook sliced chayotes until tender in boiling water. Drain well, then mash and cool. Pack into plastic containers with well-fitting lids, leaving space at the top. Freeze. Alternatively, roast the whole chayote, with seeds removed, in a moderate oven until just tender. Cool, pack in containers (leaving room at the top), then seal and label. Freeze for up to 6 months.
Chilies	Remove seeds, wash, dry, and spread on a tray in a single layer. Freeze 30 minutes, pack in freezer bags, remove air, then seal and label. Freeze for up to 6 months.
Chinese cabbage (wong bok)	Only freeze crisp and young cabbage. Wash and shred finely. Blanch for 1½ minutes. Chill in iced water for 1–2 minutes. Drain, place in freezer bags, then seal and label. Freeze for up to 6 months.
Chinese kale (gai larn)	Remove any coarse leaves and thick stems. Wash and blanch in boiling water for 2 minutes. Chill in iced water for 2 minutes. Drain and spread on a tray in a single layer for 30 minutes. Pack in freezer bags, remove air, then seal and label. Freeze for up to 6 months.
Chinese spinach (amaranth)	Wash and trim leaves off stalks. Blanch for 1 minute. Chill in iced water for 1 minute. Drain, pack in freezer bags and remove air from bags; seal and label. Freeze for up to 6 months.
Corn	Remove leaves and threads and cut off top of cob. Wash, blanch a few cobs at a time for 5–7 minutes, depending upon size. Chill in iced water for 5–7 minutes, drain, then wrap each cob in plastic wrap. Pack wrapped cobs in freezer bags, remove air from bags, then seal and label. Freeze for up to 6 months.

Vegetable	Freezing method
Cucumber	Peel and chop in food processor. Pack into plastic containers with well-fitting lids, then seal and label. Freeze for up to 3 months.
Eggplant	Cut into slices, sprinkle with salt and allow to stand for 20 minutes. Drain off excess liquid and fry eggplant gently in butter or margarine until just tender. Cool, pack in plastic containers, then seal and label. Will freeze for up to 3 months.
Endive	Do not freeze.
Fennel	Use fresh young stalks. Wash thoroughly. Blanch for 3 minutes. Chill in iced water for 3 minutes. Drain, pack in freezer bags, then seal and label. Will freeze for up to 6 months.
Garlic	Place cloves, separated from bulbs, in freezer bags. Remove any excess air from bag, then seal and label. Freeze for up to 3 months.
Ginger	Separate ginger into convenient-sized knobs. Place in freezer bags. Remove excess air from bags, then seal and label. Freeze for up to 6 months.
Jerusalem artichoke	Peel and slice. Place in cold water with the juice of ½ lemon to prevent discoloration. Blanch for 2 minutes in boiling water. Cool in iced water for 2 minutes. Drain and spread on a tray in a single layer. Freeze for 30 minutes. Pack into freezer bags, remove air, then seal and label and label. Freeze for up to 6 months.
Kohlrabi	Wash well, peel and cut into pieces. Blanch for 3 minutes. Chill in iced water for 3 minutes. Drain and spread on a tray in a single layer. Freeze for 30 minutes. Pack in freezer bags, remove air, then seal and label. Freeze for up to 6 months.
Leek	Remove tough outer leaves, wash remainder. Cut away green part of stem, slice white flesh, or cut in half lengthwise. Blanch 2 minutes (slices), or 3 minutes (halves); chill in iced water 2–3 minutes. Freeze on trays in single layer 30 minutes. Remove, pack in freezer bags, expel air, then seal and label. Freeze for up to 6 months.
Lettuce	Do not freeze.
Marrow	Peel, cut into pieces and cook in boiling water until just cooked. Cool and place in freezer bags, remove air from bags, seal and label. Alternatively, bake in oven until almost cooked. Cool, package in freezer bags, then seal and label. Freeze for up to 3 months.
Mushroom	Cultivated mushrooms need no preparation. Pack clean mushrooms in freezer bags. Remove air from bags, then seal and label. Freeze for up to 6 months.
Okra	Wash well and trim off stems. Blanch in boiling water for 3–4 minutes. Cool in iced water for 3–4 minutes, drain and pack in freezer bags. Remove air from bags, the seal and label. Freeze for up to 6 months.

Vegetable	Freezing method
Onion	Peel, chop, or cut into rings. Wrap in layers of plastic wrap, place in a plastic container. Label and freeze for up to 3 months. Alternatively, package small onions in their skins in freezer bags. Remove air from bags, then seal and label. Freeze for up to 3 months.
Parsnip	Peel and dice. Blanch for 2 minutes, chill in iced water for 2 minutes, then spread on a tray and freeze for 30 minutes. Pack into freezer bags, remove air, then seal and label. Freeze for up to 6 months.
Pea	Shell, wash, and blanch for 1 minute. Chill in iced water for 1 minute, drain, then spread on a tray. Freeze for 30 minutes. Pack into freezer bags, remove air, then seal and label. Freeze for up to 6 months.
Pepper	Wash, remove seeds, and cut into slices or leave whole. Place on a tray in a single layer. Freeze for 30 minutes. Pack in freezer bags, remove air, then seal and label. Freeze for up to 6 months.
Potato	There are a number of ways of freezing potatoes: **1** Scrub new potatoes. Cook in boiling water until almost cooked. Drain, cool, pack in freezer bags. Seal, label, and freeze for up to 6 months. **2** Prepare fries and deep fry for about 4 minutes until cooked, but not brown. Drain and cool on paper towels. Place on a tray in a single layer and freeze for 30 minutes. Pack in freezer bags, remove air, then seal and label. Freeze for up to 3 months. **3** Potatoes may also be mashed or prepared as Duchesse Potatoes and then frozen for up to 3 months.
Radish	Do not freeze.
Rutabaga	Only use tender, young rutabagas. Cut to required size and blanch for 3 minutes. Chill in iced water for 3 minutes. Drain, place pieces on a tray in a single layer, then freeze for 30 minutes. Pack in freezer bags, remove air, then seal and label. Freeze for up to 6 months.
Shallot	Separate cloves from bulb. Place in freezer bags; remove excess air. Freeze for up to 3 months.
Snow pea	Use tender pods. Wash and top and tail. Blanch for 30 seconds. Chill in iced water for 30 seconds. Drain, pack in freezer bags, remove air, then seal and label. Freeze for up to 6 months.
Spinach	Wash well and trim leaves off stalks, blanch in small quantities in boiling water for 1 minute. Chill in iced water for 1 minute, drain, then pack in plastic bags or containers; seal and label. Will freeze for up to 6 months.

Vegetable	Freezing method
Squash	Peel and cook in boiling salted water until tender. Mash, cool, and pack into freezer containers leaving room at the top for expansion. Seal and label. Freeze for up to 3 months.
Sugar snap pea	Remove pods, then wash and blanch for 1 minute. Chill, drain, and spread on a tray. Freeze for 30 minutes, then pack in plastic bags. Remove air from bags, then seal and label. Will freeze for up to 6 months.
Sweet potato	After scrubbing and peeling, bake or roast until just tender. Drain on paper towel and cool. Pack into plastic bag or container. If using plastic bags ensure that air is removed before sealing. Label and date. Will freeze for up to 3 months.
Swiss chard	Wash well and trim leaves from stalks. Blanch in small quantities of boiling water for 1 minute. Chill in iced water 1 minute, drain, then pack in freezer bags or containers. Remove air from plastic bags, label and date bags or containers, then freeze. Will freeze for up to 6 months.
Tomato	There are various ways of freezing tomatoes. **1** Wash, remove stems, then cut into halves or quarters or leave whole. Dry and pack into freezer bags. Remove air, then seal and label. Freeze for up to 6 months. **2** Dip into boiling water for 1 minute, remove, and peel. Place whole tomatoes on a tray and freeze for 30 minutes. Place in plastic bags, remove air, then seal and label. Freeze for up to 6 months. **3** Simmer chopped tomatoes in a pan for 5 minutes or until soft. Push through a sieve or food mill to remove skins and seeds. Cool, then pack in plastic containers, leaving space at the top of container. Freeze up to 6 months.
Turnip	Peel and trim young, tender turnips. Cut to required size and blanch for 3 minutes, then chill in iced water for 3 minutes. Drain, place pieces on a tray in a single layer, and freeze for 30 minutes. Pack into plastic bags, remove air, then seal and label. Freeze for up to 6 months.
Water chestnut	Bring chestnuts to the boil. Drain and peel off shells. Pack in freezer bags or plastic containers, remove air, then seal and label. Freeze for up to 6 months.
White radish (daikon)	Do not freeze.
Winter squash	Peel and cook in boiling salted water until tender. Mash, cool, then pack into plastic containers, leaving headspace. Freeze for up to 3 months. Alternatively, peel and cut into pieces. Bake until almost cooked. Pack into freezer bags when cool, remove the air, then seal and label. Will freeze for up to 3 months.
Zucchini	Slice into 1 inch slices without peeling, then sauté gently in a little melted butter until barely tender. Cool, then pack into plastic containers, leaving space at the top of the container. Freeze for up to 3 months.

The fruits of your labor finally make it to the dinner table. Your vegetables will be absolutely fresh and juicy, with all the advantages of flavor and nutrition that home-growing provides. You will definitely feel it was well worth the effort.

eat the garden

Cooking vegetables

Vegetables offer a nutritious and tasty way to balance the diet and provide many of the vitamins and minerals essential to health. Nature ensures variety because a different vegetable will reach its peak cropping time every month of the year. Let the seasons be your guide to cheap flavorsome food.

The cooking times of vegetables vary according to the method used and the quality, size, quantity, and freshness of the vegetables. Wherever possible, cook vegetables in their skins for extra good health.

Boil artichokes with the juice of 1 lemon for 40 minutes. Serve with a vinaigrette of lemon juice, olive oil, finely chopped onion, and finely chopped parsley.

Artichoke

Baby artichokes may be eaten whole, even raw in salads; a more mature bud may be stuffed, quartered, boiled, or fried; and finally, as a large artichoke, it may be boiled and eaten one leaf at a time (suck or scrape the flesh off the fibrous base with your teeth), dipped into vinaigrette or hollandaise sauce. In all but the baby artichoke, care must be taken to discard the prickly choke, above the fleshy (and delicious) base, also known as the heart. Choose heavy artichokes with firm heads and stems, and leaves that are tightly overlapping.

When preparing artichokes, rub the cut surfaces with lemon or vinegar to stop them from turning brown. Always cut artichokes with a stainless steel knife to avoid staining the flesh. It's also important to wash your hands after handling the stem as it gives off a bitter flavor.

Asparagus

Asparagus shoots need to be cooked with care so as not to damage the fragile tips: stand them upright in a special asparagus steamer (which allows the spears to cook in water and the tips to cook in steam), or lie them flat in a large pan filled with lightly salted water. Once cooked, serve asparagus with melted butter and Parmesan, or add to risottos, quiches, stir-fries, or salads. Fresh asparagus has firm, bright green spears with tight tips. Check the cut ends are not split or dried out.

Types of asparagus

Green This is the most common type of asparagus and is cut above ground when the shoots are 6 inches long.

White White asparagus is cut while the asparagus is below the ground (the lack of light prevents it from producing chlorophyll and turning green). It is more tender than the green variety and is popular in parts of Europe. Before cooking, white asparagus needs to be peeled up to the tip as the skin is tough.

Purple Purple when fresh, this type turns green when cooked.

Sprue Young, thin asparagus.

Asparagus with Parmesan

Steam or boil asparagus until tender. Serve with butter and shavings of Parmesan.

Green beans.

Beans

Green beans are native to tropical America and were cultivated in Mexico and Peru more than 7,000 years ago. There are hundreds of varieties and they can be steamed, boiled, stir-fried, or cooked for use in salads. Cook beans in plenty of lightly salted water until they are just tender.

Types of beans

Fava beans Also known as broad beans, young fava beans can be eaten in their pods like snow peas, but as they get older, the pods become tougher. Older beans need to be removed from their pods before cooking and should also be double-podded to remove the gray skins. To do this, blanch them for a couple of minutes, drain, then cool under running cold water, then slip off the skins. When buying fava beans, remember that most of the weight is the pods, which you will be throwing away. Frozen fava beans are also available.

Runner beans These flat beans should snap crisply when fresh, and most need to be stringed down each side unless they are very young. Though it is common to chop or slice the beans before cooking, this will cause the nutrients to leach out during cooking.

Yard-long beans Also known as snake beans, these long beans are like green beans and are generally sold in bundles. Often used in Asian cuisine.

Green beans Also known as French beans and string beans, these are usually fine, thin green beans, but they are also available in yellow waxy pods, purple or cream pods, and green and purple pods. Make sure the pods snap crisply to check for freshness.

Cranberry beans Popular whether dried or fresh, cranberry beans have distinguishable cream and red pods with beans the same color. Cranberry beans are popular in Italy where they are mainly used in soups or stewed with olive oil and garlic as a side dish.

Mung beans Small, olive-green beans sold dried as pulses or after the seed has sprouted as mung bean sprouts. As a pulse, mung beans may be cooked in soups and casseroles or in purées. The Chinese use the sprouts in sweet cakes or ferment them to make sauces. In Southeast Asia, mung beans are ground to make a flour used for sweets and doughs. The starch is used for making fine thread noodles.

Braised green beans

In a large frying pan, fry 1 chopped onion with 1 crushed garlic clove in 3 tablespoons olive oil, until soft. Add 1 pound green beans and fry. Add a 13 ounce can chopped tomatoes and simmer until the beans are tender. Season well. Serves 4.

Beet goes with balsamic vinegar, chives, orange, potato, sherry, and sour cream.

Beet

Native to the Mediterranean beet, or beetroot, is a root vegetable originally cultivated for its young leaves, but now grown for its sweet-flavored, purple-red root.

When cooking beets, take care to prevent them from bleeding. Don't cut or peel before they are cooked, and wash them carefully to prevent the skin breaking. Beet is remarkably versatile: grate it raw and add to salads; bake, steam, or boil it; or purée it with oil and spices to make a dip. It is also used to make the eastern European soup, borscht. Cook and use the leaves as you would spinach: blanch them and add to soups, salads, or pasta sauces. Store beets in the crisper drawer of the fridge for up to 2 weeks, and 1–2 days for the leaves.

Beet mash

Boil beets until tender (this can take up to 2 hours), rub off the skins, then mash with an equal quantity of cooked potatoes. Season. Add chopped chives and a knob of butter. Serve with fish, chicken, or meat.

Broccoli

Broccoli can be eaten raw, steamed, or boiled, and the stalks, which are quite sweet, can be peeled and diced and used in the same way as the florets. Drain well before serving as the florets hold lots of water.

Roast broccoli

Toss 1¾ pounds broccoli florets in 1 tablespoon ground cumin, 1 tablespoon ground coriander, 5 crushed garlic cloves, 2 teaspoons chlli powder, and 4 tablespoons oil. Spread out the broccoli on a baking sheet and roast at 400°F for 20 minutes, or until cooked through. Serves 4.

Brussels sprouts

Brussels sprouts can be steamed or boiled, or shredded and used in a stir-fry. To boil them, remove the outer leaves and soak in salted water for a few minutes to remove any bugs. Cooking in lots of boiling water with the lid off helps them to stay green.

Brussels sprouts with bacon

Fry 13 ounces shredded Brussels sprouts in a little oil until tender. Add 4 finely chopped bacon slices and fry together until crisp. To serve, season with pepper and sprinkle a few chopped almonds over the Brussels sprouts. Serves 4.

Cabbage

This stalwart vegetable is a member of a family that includes cauliflower, broccoli, Brussels sprouts, and many Asian greens. There are loose-leaved and -hearted varieties of cabbages. Loose-leaved cabbages tend to be green or tinged with red, and firm cabbages are red, white, or green. White-hearted cabbages are good raw and shred easily; green wrinkly savoy cabbages can be eaten steamed or boiled as a vegetable.

Cabbage can be grated finely and eaten raw in coleslaw or salads; it can be cooked in stir-fries, braised, steamed, or added to soups. Cabbage leaves can be used to wrap fillings, or the whole cabbage can be stuffed and baked. Red cabbage, when shredded and cooked with onions, stock, red wine, and vinegar, is a classic accompaniment to game and pork dishes. Cabbage is also shredded and salted to make sauerkraut. Sauerkraut should be rinsed and drained before use to remove any excess salt.

The hard white core in the center of the cabbage can be tough and should be removed before cooking. Cut into quarters, then cut off the base of each quarter to remove the core.

Red and white cabbage.

Don't cook cabbage for too long or in lots of boiling water as this causes it to lose its color and nutrients, as well as giving off a sulphurous smell. Adding a bay leaf to the cooking water may help with the smell. To prevent red cabbage from turning gray, cut it with a stainless steel knife. You can also add a little lemon juice or vinegar to the cooking water, or sprinkle it over the leaves if using raw.

Cabbages are regarded as one of the health super foods. They contain a number of therapeutic compounds. Cabbage also contains antiviral and antibacterial compounds that are useful for infection fighting.

Coleslaw

Toss together 7 ounces finely shredded white cabbage and 2 grated carrots. Mix in 5 tablespoons mayonnaise with 2 teaspoons French mustard and 2 teaspoons sugar. Season well. Serves 4.

Carrot

New crop or baby carrots are best for eating raw in salads and only need to be cleaned with a stiff brush before use. Remove their fine green tops for longer storage. Larger, older carrots are best peeled and cooked. They can be steamed and served with butter, used in soups, puréed, or added to sweet dishes such as cakes and muffins.

Vichy carrots

Peel 1¾ pounds young carrots and cut into thin rounds. Put in a shallow pan, just cover with water, and add 1½ teaspoons each salt and sugar and a knob of butter. Cover and cook over low heat until carrots are nearly tender, then remove the lid and boil until any remaining liquid evaporates. Serve sprinkled with finely chopped parsley and small knobs of butter. Serves 4.

Revive limp **carrots** by soaking them in iced water for 30 minutes.

Cauliflower cheese

Steam a whole head of cauliflower until tender, then cut into quarters and put in a baking dish. Melt 1½ tablespoons butter in a saucepan, add ¼ cup flour. Mix and cook until bubbling then add 1¼ cups milk off the heat and whisk well. Return to the heat and simmer for 2 minutes. Add 1¼ cups grated cheese to the milk and mix in. Season, then pour the sauce over the cauliflower, sprinkle with a little extra cheese, and place under a hot broiler until golden and bubbling. Serves 6.

Cauliflower

A member of the cabbage family, the cauliflower has a large head of tight flower buds (known as "curds"). Cauliflowers are usually creamy white, but there are also green and purple varieties, as well as miniature ones. Cauliflower can be eaten raw as crudités or steamed, boiled, stir-fried, pickled, or used in soups. Remove the leaves and store in the vegetable crisper in the fridge.

Prepare florets or the whole cauliflower by soaking it in salted water to get rid of any bugs. Cook in a non-aluminum saucepan (aluminum reacts with cauliflower and can turn it yellow). Cauliflower can be steamed or boiled, but steaming is better as it keeps the florets intact. If cooking a whole cauliflower, cut a cross in the base of the stalk or cut out the core to help it cook evenly.

Cauliflower contains a natural chemical that breaks down into a sulphur compound when cooked. To prevent this, cook until just tender with a bay leaf—the longer it cooks, the stronger the smell will become.

Celeriac

A winter vegetable, also known as celery root or knob celery, celeriac is a type of celery but, unlike celery, only the knobby root is eaten. To prepare celeriac, peel and cut it into cubes or strips. The flesh discolors on contact with air, so soak or cook celeriac in water with a squeeze of lemon juice to prevent this.

Celeriac can be eaten raw in salads, or used in soups and stews. Cooked and mashed with garlic and potatoes, it is perfect served with game or meat. For better storage, remove the leaves and store celeriac in the crisper drawer of the fridge for up to 1 week.

Celery

Celery is grown for its stalks, roots, and seeds. The ancient Greeks, Egyptians, and Romans used wild celery for its medicinal properties and used celery leaves, like bay leaves, to crown their victorious athletes. In the sixteenth century, the first cultivated form of celery was developed, and was usually eaten cooked.

Celery grows as a cluster of long ridged stalks, which vary in color from white to green. Celery stalks are often grown under cover to prevent them from becoming too dark and too strong in flavor. Celery stalks are eaten raw in salads, as crudités, cooked and served as a vegetable, braised in tomato or cream, or used as a base flavor in stocks and sauces. Celery leaves are used in soups, such as cream of celery, and the tender inner leaves can be used in salads or eaten with the stalk.

Celery has a high water content so it should be stored in the crisper drawer of the fridge wrapped in plastic. To revive wilted celery, sprinkle it with water and put it in the fridge until it becomes crisp again.

Celeriac remoulade

In a bowl mix 14 ounces coarsely grated celeriac, 5 tablespoons mayonnaise, 2 tablespoons mustard, and 2 tablespoons baby capers. Season; add lemon juice to taste. Serve the remoulade with bread or as a vegetable with meat dishes. Serves 4.

Celeriac root and celeriac remoulade.

Waldorf salad

Featuring celery and apples in mayonnaise, the Waldorf salad was created at the end of the nineteenth century at New York's Waldorf-Astoria hotel.

Endive

Not one but a group of leafy vegetables cultivated from European wild endive, all of which share differing degrees of bitterness. Endive vary from long-leaved varieties, through the various radicchios to the Belgian endive type, which is blanched (grown in the dark) to control the bitterness. Leafy endive is good in salads and Belgian endive can be broiled, braised in stock, and caramelized.

Cook endive in stock until tender, drain well, then barbecue or broil it until browned and caramelized, or fill a cooked pastry case with endive cooked in stock and drained, sprinkle with blue cheese, drizzle with cream and cook until heated through. All types of endive can be used as salad leaves but bear in mind their bitterness and use in moderation.

Radicchio is the Italian name for red endive. There are several varieties, but two of the most common sold in Italy are rosso di Verona, a pink, flower-like endive that looks similar to a round cabbage and is usually called radicchio in other countries, and rossa di Treviso, deep red and creamy streaked and usually called red endive elsewhere. Red endive is not as bitter as white, and it adds wonderful color to salads. Sauté lightly in olive oil and balsamic vinegar.

Belgian endive.

Corn fritters.

Corn

Corn is usually yellow but can also be blue, red, white, orange, and purple. Blue corn may be ground into flour and used to make corn chips and tortillas.

When cooking corn, do not salt the water as it stops the kernels softening as quickly. Cook in slightly sweetened water or add a little milk to retain flavor and softness.

To remove the kernels from corn, stand the cob on one end and slice downwards, as close to the cob as possible. To barbecue, strip back the husk and remove the silk, then replace the husk and soak it briefly in water. The husk will burn off as it cooks. This will stop the corn from burning.

Corn fritters

Mix 1 cup cornmeal with ¼ cup plain flour, 1 teaspoon bicarbonate of soda, and 2 cups milk. Stir in 1½ cups corn kernels, 1 tablespoon melted butter, and 1 tablespoon finely chopped scallions. Whisk 2 egg whites until soft peaks form and stir in. Season well. Heat some oil in a frying pan and fry spoonfuls of the mixture. Fry until brown on both sides and cooked through. Serve with roasted tomatoes. Makes about 30 fritters.

Cucumber

One of the oldest cultivated vegetables and, many would say, one of the most refreshing, cucumbers, like other members of the cucurbit family, have a high water content of 96 percent.

The cucumber today exists in over 100 varieties—including at least one described as "burpless"—as well as many shapes.

Cucumber can be eaten raw in salads; cooked in a soup; mixed with yogurt as raita, used as an accompaniment to curries; or added to yogurt and garlic to make Greek tzatziki.

Cucumber is the traditional accompaniment to cold salmon, and the main ingredient for a doria garnish for classic fish recipes. Sliced paper thin in white bread sandwiches, the cucumber represents the height of old-fashioned English gentility at afternoon tea.

Many varieties are grown for pickling as dill pickles, gherkins and French cornichons. Store cucumbers in the refrigerator wrapped in plastic to prevent their odor from spreading to other foods.

Cucumbers have a refreshing flavor and are a key ingredient in raita, which is a cooling side dish served with curry. **To make raita** mix 1 large grated cucumber, 1 finely chopped tomato, and 1¼ cups plain yogurt with 1 tablespoon black mustard seeds toasted in oil. Sprinkle with fresh chopped cilantro leaves.

Eggplant

Eggplants, or aubergines, can be served hot or cold, puréed, fried, stuffed, or battered, and they are the main ingredient of many famous dishes such as moussaka, imam bayildi, baba ghanouj, and ratatouille.

Eggplants vary in size and shape from small, round pea shapes to large, fat, pumpkin-shaped fruit. Their color ranges from green, cream, or yellow to pale or dark purple. Look for firm, heavy eggplants with shiny, smooth skins with no brown patches and a distinct cleft in the wider end.

Most eggplants don't need peeling or degorging (salting and draining) to reduce their bitterness, but this can reduce the amount of oil they absorb as they cook. Blanching in boiling water also helps stop this. To degorge, cut into slices and put in a colander. Sprinkle heavily with salt and weigh down with a plate (to speed up the removal of liquid). Leave for 30 minutes, then rinse in cold water. Dry well with paper towels. Always cut with a stainless steel knife to stop them discoloring.

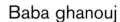

Baba ghanouj

Roast a large eggplant at 400°F for 30 minutes or until soft. Allow to cool, then peel and cut into cubes and process with 1 tablespoon tahini, 1 crushed garlic clove, and plenty of lemon juice. Season well. Serve with crackers. Serves 6.

Braised fennel

Cut 4 baby fennel bulbs into quarters and blanch them in boiling water for 5 minutes. Drain well. Fry the fennel in butter until browned, then add 1 teaspoon brown sugar and caramelize. Add 1 tablespoon white wine vinegar and 5 fluid ouces chicken stock. Cover and simmer until the bulbs are tender. Boil until the liquid is reduced and stir in 2 tablespoons heavy cream. Serves 4.

Fennel

Native to the Mediterranean but now widely grown, fennel is cultivated for its aromatic leaves and seeds, similar in flavor to aniseed. The fine feathery leaves can be snipped like dill and used to flavor fish dishes, dressings, or sauces. Florence fennel, known as *finocchio* in Italy, is cultivated for its thick stems and bulbous base, both of which may be eaten raw like celery, or the base may braised, sautéed, or added to soups.

Garlic

Each head of garlic is made up of a cluster of ten to sixteen cloves, and both head and individual bulbs are covered with a paper-like skin. There are many varieties of garlic, each differing in size, pungency, and color. In dishes such as aïoli, tapenade, and pesto, garlic is indispensable, and it adds flavor to a variety of sauces, stews, and meats. Don't be tempted to use more than the specified amount, as garlic will overpower the other flavors.

Garlic is freshest in summer when the bulbs are firm and the cloves harder to peel. Discolored garlic or bulbs that are sprouting will have a rancid flavor. The green shoots of garlic can be used like chives and snipped onto salads and stir-fries. Garlic can also be eaten as a vegetable, barbecued, or roasted whole or as cloves.

Raw garlic is more potent than cooked. When garlic is cooked, some of the starch converts to sugar, making the garlic less pungent. Be careful not to overbrown or burn it as it can become very bitter. Chopping or crushing garlic releases the flavors. Crush a whole garlic clove by putting it under the flat blade of a knife and banging the knife with your fist. If the clove has sprouted, cut out the green sprout from the center. Flavor oil with garlic by frying slices in oil, then discard the slices.

Aïoli

Place 6 peeled garlic cloves, 2 egg yolks, and a pinch of salt into a blender and blend the ingredients until a thick paste forms. With the motor running, add about 1 cup olive oil, drop by drop, until the aïoli is thick and creamy. However, it if gets too thick, add a little lemon juice. Season to taste. This recipe can also be made using a mortar and pestle. Serves. 6.

Garlic and aïoli.

Edible weeds

An amazing number of common garden weeds are gourmet foods in their own right, healthful and free for the taking. Weeding is anything but a thankless task when you know the gourmet secrets of weeds.

Types of edible weed

Among weeds well worth sampling are nettles, used as a spinach substitute; lamb's-quarters or fat hen (*Chenopodium album*), which is also excellent as a spinach substitute; corn salad, which is a superb salad green for cooler months; dandelion leaves, which are excellent sautéed as wilted greens or as a slightly bitter green in salads; wild sorrel, which makes an excellent creamed soup or salad addition; and the ubiquitous chickweed (*Stellaria media*), which is a delicious addition to salads and reputed to have a regulating effect on the thyroid gland. Succulent purslane (*Portulaca oleracea*) flourishes in sunny dry garden soils. The tender young leaves are excellent raw in salads, and can also be used like spinach as the flavor is somewhere between watercress and spinach.

A tradition of gathering wild greens exists in Mediterranean countries such as France, Italy, and Spain, as well as the Middle East, and each country has its own repertoire of dishes created from wild greens. Among Italy's favourite wild greens are borage (*Borago officinalis*), sea kale (*Crambe maritima*), wall arugula (*Diplotaxis tenuifoliia*) and wild arugula (*Diplotaxis erucoides*), wild sorrel (*Rumex acetosa*), corn salad (*Valerianella locusta*), the fresh shoots of wild hops (*Humulus lupulus*), and wild garlic or ramsons (*Allium ursinum*).

Other countries around the world have their own wild pantry. New Zealand is rich in wild foods and Maori techniques for their preparation, with foods like pikopiko and the near-asparagus-flavored fiddlehead. Australia has an ancient tradition of wild foods, many of which have gained an international reputation in recent times. Both countries are adding their indigenous wild foods to an emerging Pacific Rim cuisine.

Thinnings

Thinnings from the vegetable garden, which you remove when reducing overcrowding can also be eaten, rather than thrown away or put on the compost heap. The seedlings of endive, turnips, radish, collards, Swiss chard, sorrel, beet, and mustard can be used in salads or wilted like spinach.

Fiddleheads
the young fronds of the ostrich or oyster fern. They are boiled and served with a sauce, and added to stir-fries or salads.

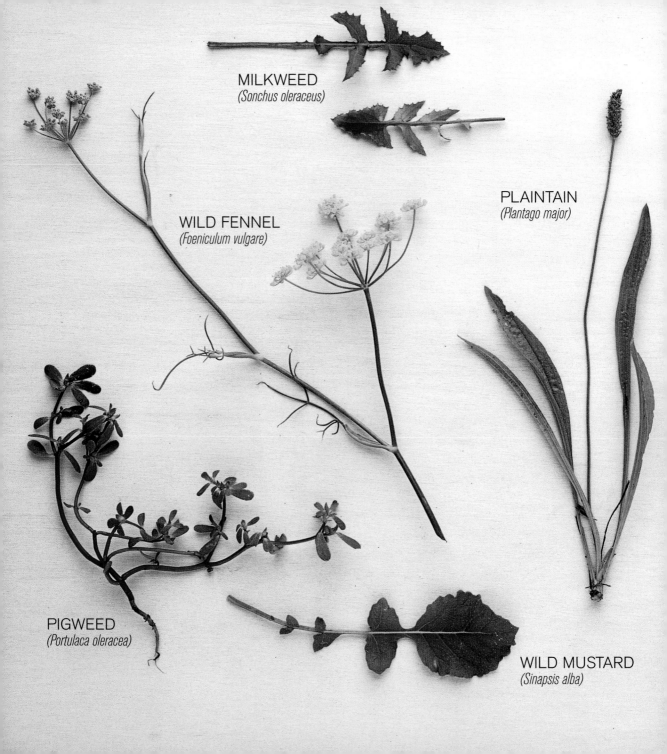

MILKWEED
(Sonchus oleraceus)

WILD FENNEL
(Foeniculum vulgare)

PLAINTAIN
(Plantago major)

PIGWEED
(Portulaca oleracea)

WILD MUSTARD
(Sinapsis alba)

MARSH MALLOW
(Althaea officinalis)

WATERCRESS
(Nasturtium officinale)

edible weeds

The term "weed" makes one think of a useless plant, but the definition is actually an "unwanted plant". Calling weeds wild plants is perhaps a better term, unless they have become an environmental menace. Many weeds are beneficial to your health and make delicious eating. Therefore, they are worth more consideration than how best to remove them.

WILD MUSTARD
(Sinapsis alba)

DANDELION
(Taraxacum officinale)

Roasted Jerusalem artichokes

Scrub 1½ pounds artichokes, then toss them in 2 tablespoons olive oil with plenty of seasoning. Put them on a baking sheet and roast at 400°F for about 40 minutes, or until tender in the center, then drizzle with a little hazelnut or walnut oil. Serve as a vegetable or for a salad, toss with arugula leaves and fried cubes of bacon. Serves 4.

Jerusalem artichoke

Neither from Jerusalem nor an artichoke, this winter root is actually a native of Peru and a relative of the sunflower (in Spanish, "girasol" — mispronounced in English as "Jerusalem"). They have a mildly sweet, smoky flavor. Finely slice and add raw to salads, boil, or roast like potatoes or use to make wonderful velvety soups and mashes. When cut, drop into water with a squeeze of lemon juice to stop them going brown. Jerusalem artichokes have a reputation for causing flatulence. This can be countered with a pinch of asafoetida.

Jicama

Jicama, or yam bean, is a bulb-like root vegetable, similar in appearance to a very large turnip, with thin, beige, leathery skin and sweetish, crisp white flesh. A native to Mexico, jicama is also eaten extensively in Southeast Asian cuisine. To use it, peel the skin including the fibrous flesh directly under it, then slice and use raw in salads, add to stews, or cut into cubes and use in stir-fries as a substitute for water chestnuts—which it resembles in flavor. Jicamas are a good source of starch and, like potatoes, if stored in the fridge for too long will convert their starch to sugar. Jicama is also known as Mexican potato or Mexican turnip.

Kale

A relative of the cabbage, with a similar but stronger flavor and, depending on the variety, dark-green or purple, smooth or curly leaves. As it grows happily in colder climates, kale has long been a popular winter vegetable in northern European countries, and is eaten widely in the southern United States as "collard greens". Use as you would cabbage or stir into soups and stews.

Kohlrabi

The bulbous stalk and the leaves of this cabbage family member are edible. The stalk is somewhat like a turnip, and can be eaten in the same way, either grated or sliced raw, added to stir-fries or stews, mashed, or cooked in chunks and tossed in butter. The flesh is crisp and mild in flavor. Kohlrabi is more popular in Asia and continental Europe, particularly Germany, than Britain and the United States.

Leeks à la grecque

In a large frying pan, simmer together 1 cup water, ¼ cup olive oil, ⅓ cup white wine, 1 tablespoon concentrated tomato purée, ¼ teaspoon sugar, 1 crushed garlic clove, a sprig of thyme, 1 bay leaf, 4 peppercorns, and 4 crushed coriander seeds for 5 minutes. Add 12 thin leeks and cook until tender in the middle. Remove leeks, add a squeeze of lemon juice and 3½ fluid ounces water and boil until the liquid thickens and forms a sauce. Stir in 1 tablespoon chopped parsley, then return to the pan. Cool before serving. Serves 6.

Leek

The leek is a mild-flavored member of the onion family. The thick white stems of cultivated leeks are blanched by piling up dirt around them as they grow. Smaller leeks are best as the green tops are still tender. Some recipes call for just the white part, but most of the leek can be used if it is young and the green leaves are not too tough.

Leeks are particularly good in creamy sauces and soups, most famously vichyssoise. Like onions, they need to be cooked for a reasonable amount of time or they will be crunchy rather than tender and sweet; if overcooked, they will go slimy. Leeks can be boiled, steamed, or braised in butter and cooked. Whole cooked leeks can be wrapped in pieces of ham or covered in a béchamel sauce and broiled. The leek is also the national emblem of Wales.

Leeks often contain soil and grit between their layers and therefore need to be washed thoroughly. Trim the roots, remove any coarse outer leaves, then wash well in a colander under running water. If using whole leeks, carefully separate out the leaves to rinse—making a cut halfway through the stalk to open the leaves. Wash the leek, leaf end down, so all the dirt runs out.

Lettuce

Lettuces vary greatly in color and texture: from light green to deep red, from those with loose, floppy leaves to those with crisp leaves and firm stems. Lettuce is mainly used fresh in salads or sandwiches but can also be cooked. In France, lettuce is cooked with baby onions and peas in stock and in China lettuce is a common cooked vegetable. In a green salad, lettuces are generally interchangeable, but when adding other ingredients, pick a leaf type that will suit them—floppy leaves won't go well with heavy ingredients like potatoes, and crisp firm leaves need a fairly robust dressing. Always dress lettuce just before you serve it.

Lettuce leaves need to be washed and dried before use. Either dry them in dish towels or paper towels or use a salad spinner, as any moisture left on the leaves will dilute the dressing. Don't leave lettuce to soak for any length of time as the leaves will absorb water and lose their flavor.

Caesar salad

Tear a large romaine lettuce into pieces and place it in a large bowl. In a blender, blend 1 egg yolk with 1 garlic clove and 4 anchovy fillets. Gradually add 5½ fluid ounces olive oil, then add 1 tablespoon lemon juice and a dash of Worcestershire sauce. Toss the dressing through the lettuce, then add some chunky croutons and Parmesan shavings. Serves 4.

Stuffed marrow

Cut a marrow into thick rings, scoop out any seeds, then blanch for 5 minutes. Fry 1 chopped onion with 8 ounces ground lamb, add heaping ⅓ cup cooked rice, 1 chopped tomato, 2 tablespoons chopped parsley, and ½ teaspoon cinnamon; season. Fill the rings and put on a baking sheet. Drizzle with olive oil, cover, and bake at 350°F for 30 minutes. Serve with yogurt. Serves 6.

Marrow

From the same family as the squash, winter squash, and cucumber, Marrows are best eaten young as their flavor deteriorates and becomes more watery as they get bigger. Marrows are best stuffed, either halved lengthwise or cut into rings with stuffing in the middle. Use stuffings that will absorb water without going soggy, such as rice or couscous. A whole marrow is baked for about 2–3 hours, depending on its size.

Mushrooms

Some of the most exciting food known to humanity is found in dark, damp habitats, on forest floors, living off live, decaying, and dead organic matter. Mushrooms are the fruit of the fungus that grows above ground. There are countless varieties of edible mushroom, some cultivated, others gathered from the wild, though this should be done by experienced people.

The most common types of cultivated mushrooms are small button mushrooms, larger open-cup mushrooms, and flat (open or field) mushrooms.

Types of wild mushroom

Chanterelle Also known as girolles, these are golden yellow with a concave cap. The underside has blunt, gill-like waves and folds. Chanterelle is a good all-round mushroom.

Enoki Also known as enokitake, these mushrooms grow and are bought in clumps. They have tiny cream caps on slender stalks, and a delicate flavor and crisp texture. The base of the clump can be sliced off or the whole clump can be cooked together.

Horn of plenty Also known as black trumpet and trompette des morts, these saggy, leather-like mushrooms have a strong, earthy taste. Slit down the side to clean them. Fry them in butter and garlic or try them in cream sauces with chicken.

Morel These short, stubby mushrooms resemble a domed sponge; usually found dried. They are good with chicken or veal and make an excellent creamy mushroom sauce.

Oyster These are wild mushrooms, now cultivated widely. Tear large oyster mushrooms into long pieces along the lines of the gills. Add to stir-fries or fry quickly and add to leafy salads.

Porcini Also known as cep or penny bun, these have a brown cap and thick white stem. They have a rich, sweet, and nutty flavor and are sold fresh and dried (usually called porcini). Porcini are good in risottos and stews or raw in salads.

Shiitake With dark-brown caps, shiitake are available fresh and dried. Dried are best with a crazed top. Fresh are best when very smelly. Cut a cross in the top of the cap of large mushrooms to allow them to cook through the thickest part.

Shimeji Also known as beech, these are small oyster mushrooms with long stalks. When cooked they retain a slightly crunchy texture and are good in mushroom mixtures, such as stir-fries.

Straw These are grown on beds of straw. They are small and globe-shaped with an internal stem. They are usually found canned.

Mushrooms do not keep for long. Wild mushrooms are best eaten on the day they are picked and will last no longer than a day in the fridge; cultivated mushrooms will last up to 5 days.

Bitter melon.

Chinese cabbage (wong bok).

Chinese keys.

Asian vegetables

Bitter melon

Used in Chinese, Southeast Asian, and Indian cooking, bitter melon, or bitter gourd, is usually sliced and salted to remove the bitter juices, then braised or stuffed with pork and served with black bean sauce or cooked in curries.

Bok choy

A member of the cabbage family with a slightly mustardy taste, bok choy is also known as Chinese chard, Chinese white cabbage and pak choy. Separate the leaves, wash well, and use both leaf and stem in soups and stir-fries; steam and serve with oyster sauce; or fry in sesame oil with garlic and ginger. A smaller type is Shanghai bok choy, or baby bok choy, which is used in the same way.

Chinese kale

Chinese kale, or Chinese broccoli or gai larn, is distinguished by its small white flowers. It can be steamed whole and served with oyster sauce, or cut up the leaves and stems and add it to soups and stir-fries. Young stalks are crisp and mild; thicker stalks need to be peeled and halved.

Chinese cabbage

A versatile vegetable with a mild, sweet flavor. It can be shredded and eaten raw; steamed; used in stir-fries, soups, and curries; or used to make cabbage rolls. Chinese cabbage is also used to make Korean kimchi. It is also known as celery cabbage, Chinese leaves, napa cabbage, Peking cabbage, and wong bok.

Finger-root

A member of the ginger family, finger-root (also known as Chinese keys) is a reddish brown root vegetable with thick, tapering roots that grow in a cluster, resembling a bunch of keys. Its spicy flavoring is used mainly in curries and pickles in Thai and Indonesian cooking.

Choy sum

Choy sum, or Chinese flowering cabbage, has mild, mustard-flavored leaves and small yellow flowers. Steam or stir-fry whole and serve with oil and garlic and oyster sauce, or chop and add to soups.

Chrysanthemum greens

The young leaves of chrysanthemum greens, or garland chrysanthemum, are used in salads and stir-fries and the edible flowers are used in Chinese cooking.

Ong choy.

Sin qua.

Tatsoi.

Gai choy

A strong, bitter cabbage that is generally pickled as Sichuan pickled cabbage or used in pork-based soups. Another variety, jook gai choy, can be used in soups and stir-fries. It is also known as mustard greens, Oriental mustard, or swatow mustard cabbage.

Hairy melon

A relative of the winter melon that looks like a cucumber covered in tiny hairs and is sometimes called fuzzy melon. It is used in Cantonese cookery. Remove the hairs by scrubbing or peeling it, then bake or boil the flesh; cut it into strips and stir-fry; cut into large pieces, core, and fill with a meat stuffing; or use in braised dishes.

Ong choy

An aquatic plant popular in Southeast Asia, which is cooked like spinach and used in soups, curries, and stir-fries. It is sometimes steamed and served as a side dish. It is also known as kang kong, swamp cabbage, water spinach, or water convolvulus.

Shiso

Widely used in Japanese cooking, shiso leaves can be red, green, or purple. Green leaves are used in sushi, battered and fried in tempura, wrapped around meat or fish, and added to salads; the red leaves are used to give color and flavor to pickled plums. It is also known as beefsteak plant or perilla.

Sin qua

Similar to a cucumber in shape, but with ridges, this vegetable tastes similar to okra and zucchini. To use, peel off the ridges and some of the skin. It can then be baked, boiled, or used in curries and braised dishes. It is also known as angled luffa, Chinese okra, or vegetable gourd.

Tatsoi

Tatsoi, or rosette pak choy, has small, dark-green, shiny leaves with a white stem. The leaves need to be thoroughly washed and can be steamed or stir-fried and are often used in soups.

Winter melon

A very large vegetable used like a squash and stir-fried or used in braised dishes or soups. It is also known as Chinese bitter melon, wax gourd, or white gourd.

Okra goes well with eggplant, onion, pepper, and tomato.

Okra

Okra, also known as bhindi, gumbo, and ladies' fingers, is a five-sided pod that contains numerous white seeds. When cooked, okra releases a sticky, gelatinous substance that is used to thicken soups and stews such as the Cajun and Creole dish, gumbo. Okra is also used extensively in India, the Caribbean, Southeast Asia, and the Middle East. It can also be eaten raw in salads, or blanched then dressed in a vinaigrette. To prepare, gently scrub with paper towel or a vegetable brush. Rinse and drain, then slice off the top and tail. If using as a thickener, blanch whole first, then slice and add to the dish about 10 minutes before the end of cooking. In some recipes, the pod is used whole, thus preventing the release of the sticky substances within.

Onion

One of the most important ingredients in the kitchen, onions are used in just about every nation's cuisine, adding a depth of flavor to dishes, although they are a delicious vegetable in their own right. Onions grow as single bulbs (globe) or in clumps (aggregate). Dry onions are left in the ground to mature where they develop a papery brown skin; green onions (scallions) are pulled out while young and the bulb is still small. Store in a cool dark place.

Red onions.

Types of onions

Yellow The most common kind of onion, sometimes called brown onion. Varieties include a sweet onion called vidalia, Spanish onions, pickling onions, and cipolline—small flat onions.

White Generally mild and slightly sweet. Can be used for cooking or salads. Pearl onions are small white onions ideal for pickling, but can also be added whole to stews and casseroles.

Red Delicious in salads, adding both flavor and color. Good for barbecues and broiling. When cooked, red onions have less flavor than other varieties, although they can be slightly sweeter.

Scallion This is an immature onion that if left in the ground would grow to full size. Depending on when it is picked, it has a small, white bulb of varying size and long green tops. There is also a variety called a Welsh onion with a papery brown skin. Scallions have a mild, delicate flavor and both the green tops and the white bulb can be sliced and added to salads or omelets, tossed into stir-fries, or shredded finely and used as a garnish on fish or in noodle dishes. Store wrapped in plastic in the fridge. Also known as salad onion, green onion, spring onion, and, erroneously in some countries, shallot.

Curried parsnip soup.

Parsnip

The parsnip is a root vegetable with a nutty, sweet flavor. It has creamy yellow flesh and can be served roasted, mashed, or added to casseroles and soups. Parsnips are a fall/winter vegetable and they become sweeter after the first frosts. Leave the skin on for cooking, then peel once cooked. If peeled before cooking, store in water with a squeeze of lemon or vinegar (acidulated water) as their flesh darkens on contact with the air. Particularly large or old parsnips may need their core removed before cooking as they can be hard, flavorless, and very fibrous. Parsnips will keep in the fridge for about 4 weeks.

Pea

The three main varieties of pea are the garden pea, the field or gray pea (these are dried and not eaten fresh), and the wild Mediterranean pea. Peas should be cooked briefly in boiling water or a little butter. They are usually served hot as a vegetable or added to soups and risottos. Both pease pudding, made from split peas boiled in a cloth, and mushy (mashed) peas are eaten in the United Kingdom.

Types of garden peas

Pea shoots (pea leaf) These are the tender leaves of the garden pea that have been prevented from flowering or shooting to encourage the growth of the small leaves. Good in stir-fries. They only last 2 days.

Petits pois Not a different variety, just peas that have been harvested young. The peas are shelled before cooking.

Snow pea A variety of pea, also called mangetout, eaten pod and all (top and tail before eating). They have a flat, thin pod and are eaten raw in salads or used in stir-fries.

Sugar snap pea Similar to snow pea, but with a more rounded pod as they are more developed. Use whole, in stir-fries or noodle dishes.

Snow pea.

Curried parsnip soup

Heat 2 tablespoons olive oil in a large saucepan. Add 2 large, peeled and chopped parsnips and 1 chopped onion. Cook over medium heat for 5 minutes. Add 2 teaspoons good-quality curry paste, such as Madras, and cook, stirring, for 1 minute. Add vegetable stock or water to cover. Cover with a lid, bring to the boil, then simmer for about 20 minutes until the parsnips are tender. Cool slightly, then blend in a food processor until smooth. Return to the pan, stir in 2 cups water and 3 tablespoons heavy cream or fromage frais. Check seasoning and serve with crusty bread. Serves 4.

If harvested too late, peas become dry and lose their sweetness.

Peppers

The fruit of a tropical plant (*Capsicum annuum*) deliberately misnamed pepper (pimiento in Spanish) by Columbus in order to sell its close relation, the chili, as an alternative to the spice pepper that was, at the time, much sought after. Although peppers are a fruit, they are treated more as a vegetable or salad ingredient. They are also known as bell peppers, capsicums, or sweet peppers.

Peppers vary in appearance but they are all basically smooth, shiny and hollow, containing thin white membranes and seeds. Most peppers are green at first, they then turn red, yellow, or orange or even purple-black, depending on the variety. Other types include wax peppers, which are yellow or white; cherry peppers, which are small, round peppers; and anaheim and poblano peppers (ancho when dried), which are usually classed as chilies although they are actually sweet peppers.

Preparing peppers

Peppers can be prepared in many ways. Simply cut into slices, chunks, or quarters, and eat raw in salads; stuff or fry; skinned peppers can be sliced and added to salads, or drizzle with olive oil for the antipasto table. Eat raw peppers as crudités or use in soups, stews, and stir-fries. Peppers feature in ratatouille, peperonata, and gazpacho.

When stuffing whole peppers, cut a slice off the top and remove the seeds and white veins. Blanch each pepper for 2 minutes. Fill the pepper with the stuffing, replace the top slice, then bake.

Roasting or broiling peppers makes them sweeter and also gives them a smoky flavor if you use a chargbroil or barbecue. To remove the skin of peppers, put whole or halved peppers under the broiler until the skin blackens and blisters. Turn the pepper so that all sides are blackened. Alternatively, roast them whole at 350°F for 15–20 minutes. Allow to cool, then peel away the skin. Peeled, seeded peppers can be kept covered in oil in the fridge for 1 week.

To make pepper sauces, broil and remove the skins (as explained above), then purée or push the flesh through a sieve.

Stuffed peppers

Fry 2 finely chopped onions in 4 tablespoons olive oil until soft. Stir in 3 crushed garlic cloves, 1 teaspoon each of cinnamon and paprika, and 2 tablespoons currants. Cook for 1 minute. Cook heaping ½ cup mixed wild rice and long-grain rice. Stir this into the onion mixture and season. Slice the tops off 4 medium red peppers, discard the seeds and fill with the stuffing. Replace the tops, stand in a baking dish, then drizzle with olive oil. Cover with foil and bake at 400°F for 1 hour. Serves 4.

Chili peppers

Cascabel.

Chilies are not merely hot, each has its own flavor and varies in its degree of "hotness", and it is important to use the right chili for the right dish. Mexican recipes usually call for the skin to be removed after roasting as it can be bitter. Roasting also gives a smoky flavor to the flesh. Drying chilies intensifies the flavor. Dried chilies are often roasted before soaking to reconstitute them (be careful not to burn them when you roast them).

Types of chilies (with heat rating from 1–10)

Anaheim (2) Come in green and red and have a mild, sweet flavor. Used to make rellenos and also used in soups and stews.

Ancho (3) A dried poblano chili, dark red, and mildly sweet. Used widely in Mexican cuisine, often with mulato and pasilla to form the "Holy Trinity" of chilies used in mole sauces.

Banana (2) These are mild and sweet, large, long chilies, creamy yellow or orange red in color. Use split in half and broiled. Also called Hungarian wax peppers.

Bird's-eye (8) Also called Thai chilies, these are tiny, either red or green, and very hot. Use in Thai curries or sliced raw onto Asian salads.

Cascabel (4) Small, plum-shaped chilies sold dried. Reconstitute and use chopped in salsas, or in soups and stews.

Habanero (10) Looks like a mini pepper and can be green, red, or orange. They are very, very hot. Use in salsas and marinades.

Jalapeño (5) Oval-shaped chili with thick, juicy flesh and a wheel shape when sliced. Very hot if seeds and membrane are used. Ripens to red and when dried is called chipotle.

Pasilla (3–4) A dried black chili often used in mole.

Pepperoncini (4–5) From south Italy, sweet and mildly hot, and usually available dried. Crumble into pasta sauces and stews.

Poblano (3) A dark green, almost black, long chili with thick flesh that ripens to red. Dried versions are mulato and ancho.

Serrano (7) A common Mexican chili, cylindrical in shape, red or green, and often used in salsas or pickled.

Habanero.

Chopping chilies

1 Wearing rubber gloves, carefully cut the chilies in half and scrape out any seeds.
2 Cut away the membrane, then chop or slice the chilies.

Banana chili.

Chili con queso

Seed 1 ancho or pasilla chili and flatten into one piece. Gently fry on both sides in 1 tablespoon oil, then allow to cool and crispen. Break the chili into small pieces. Add 1 cup sour cream to the pan and cook for 2 minutes. Add ¾ cup cubed Cheddar, stir until melted, then add the chili. Serve with corn chips. Serves 4.

PEPPERCORNS
(Piper nigrum)

GREEN
CAYENNE
(Capsicum annuum)

BIRD'S-EYE CHILI
(Capsicum annuum)

BROWN MUSTARD
(Brassica spp.)

RADISH
(Raphanus sativus)

ORANGE HABANERO
CHILI
(Capsicum annuum)

HORSERADISH
(Armoracia rusticana)

DRIED CHILI
(Capsicum annuum)

YELLOW MUSTARD
(Brassica spp.)

ORNAMENTAL
CHILI
(Capsicum annuum)

CASCABEL
CHILI
(Capsicum annuum)

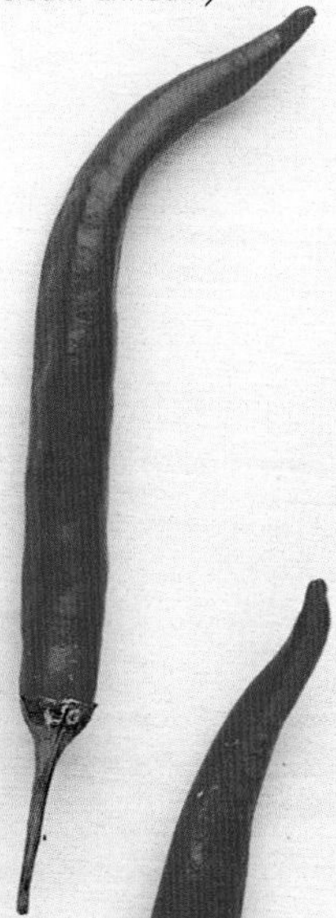

RED CAYENNE
(Capsicum annuum)

DRIED BIRD'S-
EYE CHILI
(Capsicum annuum)

RED HABANERO
CHILI
(Capsicum annuum)

hot foods

If hot and spicy is the way you like it, grow some vegetables that bite back! Radish, both red and white, has a kick. Horseradish, too, is another root crop that will add spice. Best known for heat, however, are chilies. They come in various strengths from fiery hotness to a milder intensity. The seeds and membrane are the hottest parts of the fruit.

SERRANO
CHILI
(Capsicum annuum)

RED CAYENNE
(Capsicum annuum)

WHITE RADISH (DAIKON)
(Raphanus sativus var. longipinnatus)

Potatoes Anna

Arrange thinly sliced, patted-dry potatoes in circles in a dish. As each layer is added, add butter, then season. Cover the dish with foil and weigh the top down to force the layers together. Bake until golden-brown, then turn out.

Potato

Native to South America, the potato is now a staple in the global diet. Potatoes are cheap, hardy, and easy to grow, and are high in starch, protein, and vitamins. Almost all nationalities have a traditional dish based on potatoes, such as gratin dauphinois, rösti, and Irish stew. There are thousands of varieties of potatoes, but only a hundred or so are grown for commercial use.

Potatoes can be divided into new crop (early) potatoes and old (main crop) potatoes and their texture can be floury or waxy. Some are all-round types, others are more suitable for specific recipes. Potatoes are never eaten raw but must be cooked first as they contain 20 percent indigestible starch, which, when cooked, converts into sugar.

Preparing and storing potatoes

Scrub potatoes well before preparing, to remove dirt and cut off any green parts and any "eyes". It is the thin layer immediately underneath the skin that is the most nutritious, so leave the skin on potatoes, where possible. Store potatoes in paper bags to allow moisture to escape and to keep light out. Keep in a cool and dry, dark, well-ventilated place to prevent them from sprouting. If exposed to light, potatoes turn green—these will be bitter and indigestible and can be poisonous. If stored in the fridge, potatoes become sweeter than if stored at room temperature.

Types of potatoes

Floury These have a low moisture and sugar content and are high in starch. They are good for baking, roasting, mashing, and fries, gnocchi, and in bread, but disintegrate when boiled. They include Idaho, Pentland Squire, and King Edward.

Waxy These have a high moisture content and are low in starch. They hold their shape when boiled or roasted but don't mash well. Use in salads or stews. These include Roseval, Charlotte, Pink Fir Apple, Fingerling, and Cara.

Salad These are waxy, have a distinct flavor and are not usually peeled. Boil or roast. These include Fingerling, Pink Fir Apple, Jersey Royal, and La Ratte.

All-purpose Use in recipes that don't specify the type of potato needed. These include Desiree, Nicola, Maris Piper, Romano, Wilja, Yellow Finn, Spunta, Pontiac, and Pink Eye.

Winter squash (Pumpkin)

A member of the gourd family classified as a winter squash, often with orange skin and flesh as used in Halloween lanterns. Their flesh has a pronounced sweet flavor and is used in both sweet and savory dishes. Winter squash can be boiled, steamed, roasted, or mashed. In some countries, all squashes are referred to as pumpkins; in others, only the large round segmented ones.

If boiling winter squash, remove the skin and seeds. If roasting larger pieces, the skin can be left intact for cooking. The seeds of winter squash are dried and used in both sweet and savory food. They are delicious toasted and sprinkled on salads and soups, or they can be eaten as nibbles, just like nuts. The roasted seeds are also used to make a thick, dark brown oil with a strong flavor and aroma, used as a salad dressing and seasoning. Store whole at room temperature for around 1 month. Wrap cut squash in plastic wrap and store in the fridge.

When making squash purée or mash, steam or roast it to give a better flavor as boiling it tends to make the flesh a little watery.

Radish

A peppery root vegetable related to the mustard plant, whose many varieties are grouped under red, black, or white radishes. Red are the mildest and are crisp and juicy, usually eaten raw in salads. Black radishes have a stronger flavor, and are often peeled before use to reduce their pungency. Add to stir-fries and soups.

White radish (daikon)

White radish, or daikon, has a firm, crisp flesh and a mild flavor, similar to a white turnip. Some varieties have a slight peppery taste, while others are slightly sweeter. Raw white radish can be diced and added to salads, or used like a potato or turnip and added to soups, stews, or stir-fries. In Japan, grated raw white daikon is formed into a small pile and is the traditional accompaniment to sashimi or tempura or it may be eaten as pickles.

Thai winter squash and coconut soup

Heat 2 tablespoons olive oil in a large saucepan and gently fry 1 finely chopped onion for 5 minutes. Add 1 tablespoon red curry paste and 1 tablespoon concentrated tomato purée and fry for 30 seconds. Add 3 cups cubed winter squash flesh and fry for 5 minutes. Add 13 fluid ounces coconut milk and 2 cups vegetable stock. Cover and simmer for 15 minutes. Remove lid and simmer for a further 5 minutes. Cool slightly, then purée in a food processor until smooth. Return to a clean saucepan and reheat. Stir in 3 tablespoons chopped cilantro and garnish with sliced red bird's-eye chili. Serves 4.

French shallot.

Arugula

Arugula, or rocket, is a slightly bitter salad leaf with a nutty, peppery flavor. Younger leaves are milder than the mature, which can get quite hot. Arugula is used predominantly as a salad ingredient, and is one of the traditional ingredients of Provençal mesclun salad; it can be used as a pizza topping, added to soups and purées, or served wilted as a vegetable. Arugula wilts quickly but will keep in the fridge wrapped in plastic for up to 2 days.

Shallot

A relative of the onion, but with a milder flavor, shallots grow in clusters and are joined with a common root end. There are several types including the gray or common shallot, with gray skin and a purple head; the Jersey shallot, a round bulb with pink skin; the French shallot, also called banana shallot, which has golden copper-colored skin and an elongated bulb; and Asian shallots, which are a lighter pink.

Shallots can be used as a garnish, thinly sliced and eaten raw in salads, or peeled and cooked whole as a vegetable. In France, shallots are used in sauces as the flesh dissolves well when cooked; in Asia, they are made into pickles. Store in a cool, well-ventilated place for up to 1 month. In some countries, such as Australia, scallions are erroneously called shallots.

To skin shallots, blanch them in boiling water for 1 minute, then peel. If leaving whole, then only trim the root or they will fall apart. When browning shallots, make sure they are well browned all over as the color will wash off if they are added to a liquid.

Arugula and Parmesan salad

Put 2 bunches of washed and dried arugula in a serving dish. Mix 4 tablespoons olive oil with 1 tablespoon balsamic vinegar. Pour dressing over the arugula and mix well. Use a vegetable peeler to shave off pieces from a block of Parmesan. Scatter over the arugula, sprinkle with a little coarse salt and pepper. Serves 4.

Spinach

Originally native to Persia, spinach is a green leafy plant with slender stems. The young leaves are used in salads; the older ones are cooked. It contains iron and vitamins A and C, but also oxalic acid, which is responsible for the slightly bitter taste and which acts as an inhibitor to the body's ability to absorb calcium and iron. This knowledge has somewhat diminished its famous "Popeye" reputation.

Cook spinach in the minimum of water—the water that is left on the leaves after washing is often enough. Steam or cook in a covered pan. Spinach that is to be added to dishes needs to be squeezed dry. This is best done by pressing it between two plates.

Sautéed garlicky spinach

Wash 2 pounds spinach thoroughly and shake dry, leaving just a little water clinging to the leaves. Heat 2 tablespoons olive oil in a frying pan and add 1 finely chopped garlic clove. Cook for a few seconds and then add to the spinach. Cover the pan for a minute to create some steam. Remove the lid and turn up the heat, stirring the spinach until all the liquid has evaporated. Season before serving.

Squash

Squash belong to the marrow family, which also includes cantaloupes, marrows, gourds, gherkins, and cucumbers. They come in a wide variety of colors, sizes, and shapes. Squashes are divided into winter and summer types. Generally, winter ones have hard skin and flesh and the summer ones have a softer skin and more watery flesh. Squashes are often stuffed and baked or roasted, puréed, braised, boiled, steamed, or fried in batter or breadcrumbs. Add them to soups and casseroles or gratins.

Types of squash

Pattypan A saucer-shaped squash, yellow, or green in color with white flesh. Usually picked when young and very small, it does not need to be peeled and cooks quickly.

Sweet dumpling Dark green with deep ridges and yellow markings. The flesh is yellow-orange in color.

Spaghetti Has a hard yellow skin and a flesh that is made up of fibers. Steam or bake, then gently pull out the fibers—these resemble spaghetti.

Golden nugget Small squash that look like baby Halloween pumpkins. They have a hard skin and can be baked whole or in halves. Best cooked with their skins on.

Turban A large squash with a crown at the top and a hard, dark skin that can be dark green or orange. It has a dry, sweet, orange flesh with a nutty flavor.

Hubbard Has a hard, coarse skin that may be ridged and varies in color from green to bluish-green to red. The flesh is pale orange.

Sweet potato

This is the tuberous root of a tropical vine which, although also native to Central and South America like the potato, is not a true potato. Today, sweet potatoes are an important crop in southern United States, South America, Asia, Japan, the Mediterranean, Hawaii, Australia, and New Zealand, where one variety, orange in color, is known as kumara, close to the original Peruvian name of "kumar"

There are several varieties of sweet potato and their flesh, which may be white, orange, or yellow, ranges from meaty to moist and watery, and their skins may be white, yellow, red, purple, or brown. Orange-fleshed sweet potatoes are softer when cooked.

Sweet potatoes can be cooked as you would a potato—roasted, boiled, mashed, or fried, but their soft, slightly sweet flesh makes them an ideal ingredient in cakes and sweet dishes, breads, soups, and casseroles. A simple cooking method is to sprinkle them with brown sugar and butter and roast.

Sweet potatoes will not store for as long as potatoes but will last 1 week if kept in a cool, dry place.

Clockwise from top: shelled soybeans, fermented soybean paste, dried soybeans, soybean pods, soybean sprouts.

soybeans and byproducts

The most nutritious and versatile of all beans, soybeans have been cultivated in their native China for thousands of years. Soybeans (or soya beans) contain a higher proportion of protein than any other legume, even higher than that of red meat, making them an important part of vegetarian diets and in Japanese, Chinese, and Southeast Asian cooking where little meat is used. Soybeans may be red, green, yellow, black, or brown. The beans are eaten fresh or dried but are also used as a source of oil, milk, curd, pastes,

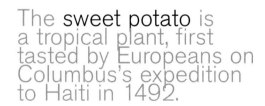

The **sweet potato** is a tropical plant, first tasted by Europeans on Columbus's expedition to Haiti in 1492.

Tofu, or bean curd, is a white, cheese-like curd made from **soybeans,** first prepared by the Chinese about 2,000 years ago.

sauces, and flavorings. They may also be cracked, sprouted, and even roasted and ground as a coffee substitute.

Dried soybeans contain a trypsin inhibitor, which must be destroyed by soaking and cooking them for a long time before they are digestible. Soak dried beans for at least 6–8 hours before use. Yellow beans need longer soaking than black. Discard the soaking water before cooking.

Preparing soybeans

Soybeans have little flavor and a slightly oily texture and benefit from being cooked with strong flavors such as chili, garlic, and soy sauce.

As with other pulses, soybeans can also be puréed, added to casseroles, or used in soups and salads. Fresh soybean pods can be rubbed with salt, then boiled. These are eaten as a snack with beer in China and Japan.

In Asian cuisine, fresh **soybeans** are boiled and salted, and then eaten as a snack.

soybean dip

Cook 3⅓ cups frozen soybeans in 2 cups vegetable stock for about 10–12 minutes. Drain, reserving ¼ cup of stock. Mix the beans in a food processor with 1 clove of garlic, ½ cup chopped fresh basil, 1 tablespoon extra virgin olive oil, and the reserved stock, occasionally scraping down the sides, until smooth. Serve warm with crostini or crusty bread. Makes 1½ cups.

Swiss chard

Swiss chard, or silverbeet, is a relation of the sugar beet and is mostly grown and eaten around the southern Mediterranean. Swiss chard has fleshy stalks and large leaves, both of which can be prepared as for spinach. The leaves may be eaten raw in salads or cooked and the stalks served in a sauce, added to soups, or sautéed.

There is a great range of chards available, many of which have colorful stalks. Ruby chard has a red stalk and can be cooked in the same way as regular Swiss chard.

Store covered and unwashed in the fridge for up to 4 days. Swiss chard is sometimes sold under the name of 'spinach' in Australia. It is also known as chard, leaf beet, seakale beet, spinach beet, and white beet.

Tomatillo

A relative of the tomato that is used as a vegetable, either raw or cooked, this fruit may be green, yellow, or purple. Tomatillos are used in Mexican cuisine in salsa verde and are essential in a proper guacamole. Like physalis, the tomatillo has a papery calyx.

Tomato

Although botanically a fruit, the tomato, another gift of inestimable value to the world's cuisines—especially Italian—from South America, is used mainly as a vegetable. So thoroughly has the tomato been assimilated that it's difficult to imagine life in the western world (no tomato sauce or pizza!) before it arrived in Naples in the sixteenth century. At first the tomato was thought of as a medicinal plant, and it took a generation before it began to appear on the table. Today, tomatoes are grown worldwide, America and Italy being the largest producers for canning, sauces, pastes, and purées. There are more than 1,000 varieties, in numerous sizes, shapes, and colors. Most varieties are red, although others are yellow or pink. Unripe green tomatoes are used in pickles and chutneys.

Pale red **tomatoes** can be left to ripen naturally on your kitchen windowsill. Tomatoes will not ripen if left in the fridge.

The best flavored tomatoes are those that are ripened on the actual vine.

For immediate use, tomatoes should be firm and bright colored, with no wrinkles and a strong tomato smell. Buy only in small quantities (unless making sauce), or buy some greener than others. For salads and pasta sauces, buy only the reddest and ripest of tomatoes. Remember, uniformity of shape or color has no relation to flavor.

Types of tomatoes

Cherry Cherry tomatoes come in various sizes but essentially are a tiny variety of tomato. Some are red, others are yellow, and some are pear-shaped and yellow. Good for salads or use whole or halved in stews and pasta sauces.

Plum Also known as egg or Roma, these are commercially used for canning and drying. They have few seeds and a dry flesh, which makes them ideal in sauces and purées. A good variety is San Marzano.

Beefsteak These are larger tomatoes, either smooth and rounded or more irregular and ridged in shape. Beefsteak tomatoes can be used for stuffing or sliced in salads. Marmande are an especially good variety.

Round This is the most common type of tomato, commercially bred to be round and red. It can be bought vine-ripened and in different varieties such as the striped tigerella or even yellow or orange colored. The round tomato is an all-purpose tomato.

Tomato salad

Slice 6 large ripe tomatoes. Arrange the tomatoes on a plate and scatter over 1 finely chopped shallot and 2 tablespoons chopped chives. Drizzle with extra virgin olive oil and top with torn basil leaves. If your tomatoes are not highly flavored, add a few drops of balsamic vinegar to the olive oil. Serves 4.

Peeling tomatoes

1 Remove the stems of the tomatoes and score a cross in the bottom of each one with a knife, cutting just through the skin. Blanch in boiling water for 30 seconds or so.
2 Test a tomato to see if the skin will come off easily, otherwise leave them to soak for a few seconds more. Don't leave them for too long or they might start to cook.
3 Transfer to a bowl of cold water then peel the skin away from the crosses—it should slip off easily.

Turnip

A relative of the cabbage, grown both for its root and the green tops, which are used as a spring vegetable. The turnip is one of the earliest cultivated European vegetables. Turnips spread across the globe early on, and appear in the cuisine of many countries: in Chinese and Japanese recipes, and as pickles in Korean and Middle Eastern cooking. In France they are eaten mostly when young. There are many varieties, long or rounded, white tinged with green or purple, but all have white flesh.

Although turnips are usually relegated to ingredient status in soups and stews, they make excellent eating on their own. When young, grate them raw into salads, braise them, or make Chinese-style turnip cake. Older turnips can be roasted, which gives them a sweeter flavor. Turnip tops (greens) are boiled as for cabbage and served with butter. Turnips are also available salted and sun-dried in Asian stores. Store unwashed and refrigerated in a perforated plastic bag for up to 2 weeks.

Navet

In France, navet is the word for any type of turnip, but it is the specific name for small, immature turnips, available in spring and summer. These are white, tinged with red, and are more delicate in flavor than winter turnips. Navets generally don't need to be peeled before cooking. If the leaves are perky and bright green, they are also edible—sauté them in a little butter with garlic and black pepper.

Glazed turnips

Peel 4 turnips and cut them into quarters, or trim 16 baby turnips. Boil for 8–10 minutes until tender but still firm, then drain well. Heat 2 tablespoons butter in a frying pan; add turnips, sprinkle on 1 tablespoon sugar and fry until turnips are golden and caramelized (be careful the sugar does not burn). Serve with roast meats or baked ham. Serves 4.

Zucchini

Zucchinis, or courgettes, are baby marrows, and are usually dark green in color, but there are also light green and yellow varieties. Young zucchini can be sliced thinly, dressed in olive oil and lemon juice, then eaten raw in salads. Use larger zucchini in stir-fries. You can also steam or boil them, coat slices in batter and deep-fry them, or hollow out, stuff and bake them. If using zucchini in fritters or frying, you should salt them first to degorge them so they soak up less oil. Storage in the fridge makes the texture of zucchinis deteriorate. Zucchini flowers are edible too, available in the male (the flower has a stalk) or female (the flower has a baby zucchini attached) form. These are usually stuffed before being baked or fried. They are sold at specialty fruit and vegetable shops. Wash them before use and make sure there are no insects hidden inside.

Marinated zucchini

Thinly slice 6 zucchinis diagonally. Heat 1 tablespoon olive oil in a frying pan and fry the slices on both sides until browned. Remove with a slotted spoon and drain. Place the zucchini in a non-metallic dish and add 1 tablespoon finely chopped parsley, 1 sliced garlic clove, and 1 tablespoon balsamic vinegar. Season with salt and pepper and leave for a few hours. Serve with broiled or roast meats or as antipasto. Serves 4.

Deep-fried zucchini flowers

For batter, whisk 2 eggs with heaping ⅓ cup flour. For stuffing, mix ½ cup ricotta with 1 tablespoon chopped basil, 2 tablespoons grated Parmesan, 2 tablespoons breadcrumbs, and an egg yolk. Season. Stuff the mixture into 10 flowers. Dip flowers in batter and deep-fry. Serves 4.

VEGETABLE

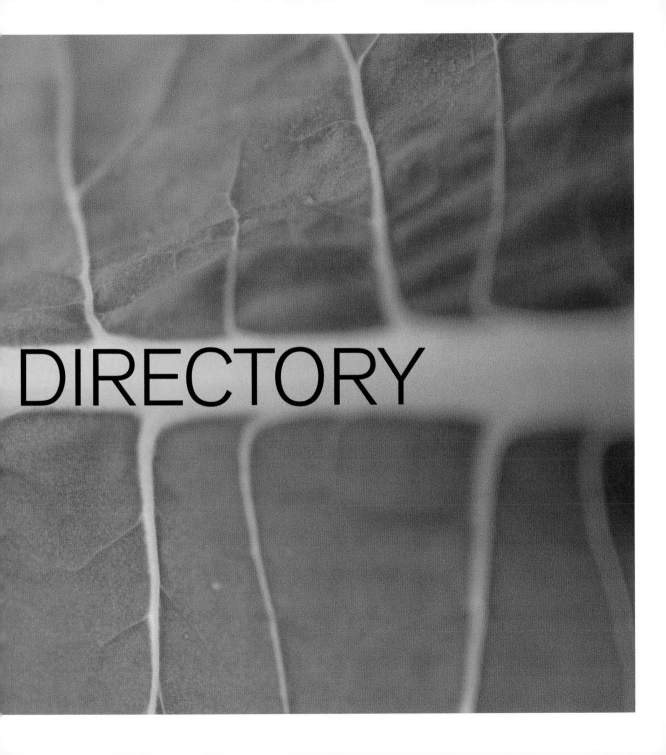

DIRECTORY

Abelmoschus esculentus, syn. *Hibiscus esculentus*

OKRA
Malvaceae

CONDITIONS
Climate. Best grown in tropical, subtropical, and hot temperate climates with long, warm growing seasons.

Aspect. Prefers to be in full sun and requires well-drained soil.

Soil. Okra likes moderation in all things. Clay or clay loamy soils with an average moisture level and neither over-fertilized nor under-fertilized are ideal.

FEATURES
Also known as gumbo or lady's finger, okra is an annual and a member of the hibiscus family. The large, yellow, hibiscus-like flowers with red-purplish centers produce edible, seed-containing pods that have an unusually high gum content. Because of this, not everyone finds this vegetable to their taste. The pod is green and grows to about $2\frac{3}{4}$–4 inches. The bush grows to a height of $6\frac{1}{2}$ feet with hairy stems and large flattened leaves. It does not grow well in containers.

GROWING METHOD
Planting. Sow seeds in spring through to early summer in cool and warm climates. Sow all year round in tropical areas. Seeds can be germinated indoors under controlled conditions and later transplanted, but in most warm climates it is better to plant directly into garden beds. Plant seeds $\frac{3}{4}$ inch deep and spaced $1\frac{1}{2}$ feet apart. Flowers take 12–14 weeks to appear.

Watering. As the plant is prone to stem rot, water sparingly around the plant and not over it.

Fertilizing. Lay a band of complete fertilizer in furrows 4–6 inches deep. Cover with soil and leave a week before planting seed. Side feed, 6 inches around the plant, when pods begin to show, to assist growth. Water in immediately. Compost to increase the water holding capacity of the soil.

Problems. Relatively few problems. Watch out for stem rot in wet conditions. Keep garden free of diseased organic plant matter. Crop rotation will prevent build-up of soil diseases.

HARVESTING
Picking. Immature pods are picked when 2–$3\frac{1}{2}$ inches long after 3–4 months. If left on the bush too long, the pods become fibrous and tough. Pick daily to lengthen cropping period.

Storing. Refrigerate for up to 3 days.

Freezing. Blanch in boiling water for 3–4 minutes, cool, pack in freezer bags, then freeze for up to 6 months.

USES
Culinary. Pods may be used fresh or dried. They are widely used as a flavoring in soups and in meat cooking, or can be fried or boiled and eaten as a vegetable. It is sometimes used as a thickening agent in soups and stews.

FEATURES

Mushroom is a fungus, the edible part of which is a spore-producing head that grows upwards from a body of filaments feeding throughout a bed of compost below. Mushrooms have no leaves or chlorophyll and absorb no carbon dioxide from the air. Young mushrooms have a small, white, rounded head that opens to a circular cap revealing ridges of pink gills beneath. These turn brown as spores develop between them. There are many poisonous forms of fungi and careful identification is recommended when collecting mushrooms in the field. Many varieties of interesting and unusual mushrooms are now available commercially. These include the pine mushroom with deep yellow to golden gills, the golden enoki, oyster, shimeji, and shiitake forms.

GROWING METHOD

Planting. The easiest way to grow mushrooms is to buy a kit with spores already in the compost medium. Simply cover tray with ¾–1½ inches of commercially available (sterilized) topsoil and keep moist. Grayish colored filaments appear in 1–2 weeks, spreading throughout the compost medium but at the same time growing together to form clumps called mycelium. Pinhead structures, which develop into the mature mushroom, grow from this mycelium forcing their way upwards through the shallow casing.

Watering. Keep compost moist but never too wet or soggy. Water 2 or 3 times a week.

Fertilizing. Do not fertilize. Initial preparation of the growing medium is satisfactory.

Problems. No serious diseases if using commercially available sterilized compost. Larvae from fly infestations, mushroom mite and nematodes can infect the mycelium and fruiting bodies. Dust beds with pyrethrum every 2 weeks to clear this up.

HARVESTING

Picking. Mushrooms take about 4 weeks to mature, in growth waves called flushes. Button mushrooms are cropped before the cap opens. Mature mushrooms are ripe when the cap opens and gills are exposed. Cut stalks at soil level and pick regularly to encourage further flushes. If, after several flushes, no mushrooms appear within 14–21 days, the bed is exhausted and the planting/cultivation cycle needs to be repeated.

Storing. Store mushrooms in the fridge for up to 5–7 days in a paper (never plastic) bag.

Freezing. Pack clean mushrooms in freezer bags and freeze for up to 6 months. They can also be dried or pickled and stored in bottles.

USES

Culinary. Use raw in salads or cook in white sauces. Closed cup mushrooms are good for stir-fries. The larger, open cup mushrooms are ideal for stews and casseroles. Flat (open or field) mushrooms are delicious broiled or stuffed and make a good, dark-colored mushroom soup, but if cooked with white meat, such as chicken, they may turn the dish gray.

Agaricus spp.
MUSHROOM
Agaricaceae

CONDITIONS

Climate. As the garden mushroom is mostly grown in temperature-controlled environments, indoors, or under shelter, all climates are suitable. High humidity with constant, cool temperatures from 54–64°F are recommended.

Aspect. Prefers the dark but will tolerate some light. Direct sunlight is not necessary for growth. The home gardener usually grows mushrooms in dark cupboards or in cellars. Good ventilation is required to remove excess carbon dioxide in the air.

Soil. Use sterilized mushroom farm compost, already inoculated with mushroom spores. Add a ¾–1½ inch layer of sterilized topsoil or peat. This is called the casing.

Allium ampeloprasum Porrum Group
LEEK
Alliaceae

CONDITIONS
Climate. Best grown in cool weather in temperatures below 77°F. Growth is slower in warm climates. During extreme drops of temperature mulch heavily with straw or pine needles.

Aspect. Prefers full sun.

Soil. Loose, rich, well-drained soil.

FEATURES
A relative of the onion, this vegetable has a long, white, underground stem and is slightly bulbous at the root end. Green, strap-like leaves protrude above-ground. Most leeks are left to grow to a fully mature state but are much tastier if cropped earlier. The flesh is thick and mildly onion-flavored.

GROWING METHOD
Planting. Plant seeds in seed-raising boxes from spring to fall in cool climates, and in late summer and fall in warm and tropical regions. In areas where winters are mild, seeds can be planted directly into the garden during late summer. When seedlings reach pencil thickness and are 8–12 inches tall, plant 6 inches deep, 6 inches apart, in rows that are a handspan apart. Roots should touch the bottom of the hole. Rather than fill the hole with soil, water regularly so as to gradually deposit soil around the roots of the young leek. Also remove the top third of the leaf structure to reduce water loss and to encourage new root growth. Alternatively, in flat garden beds, heap soil around the base of the young leek, cover stem with newspaper and pile dry soil up around it. Keep adding soil as the leek grows. A newspaper collar will prevent soil getting in among leaves.

Watering. Water regularly. Moist, fertile soil encourages strong growth.

Fertilizing. Dig in nitrogen-rich fertilizer and large quantities of animal manure and other organic material. Regular monthly applications of urea will speed up the growing process.

Problems. Very few problems. Seldom affected by specific pests and diseases in the home garden. If thrips show up, remove by hosing.

HARVESTING
Picking. Leeks take a long time to produce large stems. The growing season takes about 4–5 months from seed stage, 3 months from seedlings. It is not necessary to wait till full maturity before picking. The younger they are, the tastier and sweeter the flesh. To crop when mature, remove top half of leaves in midsummer. Crop only as required but before any frosts set in. The best way to pick is to pull the complete plant from the ground lengthwise.

Storing. Refrigerate for 7–10 days.

Freezing. Pack in freezer bags and freeze for up to 6 months.

USES
Culinary. Some recipes call for just the white part, but most of the leek can be used if it is young and the green leaves are not too tough. Leeks are particularly good in creamy sauces and soups, most famously vichyssoise. Like onions, they need to be cooked for a reasonable amount of time or they will be crunchy rather than tender and sweet; if overcooked, they become slimy. Leeks can be boiled, steamed, or braised in butter.

FEATURES

This vegetable is not to be confused with the evergreen onion, known as the scallion. Scallions are very young, green onions whereas shallots are a more mature form of onion similar to garlic in their formation. *A. ascalonicum* with its chestnut-brown skin is aptly called the golden shallot. It has small bulbs that measure ½–1½ inches in diameter when mature. It has a similar but much more delicate flavor than an onion, although elongated varieties have a stronger flavor than the rounder varieties. The bulbs are clustered at the base of the plant with narrow whitish stems and green leaves extending above-ground. This is an easy vegetable for the home vegetable gardener to grow.

GROWING METHOD

Planting. As this plant does not produce viable seeds, it is propagated by replanting small bulbs broken off from the parent plant each season. Do this from midsummer to mid-fall in cold regions; from the end of summer to the end of fall in temperate zones; and at the end of summer to the beginning of winter in warm, tropical areas. If planning to harvest in its green state, while the plant is quite young, plant the bulb quite deep to 2½ inches and hill soil around the stem as it grows. If planning for mature bulbs, plant quite shallow so that the bulblet is level with the top of the soil. In both cases, it is best to leave about 6–8 inches around each plant. Shallow, fibrous roots require light cultivation and beds need to be kept free of weeds.

Watering. Water regularly so that soil does not dry out.

Fertilizing. Apply complete fertilizer before planting and again at mid-season.

Problems. Very few pests and diseases. If thrips show up, remove them by thorough and vigorous hosing.

HARVESTING

Picking. Bulbs mature in 3–4 months, but can be harvested after 8 weeks if soft bulbs with white stalks and young green leaves are preferred. Shallots may be picked at any stage of growth, but care must be taken not to cut the main stem and hinder further development of the plant. Mature bulbs should be lifted when the top, leafy parts wither.

Storing. Store in a cool, well-ventilated place for several months.

Freezing. Place separate cloves from bulb into bags and freeze for up to 3 months.

USES

Culinary. The shallot is used a great deal in French cooking, particularly for making sauces, where its subtle flavor is an asset. Young succulent leaves may be used raw in salads or as a flavoring in the same way that chives or scallions are used. They can also be peeled and cooked whole as a vegetable. In Asia, they are made into pickles.

Allium ascalonicum, A. cepa
SHALLOT
Alliaceae

CONDITIONS

Climate. Will grow in all climates.

Aspect. Prefers full sun to partial shade.

Soil. Well-drained soil, rich in humus. Tolerates most soils but not acid. Dig in large quantities of animal manure and compost several weeks before planting.

Allium cepa
ONION
Alliaceae

CONDITIONS
Climate. All climates are suitable, but it is important to choose correct varieties to suit your local conditions. Careful planting of varieties with different maturing dates is necessary to achieve cropping over a long period.

Aspect. Onions do not like beds that get too hot. They are very temperature-sensitive. Warm weather and direct sunlight promote bulb development, so exposure to full sun will be necessary at some stage of the growth process. Cool weather promotes top growth, so green, early-maturing onions are able to tolerate partial shade.

Soil. Prefer to be in non-acidic soils about pH 6. Prepare the beds well ahead with large amounts of any form of well-decayed organic matter.

FEATURES
This versatile vegetable can be grown in most soils and climates. The edible part is the fleshy bulb, which can be white, yellow, or brown through to red. Scallions are early-maturing onions that are grown for their small white bulbs or thin stems and green tops. White and brown onions are late-maturing and keep much longer than early-maturing varieties.

GROWING METHOD
Planting. Onions are classified as early, mid-season, or late-maturing. Plant early varieties in mid- to late summer in all areas, from cold to tropical. Plant mid-season varieties in early winter in cold regions; fall to midwinter in warm areas; and in fall in subtropical to tropical areas. Plant late-maturing varieties in early winter in cold to warm zones; and in late fall to early winter in subtropical and tropical regions. Sow seeds directly in the ground or transplant seedlings from seed beds when they are $4\frac{3}{4}$ inches tall. Plant about $3\frac{1}{2}$ inches apart, in rows 12 inches apart. Control any weeds by regular, shallow cultivation. When weeding, be particularly careful not to cover the maturing bulbs with soil. The best way to do this is by hilling the soil around the bulbs rather than covering them with soil.

Watering. Water regularly and evenly. Lack of water delays growth and leads to bulb splitting.

Fertilizing. Fertilize before planting and mid-season with dressings of urea or sodium sulphate. Nitrogenous fertilizers in the form of blood and bone or animal manures are best, but complete fertilizer is satisfactory. Avoid using nitrogen as the plant approaches maturity because it promotes foliage at the expense of the bulbs.

Problems. Onion maggot thrives in fresh organic material in soil, so fertilize with well-decayed material. White stipple on leaves indicates onion thrip. Treat with an appropriate spray. Downy mildew is common and can also be chemically treated, or remove the diseased plants. Keeping your garden healthy will help prevent disease.

HARVESTING
Picking. Onions can take more than 6 months to mature, depending on the variety. Pull the plant from the ground and leave to dry in the sun, if possible.

Storing. Store in a cool, dry place, but not in the refrigerator.

Freezing. Peel, chop, or cut into rings, wrap in layers of plastic, then store for up to 3 months.

USES
Culinary. Brown onions are used in cooking sauces and stews. White onions are generally mild and slightly sweet and can be used for cooking or salads. Red onions are delicious in salads, adding both flavor and color and are good for barbecues and broiling.

Gardening. Some varieties of onion produce attractive, globular pink or white flowers.

FEATURES

A bulbous perennial (although usually grown as an annual), garlic has green, curved, flat, spear-like leaves and grows to 2–3 feet. Cloves, sheathed in a papery covering, are compacted to form a bulb and cling to a central stem. The plant has a central, rounded stalk in summer with a large, rounded flower head composed of numerous pinkish-white petals. Elephant or Russian garlic (*A. giganteum*) has huge cloves with a few segments to a bulb. It has a milder taste than common garlic, a mauve flower head, and grows to 5 feet.

GROWING METHOD

Planting. Divide bulbs into cloves in early spring. Replant the cloves in spring in very cold areas; in spring to summer in warm climates; and in winter to spring in tropical areas. Sow 1½ inches deep, 6 inches apart, in rows 12 inches apart. Keep weed-free. Left in the ground, the plant will die back in fall after flowering.

Watering. Keep soil damp but not over-wet. Be sparing with watering as the bulbs mature, and get rid of excess moisture otherwise garlic will not store satisfactorily after harvesting.

Fertilizing. Prepare beds with an application of complete fertilizer. If using organic matter, apply several months before sowing to ensure it is completely broken down.

Problems. Garlic has few problems because the strong oils and chemicals in its foliage repel insects and have antiseptic properties that deter bacteria and fungal diseases. Keep plants well spaced to reduce humidity, which can affect the plant especially in coastal areas.

HARVESTING

Picking. Harvest in summer when the flower dies and the leaves begin to turn yellow. To harvest when the plant is in full bloom, bend stems in half and leave for 8–10 days. At the end of this period ease the bulbs out of the ground with a fork, taking care not to damage them.

Storing. With leaves intact, dry in clumps in full sun for a few days. On no account let the bulbs get wet. Hang in an open mesh bag in a dry, airy position.

Freezing. Place cloves, separated from bulbs, in freezer bags. Freeze for up to 3 months.

USES

Culinary. When garlic is cooked, some of the starch converts to sugar, making it less pungent than when raw. Chopping or crushing garlic releases the flavors; over-browning or burning can cause bitterness. Garlic adds flavor to a variety of sauces, stews, and meats and it can be barbecued or roasted whole or in cloves. In dishes such as aïoli, tapenade, and pesto, it is indispensable. If used to excess, garlic will overpower the other flavors in the dish.

Gardening. Garlic is useful as a companion plant for fruit trees, tomatoes, and roses. The strong secretions of sulphur from garlic are thought to improve the scent of roses. Garlic spray is very useful as a deterrent to pests such as aphids, cabbage worm, caterpillars, spiders, and ants.

Allium sativum
GARLIC
Alliaceae

CONDITIONS

Climate. As with onions, garlic can be grown in most climates, from protected coastal positions to inland regions. It is frost-resistant at all stages.

Aspect. Prefers full sun in open position.

Soil. Soil should be well-drained sandy loam, rich in humus and not too acid, pH about 6. With strongly acid soils apply ground limestone or dolomite.

Alocasia macrorrhiza, syn. *Colocasia esculenta*

TARO
Araceae

CONDITIONS
Climate. Requires warm climate with long hot summer. Does best in tropical and subtropical areas with temperatures about 95°F. The tubers cannot be cultivated in frost-prone areas.

Aspect. Taro prefers full sun.

Soil. Fertile, friable soil containing plenty of organic material. Soil should also be moist and well drained.

FEATURES
Also known as dasheen, taro is an edible tuber with a high starch level similar to that of the potato, but with a lower water content. The flesh can be white to purplish or greenish. The tuber has a spherical shape, growing to 8 inches with a thick, fibrous, hairy, light brown skin, and characterized by divisional markings on the circumference. It is a large plant, growing to 3½–5 feet with large, light green, shield-shaped leaves resembling elephants' ears that are borne on long stalks. The leaves, sometimes called callaloo, are also edible and sometimes grown purely for their decorative quality. This vegetable is eaten in many tropical countries throughout the world, and is particularly popular in the West Indies.

GROWING METHOD
Planting. Plant fall and winter in warm zones and in midsummer to midwinter in tropical areas. If using small tubers, called "sons of taro", hived off from the parent tuber, plant during spring. Plant in furrows or trenches 6 inches deep and spaced 12 inches apart in rows about 3½ feet apart. After planting, cover tubers with 2 inches soil, and water in. Taro is best grown near an irrigation ditch so as to benefit from water run-off. Propagation may also be by stem cuttings. Sometimes the plant is "forced" in warm, dark conditions to produce blanched leaves, and these are considered a delicacy by food lovers.

Watering. Needs a great deal of regular watering during its growth cycle.

Fertilizing. Add a complete fertilizer to soil. Do not over-fertilize with nitrogen because this will promote excessive leaf growth at the expense of the tuber.

Problems. Relatively free of any specific pests and diseases.

HARVESTING
Picking. Taro matures in 3–7 months, depending on the variety. At maturity, the leaves turn yellow and the plant almost dies. When this happens, carefully lift the tubers from the soil, especially if there is any danger of a cold spell because this will cause damage to the tuber. Young leaves and stems are also edible and should be picked as soon as the leaves open. However, never strip the plant fully because some leaves are necessary for the continuing successful development of the tuber.

Storing. Will keep for several months in a cool, dry place.

Freezing. Peel and cut into pieces. Blanch for 3 minutes in boiling water. Cool and spread on a tray in a single layer and freeze for 30 minutes. Remove from the freezer, pack in freezer bags, then freeze for up to 6 months.

USES
Culinary. Taro roots can be used in a similar way to potatoes—fried, baked, roasted, boiled, or steamed. They are nuttier in flavor than potatoes when cooked.

FEATURES

One of a very large group of plants called amaranths, Chinese spinach, or amaranth, is a colorful leafy vegetable cultivated for its nutritional value. Erect and branching, this annual grows to 3½ feet or more under ideal conditions. Soft textured leaves can grow to 6 inches. The leaves are pointed or round, light to dark green and both leaves and stems have red to purple markings. The flavor is somewhat like that of an artichoke, although older plants can develop a hot taste. It grows well in containers and looks attractive.

GROWING METHOD

Planting. Plant seeds in spring and summer in warm and tropical areas, when the soil warms to about 68°F. The seeds are very small and before sowing should be mixed with coarse wet sand and set aside in a dark place for one or two days. Place the sand and seed mixture in garden trenches to a depth of ¾ inch and firm over. Keep trenches 10 inches apart and thin seedlings to 3½–4 inches apart. Successive sowings every fortnight will give a longer cropping period. Seeds can also be germinated under cover in late spring to early summer. Seedlings will appear in 2–3 weeks and can be transplanted out when about ¾ inch high and showing 2–3 true leaves. Chinese spinach can also be propagated from cuttings, which are usually taken from the areas of younger growth or sideshoots that have not flowered. The plant may bolt if left to dry out in hot weather and if it does, remove any flowers and seed heads that appear.

Watering. It is essential to keep soil moist for succulent growth.

Fertilizing. Feed occasionally with a dressing of nitrogenous liquid.

Problems. Young seedlings may become too damp and wither or flop. In warmer climates caterpillars and stem borer may also be a problem. Treat with appropriate sprays.

HARVESTING

Picking. Takes 6–8 weeks from sowing for plant to reach cropping stage. There are several ways to harvest. Tips of larger plants can be picked while quite young. Alternatively, the whole plant may be pulled from the ground, roots and all, when approximately 10 inches tall. Another method is to cut the mature plant back to 1½ inches above ground level, leaving some of the stem and a few basal leaves to promote regrowth.

Storing. The leaves will last for up to 3 days in the fridge, but will go limp immediately outside.

Freezing. Wash and trim leaves. Blanch for 1 minute, then chill, drain, pack in freezer bags, and freeze for up to 6 months.

USES

Culinary. The leaves have a slightly pungent flavor and are used in the same way as spinach. Young shoot pickings can be used in salads.

Amaranthus tricolor
CHINESE SPINACH
Amaranthaceae

CONDITIONS

Climate. Best grown in hot climates above 68°F. Will grow under cover where temperatures are controlled.

Aspect. Prefers sunny position, sheltered from winds in cool areas. Tolerates partial shade in hot areas.

Soil. Grows in light, sandy to heavy soils that are well drained. Soil must, however, be quite fertile and preferably slightly acidic. Dig in plenty of organic material in the form of compost, decayed animal and poultry manures. If the beds are well prepared in this way there will be little need for chemical fertilizers.

FEATURES

Celery is a biennial that is mostly grown as an annual. It has a tight collection of green stalks or stems that are about 10 inches tall and topped with many dividing leaves. Both stalks and leaves are edible. The seeds, produced from flowers when the plant is left to grow and not cropped, are also edible. Celery is not an easy crop for the home gardener.

GROWING METHOD

Planting. Plant in spring to summer in cool areas; winter through to summer in warm zones; and summer through to fall in tropical areas. In temperatures above 55°F, plant seed directly into open beds. Seed viability is often poor, so use fresh seeds for new plantings, sown $\frac{1}{8}$ inch deep in seed beds. Keep well-watered throughout the 2–3 week germination period. When the seedlings are about $4\frac{3}{4}$ inches high, thin and plant in the garden in trenches 4 inches deep. Leave 10 inches between plants and $1\frac{1}{2}$–2 feet between rows. Mound soil around young plants with roots well covered and thoroughly watered in. Keep beds weed-free by shallow cultivation.

Watering. Celery requires a great deal of water from seed to maturity; daily watering is needed during hot dry weather. Lack of water leads to slow growth and stringy, tasteless stalks.

Fertilizing. Enrich beds with complete fertilizer. Fortnightly side dressings are essential throughout the growing period. This is especially important because the plant is shallow rooted and the frequent watering is likely to have leached essential nutrients from the soil. Occasional dressings of sulphate of ammonia will assist growth.

Problems. A fungal disease known as leaf spot or septoria may affect this plant, producing dead spots on leaves. Control with an appropriate fungicide spray. Magnesium and calcium deficiency in soil also increases the risk of disease.

HARVESTING

Picking. Celery matures 4–5 months after planting. Cut the whole plant at ground level before seed stalks appear, or do occasional cropping by breaking off outside stems as needed.

Storing. Store in the crisper drawer of the fridge wrapped in plastic for up to 10 days. To revive wilted celery, sprinkle with water and put in the fridge until it becomes crisp again.

Freezing. Cut into 1 inch pieces. Blanch for 2 minutes in boiling water. Chill, drain, pack in freezer bags, then freeze for up to 6 months.

USES

Culinary. Celery stems are eaten raw in salads, as crudités, cooked and served as a vegetable, braised in tomato or cream, or used as a base flavor in stocks and sauces. Celery leaves are used to add flavor to stocks and soups and the tender inner leaves can be used in salads or eaten with the stalk. The seeds can be dried and used in soups and pickles.

Apium graveolens
CELERY
Apiaceae

CONDITIONS

Climate. Prefers mild to cool weather and cool nights. Very cold weather will inhibit growth. Seedlings are sensitive to temperatures below 55°F.

Aspect. Tolerates light shade and wet weather.

Soil. Soil needs neutral to alkaline pH level. Liming will reduce acidity. Prepare beds with animal manure, compost, and an addition of complete fertilizer.

FEATURES

Attractive fern-like feathery foliage is a feature of this hardy perennial which grows to 3½ feet tall. The edible part of the plant is the tender young stem or spear. Male and female flowers grow on separate plants, with male plants producing larger and better spears. Female plants, identified by their red berries, should be discarded after the second fall of growth. This delicious vegetable is easy to grow, but is not suitable for container growing.

GROWING METHOD

Planting. Plant seeds in spring in special beds. Transfer 2-year-old seedlings during winter or spring to a permanent position. Alternatively, buy and plant 2-year-old crowns in winter. Prepare permanent beds to a depth of 12 inches with plenty of organic matter and complete fertilizer. Plant in trenches that are 10 inches in width and depth. Set crowns 1½ feet apart in the trench and cover with 2 inches of soil. As the fern grows, cover with soil until the trench is filled, leaving new shoots uncovered. For "white" or blanched asparagus, mound soil over trenches to a depth of about 10 inches in late winter. The fern dies off in winter and new shoots occur in spring.

Watering. Keep soil moist, especially when spears are forming. Dry soil causes stringy stalks.

Fertilizing. Apply regular applications of high-nitrogen fertilizer in summer to encourage top growth, and late winter for spring spear growth.

Problems. Mostly problem-free. Grow rust-resistant varieties to lessen incidence of rust. Spray for asparagus beetle if this becomes a problem.

HARVESTING

Picking. Harvest 3-year-old plant in late winter or early spring. Cut when the spears are 6–8 inches long, at or just below soil level, being careful not to damage adjacent new shoots. Feathering of the spear means the harvest is too late. Harvest along the same row at 2-week intervals in season, for up to 8 weeks. For white asparagus, cut the spear 6 inches below soil level when the tip has just broken the surface. Production increases annually and maturity occurs at 4–5 years.

Storing. Refrigerate for 7–10 days. Break off the rough ends and stand upright in 1½ inches of water.

Freezing. Remove woody portions. Cut into 6 inch lengths, blanch in boiling water for 3 minutes. Cool, place on trays in a single layer, then freeze for 30 minutes. Remove from freezer, pack into freezer bags, then freeze for up to 6 months.

USES

Culinary. Cook the delicate shoots briefly and with care so as not to damage the fragile tips. Once cooked, serve asparagus with melted butter and Parmesan cheese, or add to risottos, quiches, stir-fries, or salads.

Asparagus officinalis
ASPARAGUS
Asparagaceae

CONDITIONS

Climate. Grows well in mild to cold climates and can withstand frosts, which fit in with dormancy period.

Aspect. Prefers full sun but will grow in partial shade.

Soil. Fertile, well-drained soil with a pH of over 6.

Beta vulgaris
BEET
Chenopodiaceae

CONDITIONS

Climate. Beet tolerates frost and grows best in cooler climates. However, it can grow in most climates. In regions with very hot weather, roots tend to become woody; if the weather becomes too cold, young plants may not develop roots and will run to seed. Watch planting times if you have these two extremes of temperature during the crucial stages of the growing season.

Aspect. Can tolerate both full sun and partial shade.

Soil. Prefers loose soils, which allow root to grow freely. Soils need to be high in organic matter, well limed, and with good drainage.

FEATURES

Beet, or beetroot, is mostly cultivated as an annual vegetable. The swollen edible root can be either rounded or tapered and is red, yellow (golden beet), or white. The leaves sprout as a rosette above-ground and are delicious used in salads when young. Beet is suitable for growing in either gardens or large containers; however, the *Cylindrica* variety, with its long tubular roots, is not suitable for containers.

GROWING METHOD

Planting. Sow in spring through to early fall in colder areas, during spring and fall in warm regions, and all season in subtropical climates. Sow seeds directly into garden soil and stagger planting by a month for continuous supply throughout harvesting period. Prepare trenches 4 inches deep, 3½ inches wide, and in rows 1½ feet apart. Lay a narrow band of complete fertilizer in the trench and cover with 2¾ inches of soil. Lay seeds on top, then fill the trench with soil. Alternatively, dig in a complete fertilizer throughout the bed before sowing. Thin out the very young seedlings to 1½ inches apart and later to 2½ inches as the root swells. Beets do not like weed competition, but when weeding take care not to damage developing roots.

Watering. Give young beets plenty of water to encourage larger, tender roots. Left to dry out, the vegetable becomes tough and stringy.

Fertilizing. In new beds, use a complete fertilizer. Do not over-manure or over-fertilize soils in beds that have been heavily fertilized for the previous crop because this leads to rather tasteless beets with a low sugar content.

Problems. Seldom any problems.

HARVESTING

Picking. Beets mature about 3–4 months after sowing, depending on area and seasonal conditions. Harvest before the plant goes to seed and when the root is sufficiently large.

Storing. Refrigerate the roots for up to 3 weeks. The leaves can be refrigerated for up to 1 week. Beets can also be canned or pickled.

Freezing. Only freeze tender young beets. Cook until tender and slice, chop, or leave whole. Cool and transfer to plastic containers, then freeze for up to 6 months.

USES

Culinary. Beet is remarkably versatile: grate it raw and add to salads; bake, steam, or boil it; purée it with oil and spices to make a dip; or as in Eastern European kitchens, use it to make the soup, borscht. Cook and use the leaves as you would spinach. Blanched, it can be added to soups, salads, or pasta sauces.

FEATURES

Swiss chard, or silverbeet, is a member of the beet family and is often mistakenly called spinach. Swiss chard has white to cream ribbed stems supporting large, green, crinkly leaves. All these parts are edible. Different varieties, called chards, are available and their varicolored (red, orange, gold, and yellow) stems make them attractive deep-container plants. Swiss chard is an easy vegetable to grow in the home garden.

GROWING METHOD

Planting. Plant late summer and during spring in colder areas, midwinter to early summer in temperate zones, and all year round in subtropical climates. Do not sow in winter months. Sow seeds directly into the garden in trenches ¾ inch deep, 4–6 inches apart, along rows 16 inches apart. Apply fertilizer along each side of the trench base, fill with soil, firm down, and water in. Seedlings should appear within 2 weeks. When 1½ inches high, thin so seedlings are 12 inches apart. Swiss chard should mature within 8–12 weeks of planting and may bolt to seed in hot weather. Remove flower stems as they appear and keep beds free of weeds. Mulch in hot weather.

Watering. Keep soil moist by regular waterings.

Fertilizing. Swiss chard likes a good complete fertilizer that is nitrogen-rich. Apply monthly side dressings of urea to achieve a vigorous growth.

Problems. Swiss chard is reasonably hardy but leaf spot (gray spots with brown leaf edges) can affect spring plantings. Treat with appropriate sprays, otherwise the infected leaves should be picked and burned. Aphids and leaf miners can be controlled by vigorous hosing or by picking the insects off the plant.

HARVESTING

Picking. Swiss chard will have a long cropping period if the seed is sown at the right time. Pick the mature outside leaves as the need arises and the plant will probably go on producing all season. Do not cut the stalks, but break or peel off by a downwards and sideways action. Leave younger stalks on the parent plant to encourage further growth. Alternatively, the whole plant can be cropped by cutting down to 2 inches and then left to regenerate.

Storing. Refrigerate for up to 2 weeks.

Freezing. Wash, trim leaves, and blanch in boiling water for 1 minute. Chill, drain, pack in freezer bags, then freeze for up to 6 months.

USES

Culinary. Eat cooked or raw in salads; use stalks in sauces, added to soups, or sautéed.

Gardening. Interplant Swiss chard with flowers in a mixed ornamental and edible bed.

Beta vulgaris var. *cicla*
SWISS CHARD
Chenopodiaceae

CONDITIONS

Climate. All climate zones are suitable, although it is best to avoid growing in very hot or frosty cold months.

Aspect. Prefers full sun or partial shade.

Soil. Well-drained, rich, neutral, or slightly alkaline soil. Prepare beds with plenty of compost or decayed manure.

Brassica napus Napobrassica Group
RUTABAGA
Brassicaceae

CONDITIONS
Climate. Best grown as a cool climate crop, but all climates are suitable, depending on the variety grown.

Aspect. Prefers full sun to partial shade.

Soil. Fertile, well-drained soil. Prepare beds with plenty of organic matter to assist free growth of roots. Beds that have been well fertilized and worked over for a previous crop are ideal. Do not plant in same bed as earlier crop from *Brassica* genus.

FEATURES
The rutabaga belongs to a group that includes vegetables such as cabbage, Brussels sprouts, and broccoli. Rutabaga is also known by the name of swede and is very similar to the turnip. It can be identified by the multiple leaf scars on its top and the deeply lobed structure of its grayish-green leaves. The large root, which is actually a swelling at the base of the plant's stem, sits on the soil surface as the vegetable grows. The skin is white, yellow, or purple and the flesh is creamy to yellow.

GROWING METHOD
Planting. For best results in cold regions have two plantings, one in midsummer and the other at the end of winter; plant late summer to early fall in temperate zones; and plant at the end of summer to mid-fall in hot, subtropical areas. Successive planting every 3 weeks ensures a longer cropping period. Sow seeds directly into the ground, no more than $\frac{1}{2}$ inch deep in rows 10 inches apart. Cover with compost and water in. Thin plants to $4\frac{3}{4}$ inches apart after seedlings appear, which should be within the first fortnight after sowing. Do not hill soil around exposed vegetable. Keep beds weed-free, being particularly careful not to damage the developing root.

Watering. Give vegetables plenty of water, especially through hot weather periods to avoid plant drying out. Rutabagas do not do well in dry conditions.

Fertilizing. Prepare bed with a light dressing of poultry manure plus a complete fertilizer that has a good amount of phosphorus. Apply side dressings of the same fertilizer about 4 weeks after planting.

Problems. This vegetable has no serious diseases but does suffer from various pest infestations. Aphids may be hosed off or controlled with appropriate sprays. Other pests, including caterpillars and grubs, which affect other brassicas do damage to rutabagas and turnips. Spraying with a recommended insecticide every 2 weeks from seedling stage onwards will help to control pests.

HARVESTING
Picking. This vegetable reaches maturity in about 3–4 months, or sometimes earlier in warmer areas. When harvesting the root, pull whole roots from the ground before they become coarse and woody otherwise they develop a very strong flavor.

Storing. Store in a cool, dark place. Rutabagas can be waxed with melted paraffin to prevent wrinkling during storage. They will keep in the fridge for about 4 weeks.

USES
Culinary. Use in a similar way to turnips—roast, boil, or bake—but they will take longer to cook. The leafy tops of very young vegetables can be used successfully in salads.

FEATURES

Chinese kale is known by various names such as gai larn or kailan and is often used in Asian cooking. This stout, leafy plant grows to about 1½ feet. It has thick, crisp leaves that are blue-green to gray with a waxy look. The leaves have different shapes and sizes, depending on the variety. The plant has medium-sized, attractive, white or yellow flowers. Chinese kale is cultivated as a vegetable for its chunky edible ½–¾ inch stem. It is only suitable for container growing if young plants are to be harvested. Older plants need to be grown in the garden. It has a small, shallow rooting system.

GROWING METHOD

Planting. Sow from late spring through summer to early fall in all areas. Midsummer sowings produce the heaviest yields. If harvesting young plants, scatter seed directly into the garden or a large container, thinning later to 6 inches apart. For plants that will be left to mature and have a longer cropping period, sow seeds directly into garden, spacing 12 inches apart. The plant matures in about 12–14 weeks. Secondary shoots will appear after the main flowering shoot is cut.

Watering. Keep soil moist and water frequently.

Fertilizing. Provide extra nitrogen supplements in liquid fertilizers, especially if the soil is sandy. For plants exposed to windy conditions, firm soil up around roots for strength and protection. Dig in a generous application of poultry manure and a little complete fertilizer. Side dressings of sulphate of ammonia during the growing season or weekly applications of liquid seaweed aid growth.

Problems. Susceptible to downy mildew. Treat with appropriate fungicide. Plant leaves give cover to slugs and caterpillars. Spray or dust for protection.

HARVESTING

Picking. If plant is left to mature, it can be harvested over a long period. Cut the shoots or stems when approximately 6 inches long and before the flowers open. Harvest frequently in hot climates to prevent the plant bolting and shoots becoming tough. Alternatively, the whole plant can be harvested while quite young, usually about 6 weeks after sowing.

Storing. Will keep for a long time, either in or out of the fridge.

Freezing. Cut to required size, blanch for 3 minutes, chill. Drain and place on a tray in a single layer, then freeze for 30 minutes. Remove from freezer, pack in freezer bags, then freeze for up to 6 months.

USES

Culinary. Steam whole or cut up the leaves and stems and add to soups and stir-fries. Young stalks are crisp and mild; thicker stalks need to be peeled and halved.

Brassica oleracea Alboglabra Group
CHINESE KALE
Brassicaceae

CONDITIONS

Climate. Can be successfully grown in all climatic zones, even tolerating frosts once past the seedling stage.

Aspect. Chinese kale does best in a sunny position. Needs to be protected from strong winds, which may "lift" and move the plant because of its shallow root system.

Soil. Fertile, well-drained soil. Prepare the soil with organic material such as compost and animal and poultry manure.

Brassica oleracea Botrytis Group
CAULIFLOWER
Brassicaceae

CONDITIONS

Climate. Cauliflowers can be grown in most climates but do not like extremes of temperature. Like most brassicas they do best in cooler areas, needing lower temperatures for the flower heads to form.

Aspect. Need to be protected from both full sunlight and frosts or maturing heads will discolor.

Soil. These plants are heavy feeders, requiring rich, well-drained soil with plenty of well-rotted manure or compost. They do not like acid soils, requiring a pH of at least 6.5.

FEATURES

Grown as an annual, this plant has a single stalk supporting a solid head made up of a collection of edible flower buds. Heads can be white, green, or purple, depending upon which variety of cauliflower is grown. Both quick and late maturing types are available. "Mini" varieties are now on the market and require only half the growing space of the larger cauliflowers. Cauliflowers have large rooting systems and are not suited to container growing.

GROWING METHOD

Planting. Sow from late spring through summer in cool areas; summer and fall in temperate areas; and fall in subtropical areas, to establish advanced plants before winter. Sow seeds $\frac{1}{2}$ inch deep in outdoor beds in rows 2 inches apart. Use a number of varieties with differing maturing dates so as to extend the cropping season. Seedlings take about 6 weeks to appear and are ready for transplanting when around 4–4$\frac{3}{4}$ inches high. Transplant only in cool weather and space at least 2 feet apart. To keep the cauliflower white, tie some of the largest leaves together and place them over the head. Start to do this when the head is quite small and replace the leaves as the head grows larger.

Watering. Keep soil moist and air humid around maturing plants to assist head development, but avoid watering directly over the head, which may cause damage. The head may need protection from heavy rainfalls for the same reason.

Fertilizing. Three to 4 weeks before planting, prepare bed with complete fertilizer and a good amount of dolomite or lime, which assists in the uptake of the trace element molybdenum. Apply side dressings of the same fertilizer mid-season or 4 weeks after transplanting seedlings. Cauliflowers will take more manuring and fertilizers than other brassicas. Dressings of urea will promote growth if applied when heads are starting to form.

Problems. Caterpillars of the cabbage white butterfly and aphids are a problem in warmer zones. Treat with an appropriate pesticide. Yellowing and withering of leaves is due to molybdenum or magnesium deficiency. Water seedlings with a solution of $\frac{3}{4}$ ounce sodium molybdate dissolved in 9 pints water.

HARVESTING

Picking. Harvest 4–5 months after planting. Remove heads when about 8 inches wide; cutting before they become discolored and lose their crisp firmness. Leaves can also be harvested and used as a green cooking vegetable.

Storing. Remove the leaves and refrigerate for up to 1 week.

Freezing. Divide into florets and blanch for 3 minutes. Chill, drain, and place on a tray in a single layer. Freeze for 30 minutes. Remove, pack in freezer bags, and freeze for up to 6 months.

USES

Culinary. Steam, boil, or stir-fry or eat raw as crudités. Can also be pickled or used in soups.

FEATURES

This very hardy vegetable is grown as an annual. The edible head is a large, terminal bud composed of tightly packed, overlapping leaves that form a round or sometimes pointed head. The leaves are either green or purple, depending on the variety, and have a smooth or crinkled texture. The stem is short except when the plant is left to go to seed.

GROWING METHOD

Planting. Plant in summer and spring in cool zones and all year round in other areas. Sow seeds ½ inch deep and 3½ inches apart in seed beds. Transplant into garden when seedlings are 5–6 weeks old, with 4 to 5 true leaves in evidence. Plant seedlings deeply, up to first leaves, 2 feet apart, in rows 2¾ feet apart, depending on variety. Sugar loaf cabbages need just 12–16 inches between plants. Harden off seedlings by withholding water for a couple of days just before transplanting.

Watering. Cabbages like a lot of watering, so keep topsoil moist at all times.

Fertilizing. Prepare bed several weeks before planting with a complete fertilizer and a good amount of dolomite. Spread small amounts of the same fertilizer over the garden bed one month after planting and water in at once. When cabbages start to form firm hearts, apply a light dressing of urea, especially if soils are sandy.

Problems. Cabbage white butterfly caterpillars, center grubs, and corn ear worms attack cabbages and destroy the growing buds. Spray every 2 weeks from seedling stage onwards with an appropriate insecticide. Downy mildew and magnesium deficiency are common.

HARVESTING

Picking. Harvest between 14 and 16 weeks when the head is firm. Remove from the stem by cutting, leaving the outer leaves attached to the stem. In cool areas, harvest summer through to fall; in warm areas, harvest late spring through to early summer; and in subtropical zones, harvest in fall and winter.

Storing. Refrigerate for several weeks. Can also be pickled as sauerkraut.

Freezing. Remove outer leaves. Cut into thin wedges or shred. Blanch for 2 minutes. Chill, drain, pack into freezer bags, then freeze for up to 6 months.

USES

Culinary. White-hearted cabbages are good raw and can be shredded finely in coleslaw or salads; all cabbages are good in stir-fries, braised, steamed, or added to soups; cabbage leaves can be used to wrap fillings; or the French are known to stuff a whole cabbage with sausage. Red cabbage shredded and cooked with onions, stock, red wine, and vinegar, is a classic accompaniment to game and pork dishes. Shredded and salted cabbage is used to make sauerkraut, which should be rinsed and drained well before serving.

Brassica oleracea Capitata Group
CABBAGE
Brassicaceae

CONDITIONS

Climate. Adaptable to a wide range of climates but best as a cool weather crop. It is frost-tolerant but not tolerant to extremes of heat, which cause the head to split.

Aspect. Prefers a sunny position.

Soil. Well-drained soil with a pH of 6.5 to 7.5 that has been made fertile with the addition of decomposed animal or poultry manure and compost. Keep garden beds well mulched.

Brassica oleracea Gemmifera Group
BRUSSELS SPROUT
Brassicaceae

CONDITIONS
Climate. Cool growing season is preferable. This hardy brassica tolerates frosts but does not like either extended cold or hot periods. Not suitable for growing in hot, subtropical climates. Areas with a temperature range between 77°F by day and 50°F at night are ideal.

Aspect. Garden beds should have a sunny aspect and be adequately drained.

Soil. Most soils are suitable except sandy soils, which produce loose, leafy vegetables with no heart. Young plants will do best in soils with pH of 6.5–7.5. Brussels sprouts will not grow in waterlogged soils.

FEATURES
The Brussels sprout is a member of the cabbage family with similar requirements to those of cabbages. The small heads measure about 2 inches in diameter, resemble cabbages and sprout from a tall, main stem among large, green leaves.

GROWING METHOD
Planting. Plant during summer through fall in cooler climates; during summer and early fall in temperate zones. Sow seeds ½ inch deep, well spaced, in seed boxes. Transplant seedlings 1½ feet apart, in rows 2 feer apart, when 4 inches tall. Protect plants from wind damage by hilling soil around plants. Removal of the terminal bud when the plant is about 16 inches encourages sprouts to mature all at the same time.

Watering. Plants need a great deal of water as well as cool, moist air to encourage growth. Ease off on watering a week or two before harvesting.

Fertilizing. Prepare beds some weeks ahead of transplanting by digging in a good amount of poultry manure combined with a complete fertilizer. Add extra nitrogen during picking times; if heavy rains have leached the soil, apply ⅕ ounce of nitrate of potash to each plant.

Problems. This vegetable is very prone to pests and diseases. Cabbage white butterfly caterpillars cause problems early in the season and later aphids, slugs, and snails may damage sprouts. Control these pests with commercial and/or organic sprays. Downy mildew and club root (intensified by acidic, moist soil conditions) should be treated with constant applications of fungicide. Yellowish areas around leaves are indicative of magnesium deficiency. Water soil around plant with a solution of 1 ounce magnesium sulphate (Epsom salts) in 9 pints water. Remember, many of these conditions can be avoided if proper drainage is provided in the first place. Proper preparation will prevent later problems.

HARVESTING
Picking. The growing season is 5–6 months. Harvest period is late summer through spring, unless the weather is too hot in which case the harvest time will be shorter. Mature sprouts are harvested frequently, especially in warmer zones, and are picked before they burst, starting at the bottom of the stem where mature sprouts first develop.

Storing. Refrigerate for 7–10 days. Early winter sprouts left on the stem and hung in a cool, dry place will keep for up to a month.

Freezing. Remove outer leaves and cut a cross at the stem end. Blanch for 3 minutes, then cool and drain. Spread on a tray in a single layer and freeze for 30 minutes. Remove from tray, pack in plastic bags, then freeze for up to 6 months.

USES
Culinary. Brussels sprouts can be steamed or boiled, or shredded and used in a stir-fry.

FEATURES

Kohl is the German word for cabbage and *rabi* means turnip, and these two words perfectly describe kohlrabi. It is a cabbage-like root producing a swollen white, purple or green, turnip-shaped stem above-ground. Circles of edible green leaves grow from the stem. The taste is somewhere between a cabbage and a turnip, not as strong and slightly sweeter than either. This is a favorite vegetable in Asian cuisines.

GROWING METHOD

Planting. Sow from midsummer to fall in all areas. Early spring sowings are also viable in regions with cooler temperatures. Seedlings do not transplant readily, so it is preferable to plant seeds directly into prepared garden beds. Sow seeds in rows 1½–2 feet apart and cover with no more than ½ inch of soil. Thin seedlings to 4 inches apart when about 2 inches high. Like other brassicas, kohlrabi has a shallow root system, so keep bed free of weeds by shallow cultivation.

Fertilizing. Prepare beds several weeks before sowing with complete fertilizer and a good amount of lime or dolomite. Spread small amounts of the same fertilizer over the garden bed 1 month after planting and water in immediately. Light side dressings of urea help growth as the vegetable matures. Fortnightly applications may be necessary in sandy soils.

Watering. Keep topsoil evenly moist at all times otherwise the texture of the vegetable will turn toward woodiness.

Problems. Common pests are the same as those that attack cabbages, including caterpillars of the cabbage white butterfly and center grub. Spraying with an appropriate pesticide is recommended every 2 weeks from seedling stage onwards. Downy mildew and magnesium deficiency are common.

HARVESTING

Picking. The growing season for this vegetable is short at about 8–10 weeks. Always aim to harvest during cool weather when the vegetable has reached 2–2¾ inches in diameter. Kohlrabi has a tendency to bolt in cooler areas where growing season temperatures fall below 66°F.

Storing. Refrigerate for 7–10 days.

Freezing. Wash, peel, and cut into pieces. Blanch for 3 minutes, chill, drain, and spread on a tray in a single layer and freeze for 30 minutes. Remove from tray, pack in plastic bags, then freeze for up to 6 months.

USES

Culinary. Can be either grated or sliced raw, added to stir-fries or stews, mashed, or cooked in chunks and tossed in butter.

Brassica oleracea Gongylodes Group
KOHLRABI
Brassicaceae

CONDITIONS

Climate. All climates from sub-zero to subtropical are suitable for growing this vegetable.

Aspect. Prefers sunny, well-drained beds with cool, moist soil.

Soil. Soil should be well drained and rich in organic matter. Dig in plenty of well-rotted animal manure. This will help to retain moisture levels in the soil, but do not hill soil around the vegetable as it matures. Aim for a pH range of 6.5–7.5.

FEATURES
Grown as an annual, broccoli looks like green cauliflower. Flower stalks are green, purplish to white in color and the plant has tiny yellow flowers. The edible part of broccoli is the head, which is eaten when it is green and in bud, not when yellow flowers are showing.

GROWING METHOD
Planting. Sow seeds $3\frac{1}{2}$ inches apart, $\frac{3}{4}$ inch deep, during late spring to early summer in cold climates; in late summer to fall in warmer zones; and in fall to winter in tropical areas. Successive sowings 1 month apart will produce a longer cropping period. To raise seedlings, grow in punnets or small 4 inches pots. After about 6 weeks, when seedlings are 4 inches tall and at least four true leaves have appeared, transfer to garden beds planting 20 inches apart, in rows 2 feet apart. After initial rapid leaf growth, the edible head develops in about 3–4 months. Sideshoots develop after the central head has been harvested. To encourage new growth, leave base of plant and some outer leaves on the plant after cropping.

Watering. Plant grows quickly, so keep soil moist by constant watering, if necessary. Cut down on watering as heads mature. Lack of moisture leads to seeding without head formation.

Fertilizing. Dig in a good amount of poultry manure with complete fertilizer to prepare beds. Side dressings of sulphate of ammonia during the growing season will produce healthy plants. Weekly applications of liquid seaweed fertilizer also improve crops.

Problems. Broccoli is quite prone to disease, but the risk can be reduced by seasonal crop rotation. Larvae of the cabbage white butterfly are the main pests. Control with commercial and/or organic sprays. Curling of the leaf indicates a shortage of molybdenum. Water seedlings either before or after transplanting with a solution containing $\frac{1}{5}$ ounce sodium molybdate in 9 pints water. In moist, cool areas, the plant is prone to downy mildew. To prevent, make sure plant is well aerated and has maximum sunlight penetration.

HARVESTING
Picking. When buds are large and firm but not yet flowering, cut the large central head leaving about 6 inches of stalk attached.

Storing. Refrigerate for up to a week.

Freezing. Choose tender young heads and divide into sprigs. Blanch for 3 minutes, chill, then drain. Spread on a tray in a single layer and freeze for 30 minutes. Remove from tray, pack in plastic bags, then freeze for up to 6 months.

USES
Culinary. Broccoli can be eaten raw, steamed, or boiled, and the stalks, which are quite sweet, can be peeled and diced and used in the same way as the florets.

Brassica oleracea Italica Group
BROCCOLI
Brassicaceae

CONDITIONS
Climate. Can be grown anywhere except in the hottest and coldest climates, but does require a cool winter to reach maturity. Temperate and cold climates are therefore best with day temperatures not exceeding 77°F and night temperatures not below 59°F.

Aspect. Broccoli can be grown in containers on verandahs, or even indoors, as well as in garden beds that have a sunny position.

Soil. Likes well-drained soil with a pH range of 6.5–7.5. Prepare garden beds with manures and fertilizers, providing an extra nitrogen supplement if soil is sandy.

FEATURES

Chinese cabbage has many names including wong bok and celery cabbage. It has wide, thick, crisp leaves with a prominent, broad-based midrib. The upright heads are either loose or tight, depending on variety. Leaf color varies between dark and light green with inner leaves having a creamy-white color. Plant grows 12–18 inches tall. Flavor ranges from mustardy to sweet and is rather like a lettuce. It is not suitable for containers.

GROWING METHOD

Planting. Plant spring through summer in cold regions, winter through spring in warm zones, and all year round in tropical and subtropical climates. Most importantly, plant to avoid the vegetable reaching maturity in periods of frost. Plant seeds directly into the garden because seedlings do not transplant well. Sow seeds ¼ inch deep, in clumps along the row so that when the seedlings are thinned out plants are 12–16 inches apart. Allow 14–16 inches between rows. Seedlings will emerge 1–2 weeks after planting. Slow growth leads to plant going to seed; plants may bolt in hot, dry weather and where days are long. Select varieties to suit local conditions to lessen these risks. Mulch heavily to retain soil moisture and ward off bacterial rot. Bind heads with string or elastic bands as heads reach maturity to protect tender, white, inner leaves.

Watering. These shallow-rooted vegetables require a great deal of watering to encourage fast growth. Irrigate between rows and keep water off leaves to reduce risk of fungal diseases.

Fertilizing. Dig in a complete fertilizer 1 week before planting. One month after planting, spread small amounts of the same fertilizer around the plants and water in immediately. When cabbages start to form heads, apply a light dressing of urea.

Problems. This cabbage is prone to soil diseases such as club root and bacterial soft rot. Protect the crop by liming and rotating with an unrelated crop several times over a few years. Dust or spray against caterpillars and aphids, which frequently affect this plant.

HARVESTING

Picking. Pick matured crop in dry conditions, 2–3 months after planting. Cut when heads feel solid; if left till seed stalks appear, the heads will split. Cut the heads just above soil level.

Storing. Can be refrigerated or kept in a cool, dry place, such as a cellar, for several weeks or even a few months.

Freezing. Only freeze crisp, young cabbage. Wash and shred. Blanch for 1½ minutes. Chill, drain, place in freezer bags, then freeze for up to 6 months.

USES

Culinary. Shred and eat raw; steam or use in stir-fries, soups, and curries; or use to make cabbage rolls.

Brassica rapa Pekinensis Group
CHINESE CABBAGE
Brassicaceae

CONDITIONS

Climate. Best in cool temperatures from 55–68°F. Tropical varieties have also been developed.

Aspect. Prefers open, sunny position but tolerates partial shade. Shelter from cold winds and frost.

Soil. Deep, well-drained soils, high in organic matter will retain soil moisture and lessen soil compaction. Avoid both light and heavy soils and lime if necessary so that pH range is between 6.5 and 7.

Brassica rapa Rapifera Group
TURNIP
Brassicaceae

CONDITIONS
Climate. Best grown as a cool climate crop, but all climates suit, depending on variety.

Aspect. Prefers full sun to partial shade.

Soil. Well-drained, loose, deep soil. Garden beds should be well prepared with plenty of organic matter before planting to assist free growth of roots. Beds that have been well fertilized and worked over for a previous crop are ideal as long as the earlier crop did not belong to the *Brassica* genus.

FEATURES
Closely associated with the rutabaga, the turnip is a large root, or more precisely, a swelling at the base of the stem, which sits on the soil surface as the vegetable grows. The turnip comes in a variety of shapes and sizes. It has a white flesh and skin supporting a rosette of green feathery leaves. Both the leaves and root are edible.

GROWING METHOD
Planting. Two plantings are possible in cold regions, one in late summer, the other winter to early spring. Plant midsummer to mid-fall in temperate zones and late summer to early fall in hot, subtropical areas. Successive planting every 3 weeks ensures a longer cropping period. Sow seeds directly into the ground no more than ½ inch deep, in rows 10 inches apart. Cover with compost and water in. Thin plants to 4 inches apart after seedlings appear, which should be within the first fortnight after sowing. Keep free of weeds, being careful not to damage the developing root. Do not hill soil around the exposed vegetable.

Watering. These vegetables require plenty of water, especially through periods of hot weather.

Fertilizing. Prepare bed with a light dressing of poultry manure plus a complete fertilizer that is high in phosphorus. Apply side dressings of the same fertilizer about 4 weeks after planting.

Problems. Turnips have no serious diseases but do suffer from pest infestations. Aphids may be hosed off or controlled with appropriate sprays. Caterpillars and grubs that affect other brassicas can also do damage to rutabagas and turnips. To control, spray with a recommended insecticide every 2 weeks from seedling stage onwards.

HARVESTING
Picking. The vegetable reaches maturity in 2–3 months, sometimes earlier in warmer areas. Pull whole roots from the ground before they become coarse and develop an over-strong flavor. If the seeds have been sown thickly there will be an abundance of extra seedlings, which can be harvested within 8 weeks of planting. The root and leaf are tender and sweet to eat at this young age.

Storing. Turnips have a long storage time, in or out of the refrigerator.

Freezing. Peel and trim tender, young turnips. Cut to required size. Blanch for 3 minutes. Chill, drain, then spread on a tray in a single layer and freeze for 30 minutes. Remove from tray, pack in plastic bags, then freeze for up to 6 months.

USES
Culinary. When young, grate raw and chop leafy tops into salads; braise; or make Chinese-style turnip cake. Use older turnips in soups and stews, or roast, which gives them a sweeter flavor. Boil turnip tops as you would cabbage and serve with butter.

FEATURES

Peppers (also known as capsicums) and chilies are perennial, but are often grown as annuals. The pepper plant grows to an erect, compact bush and the fruits may be a variety of shapes and colors. Chilies, a small form of pepper, produce green or purple fruit, which changes to bright red, yellow, or orange at maturity. Peppers and chilies make excellent container plants. The chili is known for its fiery hotness, whereas peppers have a delicate, rather sweet, flavor.

GROWING METHOD

Planting. Sow during spring to early summer in cooler and temperate regions; all year round, but mainly in fall, in warmer tropical and subtropical zones. Sow seeds in the open garden, especially in colder regions, 8–10 weeks before planting out. In warm climates, direct-seeding into garden beds is possible. Plant successively every 2 months to give a continuous crop. Transplant into fertilized furrows when seedlings are about 16 inches tall, space 20 inches apart, in rows 2 feer apart. Support mature plants in wind-prone areas. Fruits usually develop after insect pollination of flowers. Rotate crops over several seasons. Do not plant in beds in which vegetables from the same family, such as tomatoes, have been grown.

Fertilizing. Prepare beds with plenty of organic matter and apply complete fertilizer 1 week before planting. Lay in furrows 6 inches deep and cover with soil to ground level. After flowering and when fruit has set, apply urea monthly, 6 inches away from the plant. Water in straight away. Do not over-fertilize; too much nitrogen leads to large plants but no fruit.

Watering. To prevent flower drop, water plants so that soil is evenly moist. Over-watering can lead to waterlogging and cold soils. Carefully monitor moisture level in containers.

Problems. Aphids, fruit fly, and cutworm are the main pests. Hose off aphids or spray with the appropriate insecticides that also control fruit fly and cutworm. Watch out for powdery mildew in climates that are hot and humid.

HARVESTING

Picking. Peppers and chilies take 3–4 months to mature. Peppers are sweeter if left to ripen on the vine. Cut to remove, leaving a small brittle stem attached to fruit. Chilies may be picked at any color stage but will be hotter if left to ripen fully.

Storing. Refrigerate peppers for up to 1 week; chilies for 2 weeks or more in a sealed container. Thick-fleshed chilies can be frozen or pickled; thin-fleshed chilies can be dried.

Freezing. Wash, remove seeds, then cut into slices or leave whole. Spread on a tray in a single layer and freeze for 30 minutes. Remove, pack in plastic bags, then freeze for up to 6 months.

USES

Culinary. Remove seeds and eat peppers raw in salads; broiled or baked; or preserved in vinegar. Use chilies raw, roasted, or dried. Mexican recipes usually call for the skin to be removed after roasting because it can be bitter. Drying chilies intensifies the flavor.

Capsicum annuum
PEPPERS AND CHILIES
Solanaceae

CONDITIONS

Climate. Chilies will tolerate hotter climates than peppers but, overall, peppers are best grown as warm season plants. Die-back may occur during winter, but plants shoot again in spring revealing the true perennial nature of the plant.

Aspect. Need plenty of warmth and full sun; not suitable for growing in frost-prone areas. Ideal for container growing in sunny positions and protected from strong winds.

Soil. Light, well-drained soil. Grow chilies in lots of nitrogenous organic matter, rather than running the risk of over-fertilizing with chemical substitutes.

Cichorium endivia

ENDIVE
Asteraceae

CONDITIONS
Climate. Best as a cool season crop. Curly endive is the most cold-tolerant of the two varieties.

Aspect. Prefers direct or partial sun. In hot weather, shade transplanted seedlings, if necessary.

Soil. Prefers neutral to slightly acidic soils, pH range 5–6. Make sure garden bed has good drainage and previously has been well worked and manured.

FEATURES
Endive, or chicory, is similar to lettuce but is chewier and more substantial with slightly bitter leaves. There are two frequently grown varieties: curly endive or frisée is green, has a loose head, finely serrated or frilly leaf edges, and white midribs; escarole or Batavian endive has broad leaves that are thick, smooth, and light green.

GROWING METHOD
Planting. Sow seeds late summer and early fall to give a winter crop. In warmer climates sow from fall to spring. If growing from transplanted seedlings, plant out well before the weather gets hot. Hot summers will force the plants to bolt and go to seed. If intending to crop when young, sow seed thickly in containers to produce less bitter endive. Do not leave to mature in these overcrowded conditions because plants tend to bolt and are more susceptible to disease. In soil, sow seeds ¼ inch deep in rows 20 inches apart, in soil that is rich in humus and which has been thoroughly watered beforehand. Germination takes 10–14 days. Later, thin 4-week-old seedlings out to 12 inches apart. Best treated as an annual. Endive will sometimes grow back after cropping but the quality is usually not good.

Watering. Water endive regularly to encourage growth. Lack of water will prevent growth and cause bitterness in leaves. Sprinklers are not recommended because surplus water trapped inside the endive head may cause rot.

Fertilizing. Two weeks before planting, prepare garden bed by digging in complete fertilizer and a plentiful amount of poultry manure. Dig manure into the top 8 inches of soil because the rooting system is shallow and food needs to be close to the surface.

Problems. Has no serious diseases, but insect pests such as snails, aphids, and cutworm can be a problem. Organic gardeners trap snails by sinking small containers, such as saucers, of stale beer to soil level. Hose off aphids or use an appropriate insecticide; use plant collars to discourage cutworm.

HARVESTING
Picking. If not cropping very young leaves, endive will reach maturity in 2–3 months. Cut plant off at soil level. To reduce bitterness in leaves, cover with layers of straw several weeks before cropping. The exclusion of sunlight, or blanching, slows down production of chlorophyll in the leaves.

Storing. Keeps in the refrigerator for 2 weeks.

Freezing. Do not freeze.

USES
Culinary. Use fresh in salads mixed with other salad greens to add flavor.

FEATURES

Variously known as witloof or Brussels chicory, Belgian endive is the blanched, lettuce-like heart of the endive plant. During growing, the head is forced to grow into a compact form with pointed leaves that are white with green or yellow tips. Belgian endive has a characteristic bittersweet taste; the greener the leaves the more bitter the taste.

GROWING METHOD

Planting. Sow seeds during spring through to early summer directly into garden beds. Plant seeds ½ inch deep, in rows 12 inches apart. Plant closely together, then thin to 10 inches apart when seedlings appear in 10–14 days. Mulch around young plants to keep weeds down and to keep soil moist. Seeds planted in spring may require heavier feeding to produce advanced growth by fall. At this point, about 4 months from the time of planting, the endive should be mature and ready for the second stage of cultivation, that is, the forcing and blanching of the plant. "Lift" plants by cutting off tops to within 2 inches of the root just above the crown. Place upright in a box or container, and cover to exclude sunlight. Top with 6 inches of loose soil to prevent bitterness developing in the leaves. Keep container in a dark place at not less than 50°F. Although the growth process may sound complex, Belgian endive is surprisingly easy for the home gardener to cultivate.

Watering. Water regularly to keep soil moist, especially through the hot summer months of growth to encourage development and to help prevent any bitterness developing in the leaves.

Fertilizing. Prefers previously fertilized beds from another crop. Freshly manured soil is likely to cause forking of the roots. If extra feeding is required, use a modest amount of complete fertilizer.

Problems. Belgian endive is generally not bothered by pests and disease.

HARVESTING

Picking. The second stage of cultivation, or blanching process, takes 8–12 weeks by which time the endive is 6–8 inches long and ready for cropping. Harvest only as necessary because once picked it will become bitter if exposed to light. A second crop can be encouraged if Belgian endive is broken off, rather than cut, when picked.

Storing. Refrigerate for up to 3 days. Store in paper or a brown paper bag to prevent exposure to light.

Freezing. Wash well. Blanch for 3 minutes, chill, drain, and spread on a tray in a single layer and freeze for 30 minutes. Remove from tray, pack in plastic bags, then freeze for 2–3 months.

USES

Culinary. Belgian endive can be broiled, braised in stock, or caramelized. It is popularly used in salads with peppers, artichoke hearts, and sardines.

Cichorium intybus
BELGIAN ENDIVE
Asteraceae

CONDITIONS

Climate. Best grown as a cool season crop.

Aspect. Prefers direct or partial sunlight until put in controlled dark environment for blanching.

Soil. Well-drained, moderately fertile soil.

Cucumis sativus
CUCUMBER
Cucurbitaceae

CONDITIONS
Climate. Best in warm zones. Grows in most areas with a shorter growing season in cold areas.

Aspect. Full sun. To save space in the garden, vine varieties can be trained up a trellis, resulting in cleaner, better-formed fruit than those grown on the ground.

Soil. Light soil. Beds need to be well prepared with compost and animal manures. Heavily mulch soils to avoid compaction and to compensate for the heavy watering cycle, which is essential for successful growth.

FEATURES
Many types of cucumber are available, including long and short green varieties and the round and whitish apple cucumber. An easily digestible, "burpless" variety is also popular. Some cucumber plants grow as a bush and are suited to container growing, others grow as a vine.

GROWING METHOD
Planting. Plant late spring through to summer in cold climates, spring through to summer in warm zones, and from midwinter to mid-fall in tropical and subtropical areas. Sow seed directly into garden bed to a depth of ¾ inch, 20 inches apart, in rows 3½ feet apart. Alternatively, sow several seeds in shallow craters spaced 20 inches apart. When seeds germinate, cull seedlings to 2 or 3 healthy ones.

Watering. Water regularly during growing cycle for plants to thrive. Drooping leaves during the hottest part of the day may be a temporary reaction to extreme conditions and not necessarily a sign of water deprivation.

Fertilizing. One week before planting, thoroughly dig in complete fertilizer to promote successful early growth. When the vines start to show signs of vigorous growth, use side dressings of urea and water in immediately. Repeat at monthly intervals when the vine commences to fruit. Add lime to acidic soils or in areas of high rainfall to prevent molybdenum trace-element deficiency, which causes mottling or yellowing and upward curling of leaves. Spray young plants with a solution of sodium molybdate to rectify the deficiency.

Problems. The banded squash beetle attacks foliage and flowers. Treat with appropriate insecticide. Spray aphids and red spider mite if natural predators cannot control infestations. Powdery mildew is common. To control, spray both upper and lower surfaces with an appropriate fungicide.

HARVESTING
Picking. Pick fruit at optimum time for the variety and climate. As a general rule, when the small, spiny hairs on the fruit are easily brushed off, the fruit is ripe and ready for harvest. Leave too long and the fruit becomes tough, the seeds large, and the taste bitter. Frequent harvesting will lead to greater flower production and subsequent fruiting.

Storing. Choose firm cucumbers with no signs of bruising and store them in the refrigerator wrapped in plastic for 7–10 days.

Freezing. Peel and chop in a food processor. Pack into plastic containers with lids and freeze for up to 3 months.

USES
Culinary. Eat raw as crudités or in salads; cooked in soups; mixed with yogurt as Indian raita to accompany curries; or added to yogurt and garlic to make Greek tzatziki.

FEATURES

Summer squash are a warm weather crop that is picked when immature. Left to ripen, the skin hardens, and we then refer to the vegetable as winter squash. In its immature stage, the plant grows as more of a bush than a vine. Zucchini, a member of the summer squash family, are listed separately. Summer squash can be grown in a sunny position indoors.

GROWING METHOD

Planting. In cold regions, plant seeds in early summer only. Plant in spring in temperate zones and all year round in hot, subtropical climates. Plant seeds ¾ inch deep in seed-raising mix, in pots, 4–5 weeks ahead of planting out. Alternatively, sow directly into garden soil in final growing position. Place several seeds ¾ inch deep in wide, hollow, saucer-shaped depressions that are 8 inches deep. "Hill up" the excavated soil as a rim around the edge of the depression. Leave 3½ feet of garden space between hills. Thin to 2 or 3 plants at seedling stage and to one healthy plant when true leaves appear. Remove seedlings by cutting stems at ground level, being careful not to disturb root structure. If planting in rows, allow a clear 5–6½ feet space around each plant. Keep areas around bush free of weeds and other decaying matter. Shallow-cultivate so as not to disturb delicate root structure. If no fruit develops hand-pollinate male and female flowers, as for zucchini.

Watering. Keep water up to plant but away from stems and foliage, especially when the fruit is setting. Sandy soil requires more watering than heavier soil. Lack of water may cause partly formed fruit to fall. Large leaves may wilt in hot weather but will recover if soil is moist.

Fertilizing. Dig in complete fertilizer just before sowing. Apply side dressings of urea when fruit first sets and water in immediately. Too much fertilizer will promote vigorous green growth at the expense of fruit development.

Problems. Powdery mildew and bacterial wilt are common. Prevention is important. Do not handle fragile vines while wet and keep garden clean. Insects spread diseases such as viral mosaic. Infected plants should be sprayed on upper and lower leaves or removed altogether. Aphids and squash beetle affect early growth, especially in spring, and should be sprayed.

HARVESTING

Picking. Harvest when young before skin hardens. Regular picking will prolong flowering.

Storing. Store in the crisper drawer of the refrigerator for up to 1 week.

Freezing. Peel and cook until tender. Mash, cool, and pack into freezer containers. Freeze for up to 3 months.

USES

Culinary. Stuff and bake, purée, braise, boil, or steam this vegetable. It is also delicious sliced and fried in batter or breadcrumbs and works well in soups and casseroles or gratins.

Cucurbita pepo var. *melopepo*
SUMMER SQUASH
Cucurbitaceae

CONDITIONS

Climate. Summer squash is a warm weather crop, sensitive to cold and frosts. Can be grown in most areas but the colder it gets, the shorter the season.

Aspect. Prefers to be grown in full sun to partial shade

Soil. Grows in a wide range of soils. Good drainage is essential. Summer squash are heavy feeders and like heavily fertilized soil, so dig in plenty of well-rotted manure and compost several weeks ahead of planting.

Cucurbita pepo var. *melopepo*
ZUCCHINI
Cucurbitaceae

CONDITIONS

Climate. Zucchini likes warm weather and is sensitive to cold and frosts. It can be grown in most areas but the colder it gets the shorter the growing season will be. Zucchini also does well when grown indoors in containers and in locations where conditions can be controlled to suit the growing plant.

Aspect. Can be grown in full sun to partial shade.

Soil. Grows in a wide range of soils, but good drainage is essential. Zucchini is a heavy feeder and likes heavily fertilized soil, so dig in plenty of well-rotted manure and compost several weeks ahead of planting.

FEATURES

Zucchini, known as courgette in Europe, are a type of summer squash or young marrow. Generally they are picked quite young, when about 6–8 inches long. Zucchini grow on bushes and are quite prolific. They are ideal specimens for container growing. The vegetable is elongated in shape (although tear-shaped varieties exist) and dark green through to yellow.

GROWING METHOD

Planting. In cold regions, plant seeds in early summer only. Plant in spring in temperate zones and all year round in hot, subtropical climates. Plant seeds following the method specified for summer squash. If planting in rows, leave about 3½ feet between plants. Keep areas around bush free of weeds and other decaying matter that might harbor disease. Shallow-cultivate so as not to disturb delicate root structure. If no fruit develops it may be because of unsuitable weather or lack of bee activity around flowers, which is often the case indoors. Should this occur, hand-pollinate male and female flowers using a soft-bristled brush. Dust the male flower (the one with a flower but no fruit on the stem), then dust the inside of the female flower.

Watering. Keep water up to plant but off stems and foliage, especially when fruit is setting. Moisture retentiveness of soil depends on structure: sandy soils need more water than heavier soils. Lack of water may cause partly formed fruit to fall. Leaves wilt during hot weather but recover if soil is kept moist.

Fertilizing. Dig in complete fertilizer just before sowing. Apply side dressings of urea when fruit first sets and water in immediately. Too much fertilizer will promote vigorous green growth at the expense of fruit development.

Problems. Powdery mildew and bacterial wilt are common. Treat with appropriate sprays. To prevent, do not handle fragile vines while wet and keep garden clean. Insects spread diseases such as viral mosaic. Spray infected plants on upper and lower leaves or remove altogether. Aphids and squash beetle affect early growth, especially in spring, and should be sprayed.

HARVESTING

Picking. Harvest when 4–6 inches long and skin is soft. Regular picking will prolong flowering.

Storing. Refrigerate for up to 1 week. Can be pickled.

Freezing. Slice into 1 inch slices, sauté gently in a little melted butter until tender. Cool, then pack into plastic containers and freeze for up to 3 months.

USES

Culinary. Young zucchini can be sliced thinly, dressed in oil and lemon juice, then eaten raw in salads. Use larger ones in stir-fries; steam or boil them; coat slices in batter and deep-fry; or hollow out, stuff, and bake them. Zucchini flowers can also be lightly battered and fried.

FEATURES

The vegetables we commonly refer to as pumpkins include small to medium-sized winter squash varieties, which belong to the species *C. pepo,* and a mammoth variety of winter squash, *C. maxima.* They are grown on long, rambling prostrate vines of 20 feet or more. Large male and female yellow flowers appear on the same vine. Female flowers have short, thick stems showing immature fruit just below the petals. The fruit has a dry texture and sweet taste, and ranges from yellow to orange-gold. Skins vary from dark green, through whitish-gray to creamy-yellow, depending on variety. The so-called spaghetti squash is a member of the *C. pepo* pumpkin species.

GROWING METHOD

Planting. Sow seeds in early summer in cold regions, throughout spring in warm zones, and all year round in hot, subtropical climates. Prepare seeds for planting as for summer squash. Alternatively, sow directly into garden soil. Place several seeds 1 inch deep in wide, hollow, saucer-shaped depressions, 8 inches deep. "Hill up" excavated soil around rim. Leave 6½ feet between hills and if planting in rows leave 5–6½ feet around each plant. Thin to 2 or 3 plants at seedling stage and to a single plant when true leaves appear. Remove seedlings by cutting stems at ground level. Lightly cultivate to keep area free of weeds and other decaying matter. If necessary, hand-pollinate male and female flowers.

Watering. Water well but keep off the stems and foliage. Large leaves wilt during hot weather but will recover if soil is kept moist.

Fertilizing. Dig in complete fertilizer just before sowing. Apply side dressings of urea when fruit first sets and water in immediately. Do not over-fertilize.

Problems. Powdery mildew and bacterial wilt are common. Treat with an appropriate spray. To prevent, do not handle fragile vines while wet and keep garden clean. Insects spread diseases such as viral mosaic. Spray infected plants on upper and lower leaves or remove altogether. Aphids and squash beetle affect early growth, especially in spring, and should be sprayed.

HARVESTING

Picking. Maturity is reached in 14–16 weeks. Crop before frosts. Vine dies down leaving hard, dry stalks. Cut free of the vine, leaving a portion of stem on the vegetable.

Storing. Keeps for several months in a cool, airy place. Wrap cut vegetable in plastic wrap and store in the refrigerator.

Freezing. Peel and cook until tender. Mash, cool, then pack into plastic containers and freeze for up to 3 months.

USES

Culinary. Can be boiled, steamed, roasted, or mashed.

Cucurbita spp.
WINTER SQUASH (PUMPKIN)
Cucurbitaceae

CONDITIONS

Climate. Winter squash likes warm weather and is sensitive to cold and frosts. It can be grown in most areas but the colder it gets, the shorter the season.

Aspect. Winter squash prefers to be grown in full sun to partial shade.

Soil. Rich, well-drained soil. Good drainage is essential. A long growing season is needed for winter squash, so dig in plenty of well-rotted manure and compost several weeks ahead of planting.

Cucurbita spp.
MARROW
Cucurbitaceae

CONDITIONS
Climate. Marrow like warm weather and are sensitive to cold and frosts. They can be grown in most areas but the colder it gets the shorter the season.

Aspect. Prefers full sun to partial shade.

Soil. Grows in a wide range of soils. Good drainage is essential. Dig in plenty of well-rotted manure and compost several weeks before planting.

FEATURES
Marrow is a type of bush pumpkin or summer squash. The skin is mostly white and turns slightly yellow when mature. There is little difference in taste between varieties, although the cooked texture of the flesh varies. Male and female yellow flowers appear on the same vine. Female flowers have short, thick stems showing immature fruit just below the petals.

GROWING METHOD
Planting. Plant seeds in early summer in cool regions; in spring in warm zones; and all year in hot, subtropical climates. Plant seeds $\frac{3}{4}$ inch deep in seed-raising mix in pots, 4–5 weeks ahead of planting out. Alternatively, sow directly into garden soil in final growing position. Place several seeds $\frac{3}{4}$ inch deep in wide, hollow, saucer-shaped depressions that are 8 inches deep. "Hill up" the excavated soil as a rim around edge of the depression. Leave $3\frac{1}{2}$ feet between hills. Thin to 2 or 3 plants at seedling stage and to one healthy plant when true leaves appear. Carefully remove seedlings by cutting stems at ground level. If planting in rows, allow a clear 5–$6\frac{1}{2}$ feet space around each plant. Keep areas around bush free of weeds by shallow cultivation. If no fruit develops, hand-pollinate male and female flowers, as for zucchini.

Watering. Keep water up to plant but away from stems and foliage, especially when the fruit is setting. Sandy soil requires more watering than heavier soil. Lack of water may cause partly formed fruit to fall. Large leaves may wilt in hot weather but will recover if soil is moist.

Fertilizing. Dig in complete fertilizer just before sowing. Apply side dressings of urea when fruit first sets and water in immediately. Do not over-fertilize.

Problems. Powdery mildew and bacterial wilt are common. Treat with appropriate sprays. To prevent, do not handle vines while wet and keep garden clean. Insects spread diseases, such as viral mosaic. Spray infected plants on upper and lower leaves or remove altogether. Aphids and squash beetle affect early growth, especially in spring, and should be sprayed.

HARVESTING
Picking. Marrows reach maturity in 2–3 months, depending on variety. Crop before frosts set in and before skin hardens. Fruit is usually about $2\frac{1}{2}$ inches in diameter, but can grow much larger.

Storing. Store in the crisper drawer of the refrigerator for up to 1 week.

Freezing. Peel, cut into pieces, then cook in boiling water until just cooked. Cool, place in freezer bags, then freeze for up to 3 months.

USES
Culinary. Marrows are best eaten young because their flavor deteriorates and becomes more watery as they get bigger. Marrows are best stuffed: either halved lengthwise or cut into rings with stuffing in the middle.

FEATURES

The artichoke is a gray-green perennial, 3½–4 feet tall with decorative, compound leaves resembling those of the Scotch thistle. Edible parts are the young, tender, globe-shaped flower buds, which are harvested and eaten before opening. These attractive plants require plenty of space.

GROWING METHOD

Planting. Plant in midwinter in cooler climates, in late winter in warm regions, and in spring in subtropical areas. For best results buy shoots or suckers of disease-resistant varieties from a good nursery. Planting seed is possible, but success is variable and the plant takes about 1 year from sowing to harvesting. Place shoots or suckers in beds 3½ feet apart, in rows about 3½ feet apart. Apply half a cup of fertilizer around each and water in. In cool areas, cut back to 10–12 inches in fall and heavily mulch to protect the root structure in winter.

Watering. Keep soils evenly and constantly moist, carefully monitoring this throughout the spring and summer months.

Fertilizing. Prepare garden beds with low-nitrogen fertilizer. Repeat this application again at mid-season.

Problems. Good drainage during growth is essential otherwise crown rot may develop, principally as a result of the heavy mulching requirement during winter. Handle the plants as little as possible and remove any infected or diseased specimens immediately.

HARVESTING

Picking. Artichokes take 2–3 months to reach maturity when grown from shoots or suckers. In many areas, harvesting takes place from mid to late spring when buds are tight and about 3½ inches across. Cut well below the bud with 1½ inch of stem still attached. The optimum bearing period is the second year after planting. Every third year, divide adult plants and replant.

Storing. Sprinkle with water, seal in a plastic bag, then store in the vegetable crisper of the fridge for up to 2 weeks. Alternatively, store upright in water, like flowers, for several days.

Freezing. Remove outer leaves, wash, trim stalks, then remove "chokes". Blanch for 7 minutes. Cool, drain, pack in freezer bags, then freeze for up to 6 months.

USES

Culinary. When very young the artichoke can be eaten whole and even raw in salads. When buds are more mature, stuff, boil, or fry. For large artichoke, boil and eat one leaf at a time, sucking or scraping the flesh off the fibrous base with your teeth. Dip into vinaigrette or hollandaise sauce if desired.

Cynara scolymus
ARTICHOKE
Asteraceae

CONDITIONS

Climate. Best grown in areas with mild, relatively frost-free winters and damp cool summers. Ideal range is 50°F at night to 73°F by day.

Aspect. Prefers full sunlight.

Soil. Rich, well-drained soils. Garden beds should be enriched and prepared with fertilizer and animal compost to improve drainage. Keep mulch and water up to plants in growing season and especially in summer after harvesting.

Daucus carota
CARROT
Apiaceae

CONDITIONS

Climate. Cold tolerant and preferring cooler zones, carrots can nevertheless be grown in most climates.

Aspect. Likes full sun but tolerates partial shade. Above all, prefers a garden bed positioned for coolness.

Soil. Deep, light soil. Older garden beds that have friable soils and where organic matter has decayed offer best results. Roots can grow deep and smooth without blemishes in these sandy to loamy soils. Add lime if soils are acidic. This improves root color. In subtropical zones, it may be necessary to mulch to keep soil temperatures cool.

FEATURES

This hardy plant is grown as an annual. A feathery, green rosette of leaves above soil level grows from an edible, underground taproot that is golden-orange in color. Round and short varieties may be grown in a container but the long, tapering variety, which grows to about 8 inches, requires friable soil in the open garden. "Baby" carrots grow no more than 4 inches in length and $\frac{3}{4}$ inch in diameter. Carrots are easy to grow in the home garden.

GROWING METHOD

Planting. Sow carrot seeds from spring to the end of summer in cold regions; mid-spring to the end of summer in warm zones; and throughout the year in subtropical regions, except at the height of summer. Prepare furrows 10 inches apart and sow seeds $\frac{1}{4}$ inch deep. Cover with seed-raising mix and water lightly. When seedlings are about 2 inches high, thin out to $\frac{3}{4}$ inch apart. When remaining seedlings reach 6 inches, thin out again to 2 inches apart. Companion planting with quick growing radishes in alternate rows will protect young seedlings from burn off.

Watering. Watering is important, but during the first 8 weeks of seedling growth use only small amounts to encourage the desirable downwards growth of roots. As the crop matures, water heavily only when soil dries out. Too much water induces root crack.

Fertilizing. Beds that have been heavily manured the previous season work best. If necessary, dig in a complete fertilizer 1 week before sowing. Do not over-fertilize; too much nitrogen leads to excessive leaf growth and poor-colored roots.

Problems. Control carrot aphids with a registered pesticide. Root nematodes cause leaves to curl and turn deep red or yellow. Pull out diseased plants immediately and burn. Fumigate bed.

HARVESTING

Picking. The good thing about carrots is they can be cropped at whatever size you want them. Full maturity is reached approximately 4 months after planting, depending on variety and area. To harvest, use a garden fork and lift carrots gently out of the ground when soil is moist, to prevent the roots from snapping.

Storing. Store for several weeks in the refrigerator in plastic bags. Don't store carrots near apples, pears, or potatoes as the ethylene gas produced by these fruit and vegetables causes carrots to turn bitter. Carrots can also be pickled or bottled.

Freezing. Scrub and slice. Blanch for 3 minutes, chill, drain, then spread on a tray in a single layer and freeze for 30 minutes. Remove, pack in plastic bags, then freeze for up to 6 months.

USES

Culinary. Eat raw, steam and serve with butter, use puréed in soups, or add to sweet dishes such as cakes and muffins. Use in Indian desserts, such as halwa.

FEATURES

This is a root vegetable, which does not belong to the chestnut family at all. A perennial, reed-like plant, the slender cylindrical and thinly hollow leaves, 3½–5 feet in length, act as air pumps, taking oxygen to the roots and helping to purify the water in which the plant grows. The edible corm, about the size of a walnut, grows underwater at the end of horizontal rhizomes (underground stems). The corm changes from pale to dark mahogany-brown as it matures. The whitish flesh has a sweet, nutty flavor, which is similar to the flavor of coconut or macadamia. Corms are peeled before eating, whether raw or cooked. They have a firm crisp texture. Water chestnuts are the only nuts that are known as vegetables.

GROWING METHOD

Planting. Plant in spring after any cool snaps have passed. Place corms into any shallow, freshwater aquatic environment—such as dams, small garden ponds, aquariums, or containers that will hold water—and heap soil around, holding or fixing in place with small stones. Add at least 4 inches of soil and cover with 1¾ inches of water. Very little care is needed except to make sure that the water in the container or pond does not dry out. Rhizomes spread horizontally under the soil surface, turning up to form suckers and new plants. Later, food-producing rhizomes or corms develop. After summer harvest, store some corms for the following season in moist sand or loose, damp soil.

Watering. Not essential when in aquatic environment.

Fertilizing. No chemical fertilizing is required as long as soil used has been enriched with a lot of well-composted organic matter and old animal manure.

Problems. No diseases are known. The plant is very hardy but because it is grown in water, mosquito larvae may be a problem. Introduce goldfish or tadpoles into the aquatic environment or sprinkle quassia chips over the water surface.

HARVESTING

Picking. After about 6 months, the stem tops of the water chestnut turn brown and die down, which means they are ready to pick. The darkish skin should be tight and taut; if the flesh texture is mushy, the nut is too old.

Storing. Refrigerate in plastic bags for up to 2 weeks.

Freezing. Bring to the boil, drain, then peel off shells. Pack in freezer bags or containers and freeze for up to 6 months.

USES

Culinary. Water chestnut corms are first peeled and can then be eaten raw or cooked. They are excellent in stir-fries.

Eleocharis dulcis
WATER CHESTNUT
Cyperaceae

CONDITIONS

Climate. Best grown in climates with hot summers—ideally, above 86°F during leafy stage of growth and above 68°F when corms are forming.

Aspect. Grows in shallow water containers or ponds and usually is not affected by weather extremes.

Soil. Use only rich, clay or peaty, fertile soils. The ideal pH range is 6.9–7.3, so add a couple of handfuls of lime or dolomite, if necessary. Water chestnuts, however, will tolerate a variety of conditions, even those of slight salinity.

FEATURES

Arugula, or rocket, is an annual with long, deeply lobed, dark green leaves that are often tinted red, and simple, cross-shaped, creamy white flowers. The leaves have a pleasant, peppery, nutty flavor. The leaves form a dense rosette at the base of the plant, from which rise branching flower-bearing stems up to 3 feet tall. Plump seed heads shatter when dry, each dispersing hundreds of seeds. Arugula grows very fast and several crops may be raised during spring and summer.

GROWING METHOD

Planting. In cool regions, sow seeds in early spring and continue sowing until about mid-fall; in the tropics, start sowing in late fall and continue until the end of winter. Sow seeds 1 inch deep and thin the young plants to about 6 inches apart. If sharp frosts are likely, sow indoors in trays or punnets of seed-raising mix placed in a sunny window. Plant out when the seedlings are big enough to handle light frosts or when frosts have passed. Arugula grows fast and young leaves are the most palatable, so pick regularly and make new sowings approximately every 4 weeks. When the latest batch of seedlings is big enough to pick from, pull out the previous batch.

Watering. For the fastest growth and the sweetest-tasting leaves, keep the plants well watered. Plants enjoy consistent moisture but do not like waterlogged roots, so make sure soil drains well.

Fertilizing. Dig in a ration of complete plant food at sowing time and then water the plants every 2 weeks or so with a soluble, high-nitrogen fertilizer.

Problems. Snails and slugs may damage the leaves of freshly sown plants in early spring and fall. Either pick them off by hand or lay snail bait. As arugula can quickly become an invasive weed, it is important to prevent flowering except to provide seeds for resowing. On most plants, snap off flower stems as they rise or, better still, replace flowering plants with new, young plants.

HARVESTING

Picking. Start picking young leaves about 5 weeks after seedlings have emerged, sooner in summer when growth is faster. Harvest seeds when the pods have plumped out and are beginning to look dry.

Storing. Seeds may be stored in airtight jars but leaves must be used fresh.

Freezing. Do not freeze.

USES

Culinary. Young leaves give green salads an appealing piquancy. Add them to stir-fries.

Eruca vesicaria subsp. *sativa*
ARUGULA
Brassicaceae

CONDITIONS

Climate. Best suited to cool and warm climates but grows reasonably well in tropical winters.

Aspect. During spring, grow arugula in full sun but in summer and in the tropics, a cooler, partly shaded spot helps slow the plant's rush to seed and thus lengthens its useful life.

Soil. Grow in fertile, well-drained soil enriched with rotted manure or compost. Arugula will grow in poor soils too, but its leaves will be tough and more bitter.

FEATURES

A lovely plant with attractive, feathery leaves, this hardy perennial can grow to 5 feet. Small clusters of yellow flowers appear in summer and produce oval-shaped, ribbed, brown seeds about ¼ inch long. The whole plant has an aniseed flavor. Commonly cultivated varieties include *F. vulgare* var. *dulce*, sweet fennel, which has a large celery-like stem, and *F. vulgare* var. *azoricum*, Florence fennel or finocchio, which has a large, swollen leaf base. The seeds and leaves of both are used for seasoning in cooking; and the leaf base and stems of the Florence fennel are eaten as vegetables. A third variety, much admired for its reddish-brown foliage, is *F. vulgare* "Purpureum, bronze fennel. The subspecies *F. vulgare vulgaris*, wild fennel, is now a roadside weed in some regions.

GROWING METHODS

Planting. Plant during spring in colder regions and fall in warm and tropical zones. Sow seeds in furrows about 2 inches deep. Keep rows 20 inches apart and when seedlings appear, thin out to 1½ feet apart. Pick a permanent position in the garden because the plant will self-sow if left to its own devices. Mature plants can be lifted during spring, root cuttings taken and replanted. In cooler regions, cut the plant back to a handspan above ground level as winter approaches. Blanch the swollen leaf bases of Florence fennel by hilling soil around the base of the plant to exclude any sunlight.

Fertilizing. Add a complete fertilizer once or twice during the growing season.

Watering. Do not water excessively.

Problems. No specific pests and diseases.

HARVESTING

Picking. Plants take several months to mature. Pick fresh leaves as required. Gather seed heads while still slightly green and before they turn brown and dry in a cool, shady place.

Storing. Refrigerate, wrapped in plastic, for up to 2 days.

Freezing. Use fresh young stalks and wash thoroughly. Blanch for 3 minutes, chill, drain, pack in plastic bags, then freeze for up to 6 months.

USES

Culinary. Snip leaves from fennel as you would dill and use to flavor fish dishes, dressings, or sauces. Florence fennel is cultivated for its thick stems and bulbous base—eat raw, like celery; braise, sauté, or add to soups.

Gardening. Plant toward the back of garden as a backdrop for other plants.

Foeniculum vulgare
FENNEL
Apiaceae

CONDITIONS

Climate. Best in hot, dry climates but will grow in practically all climates.

Aspect. Prefers plenty of sun. The feathery leaves may require tying and support against wind.

Soil. Will grow in most soils (pH range of 6–7 preferred), but beds should be well-drained and contain plenty of compost and decayed animal manure. Apply lime or dolomite if soil is too acidic.

Helianthus tuberosus
JERUSALEM ARTICHOKE
Asteraceae

CONDITIONS
Climate. Most areas are suitable, but special care needs to be taken during very cold winters or if frosts abound.

Aspect. Prefers dry, sunny to semi-shaded locations. The plants will require staking if conditions are windy.

Soil. Dig in plenty of organic matter and complete fertilizer. Add a little lime just before planting.

FEATURES
A very hardy perennial belonging to the sunflower family, the Jerusalem artichoke (sometimes known as the sunchoke), has edible tubers resembling young, gnarled potatoes. Although perennial by nature, this vegetable may be planted as an annual, with the mature tubers lifted during winter and then replanted. Above-ground, the plant can grow to 8 feet and produces attractive dark-centered yellow flowers with small seeds. As a crop, it has a tendency to take over the garden if it is not checked. It can be cooked the same way as potatoes, but is rather sweet to taste. It is not related to the globe artichoke.

GROWING METHOD
Planting. Plant late winter to mid-spring in cool regions, midwinter in warm areas, and winter through to mid-spring in tropical areas. Purchase new bulbs or tubers or plant saved ones from the previous year's crop. Plant 4–6 inches deep, 2 feet apart, in rows 3 feet apart. Shoots should appear within 2–4 weeks. The plant needs little attention throughout the growth period, but bigger tubers will result if the garden bed is well prepared before planting. To improve quality, nip out flower heads at the bud stage. Just before harvest, the tall flower stems should be cut off close to the ground. In cold climates cover with mulch to keep an even soil temperature.

Watering. Do not water too much. It may be necessary to keep the soil moist during seasonal dry spells.

Fertilizing. These hardy plants require little help, but better yields are obtained if some animal manure is dug into the soil and a complete fertilizer is added before planting.

Problems. Snails and slugs may appear as shoots form. Use commercial preparations to remove them or trap snails in small containers of stale beer sunk to soil level.

HARVESTING
Picking. Harvest the plants in 4–5 months in most areas, after the leaves wilt and the stalks begin to die back.

Storing. As with other root crops, the simplest method of storing is to leave the tuber in the ground, digging up only when necessary. Store in the refrigerator for several days.

Freezing. Peel and slice. Blanch for 2 minutes, chill, drain, then spread on a tray in a single layer and freeze for 30 minutes. Remove from tray, pack in plastic bags, then freeze for up to 6 months.

USES
Culinary. Finely slice and add raw to salads; boil or roast like potatoes; or use to make soups and mashes.

Garden. Leaves and stalks are good for mulching.

FEATURES

This frost tender, warm-season perennial, grown as an annual, is an ornamental vine with small, white or pink to dark purple flowers. Edible parts are the thick, elongated tubers that can have white, creamy-yellow, or deep orange flesh. Sweet potatoes are classified as being moist or dry, depending on their cooking texture. Those with moist flesh are sometimes called yams. Sweet potato is also known as kumara, particularly in New Zealand. This sweet-tasting vegetable may be cooked in a variety of ways and is an excellent vegetable to have in the home garden. It is not suitable for container growing.

GROWING METHOD

Planting. Plant from spring to midsummer in subtropical and warm, coastal regions; and throughout the year in tropical zones. Sweet potatoes are grown from rooted sprouts or shoots, called slips, which are taken from mature, healthy tubers. Place tubers in propagating beds and cover with 3½ inches of sand or light soil. Keep the bed moist and warm. When shoots appear and have grown to 6 inches, gently pull out and transplant. Tubers will usually produce a second lot of slips for transplanting. Plant slips, not too deeply, in open garden beds 14 inches apart, with 3½ feet between rows. The rows should be ridged or hilled to a height of 10 inches for best results. Water the plants immediately.

Watering. Water well at the initial planting stage and maintain even soil moisture levels throughout the growing period. Do not over-wet or tuber rot may set in. Stop watering 1 month before harvesting.

Fertilizing. Before planting, dig in a complete fertilizer. A side dressing of urea 2 months after planting can be beneficial. Do not fertilize with poultry manure or nitrogenous fertilizers because this promotes leaf growth instead of tuber development.

Problems. There are generally no problems, but it is advisable to rotate sweet potato crops every 2–3 years. Maintaining general garden health is a wise preventative measure.

HARVESTING

Picking. Pick in 5–6 months when tubers reach maturity, bearing in mind that white-fleshed tubers take longer to mature than orange-fleshed varieties. Harvest the tubers before any cold snaps set in and be careful not to damage the thin skins when lifting them from the ground.

Storing. Sweet potatoes will keep for up to 4 months if stored unwashed. Do not refrigerate.

Freezing. Scrub and peel, then bake until just tender. Drain and cool, pack into plastic bags, then freeze for up to 3 months.

USES

Culinary. Sweet potatoes can be cooked as you would a potato—roasted, boiled, mashed, or fried, but their soft, slightly sweet flesh makes them an ideal ingredient in cakes or sweet dishes, in breads, soups, and casseroles.

Ipomoea batatas
SWEET POTATO
Convolvulaceae

CONDITIONS

Climate. Needs warm days and nights and to be free of frosts for at least 4–6 months during the growing season. Sweet potato is hard to grow in cool to cold climates.

Aspect. Prefers to be grown in full sun. It does not like cool soil.

Soil. Grows best in sandy or sandy loam soils. It is important to control weed growth before vines start rapid growth. Sweet potatoes have a deep root system so garden beds may need to be raised, especially when grown in areas where there are heavy clay soils.

Lactuca sativa
LETTUCE
Asteraceae

CONDITIONS
Climate. Because there are many different varieties, lettuce can be grown in all climates at any time of the year.

Aspect. Prefers sun to partial shade. Lettuces do not like excessively hot beds and in cold climates a protective cloche may be needed to help the vegetable mature.

Soil. Lettuces like non-acidic soils, enriched with decayed animal or poultry manure. Dig in a good quantity 2 weeks ahead of planting. Apply lime or dolomite to neutralize soil acidity. Beds should be well drained.

FEATURES
Lettuce is a cool season crop, but it is in greatest demand as a salad vegetable during hot months. New varieties to suit all seasons are now available. Lettuce has either compact or loosely arranged leaves forming a light green to reddish-brown head. The commonly available iceberg lettuce and brown and green mignonettes are compacted forms. Butterhead and oak-leaf varieties have soft, loose leaves whereas romaine has strong rigid leaves and a distinctively elongated head. Loose-leaf lettuce, or any small varieties, grow well in containers and make a handy and attractive show near the kitchen.

GROWING METHOD
Planting. Plant year round in all areas, depending on variety. Grow quickly for best results. If a variety is planted out of season it will run to seed, especially in hot weather. Succession sowings from early spring to midsummer will ensure a continuous crop. Avoid sowing during very hot weather. Seeds can be raised in containers for later transplanting, but direct sowing into garden beds is preferred. Sow several seeds in a shallow depression 10 inches apart and lightly cover with no more than ½ inch of compost or seed-raising mix. Keep soil moist. Thin out to single plants when seedlings are 2½–3½ inches tall with rows 12 inches apart. Mulch will keep weeds under control and help keep the shallow roots cool.

Watering. Keep evenly moist. Over-watering may cause fungal diseases. Lack of water can reduce head size, cause bolting in hot weather, and increase bitterness in leaves.

Fertilizing. A week before planting, dig in complete fertilizer. Side dress with a small amount of urea twice during the growing cycle, first after thinning seedlings and later when plant is half-grown. Do not let fertilizer touch leaves. Wash off if necessary.

Problems. Aphids appear early and slow plant growth. Control with appropriate sprays. Sclerotinia rot, which develops in wet, shaded conditions, is a white, cottony fungal growth that appears around the stem at ground level. Treat with suitable sprays, fortnightly. Treat downy mildew and septoria, or leaf spot, with appropriate sprays. Burn dead leaves. Keeping plants well spaced during the growing period with access to full sun, especially where ground tends to be soggy, will help keep plants healthy.

HARVESTING
Picking. Lettuces take 8–10 weeks to reach maturity, depending on climate. Pick early when hearts start to form. Loose-leaf lettuce can be harvested a few leaves at a time. Snap off mature outer leaves as needed.

Storing. Store in the crisper drawer of the refrigerator for up to 7 days.

Freezing. Do not freeze.

USES
Culinary. Lettuce is mainly used fresh in salads or sandwiches but can also be cooked.

FEATURES

Tomato has a weak, soft-stemmed structure with alternate lobed and toothed leaves. Mature plants have a vine-like or bush-growing habit. Yellow flowers grow in clusters and produce fruit of varying size, which may be red, yellow, or orange to creamy white, depending on the variety. Tomatoes are a heavy-yielding crop and a favorite of home gardeners. They are also well suited to container growing.

GROWING METHOD

Planting. Sow seeds during spring in cold regions, late fall to early summer in temperate zones, and all year round in warm and tropical climates. Seeds are usually germinated in seed boxes, but can be planted directly into the garden, ¼ inch deep. Seedlings will appear in about 14 days and when 4 inches tall, transfer into smaller containers and harden for a fortnight. When seedlings are 8–10 inches tall, transplant into the open garden 2 feet apart, in rows 2 feet apart. Weak stems will need securing against possible wind damage and to support heavy fruit. Use 6½ foot stakes and fix firmly in soil at the time of planting seedlings. As the plant grows, secure the stem to the stake with soft ties at 12 inch intervals. Prune by picking out lateral shoots that appear at junctions of leaf stalks and main stem. Single lateral shoots can be left to elongate and form another stem.

Watering. Do not let soil dry out; plenty of water is needed during the growth cycle. Uneven watering leads to blossom-end rot. Do not water over the plants with sprinklers. Instead, irrigate along furrows between the rows.

Fertilizing. Phosphorus must be provided, especially at seedling stage. Lack of it leads to low yields. Dig in complete fertilizer before planting, or fertilize under seedlings.

Problems. Prone to spotted wilt, spread by thrips. Immature fruit becomes blotched or mottled and stunted foliage turns purplish. Leaf or target spot is common in wet seasons but is also caused by excessive use of nitrogen. Mites, tomato caterpillar, and fruit fly are other pests. All can be controlled by appropriate dust or sprays. Rotate crops if soil disease is endemic.

HARVESTING

Picking. Crop matures in 3–5 months, depending on variety. Pick fruit when ripe on the bush or when mature and green and ripen indoors.

Storing. Store tomatoes at room temperature for up to 3 days, or refrigerate for up to 3 weeks. They can also be bottled.

Freezing. Wash, remove stems, cut in half or leave whole, dry, pack into freezer bags, then freeze for up to 6 months.

USES

Culinary. Use raw in salads, or cook this versatile vegetable in sauces, especially pasta sauces, soups, and stews. Tomatoes are an excellent base for pickles and chutneys.

Lycopersicon esculentum
TOMATO
Solanaceae

CONDITIONS

Climate. Varieties of tomato have been developed that are suitable to all climatic conditions. However, this is naturally a warm-season vegetable (technically a fruit), susceptible to frosts.

Aspect. Prefers full sun to partial shade, although can be affected by sunscald in very hot climates. These plants require protection from strong winds.

Soil. Fertile, deep, well-drained soil. Prepare the garden beds with plenty of animal manure about a month before planting time. Dig in thoroughly to spade depth.

Nasturtium officinale
WATERCRESS
Brassicaceae

CONDITIONS
Climate. Warm, moist climates are ideal.

Aspect. Prefers a wet shady place that is protected from both strong winds and winter frosts. A pot or tub that can be kept damp is also suitable.

Soil. Wet, well-limed soil, rich in humus. For container growing, use very damp, rich soil and top it up occasionally with well-rotted garden compost.

FEATURES
Although European in origin, watercress is now widely used in Asian cuisines. It is a perennial that grows to just 8 inches with a spreading habit. Round, dark green leaves composed of several leaflets have a peppery mustard flavor and are carried on fleshy stems. The plants usually grow in water and clusters of small, white flowers appear in early summer.

GROWING METHOD
Planting. Plant through spring and fall in cool zones and mostly in winter in warm zones. Sow seeds by placing them on a constantly damp seed-raising mix. Transplant seedlings to a permanent position when they are about 3½ inches tall. Either float or submerge in shallow, moving water or root in rich, wet soil. Watercress can also be grown by root division of a mature plant or propagate from stem pieces in temperate climates. Stem pieces will root easily in wet soil; place into a container with good quality potting mix and then lower it into a waterbed. Do not let the water stagnate: drain off some of the water once a week and top it up with fresh water each time. The water should be alkaline and at a temperature of around 50°F. Pick leaves regularly and do not leave to flower.

Watering. Requires a great deal of water.

Fertilizing. Apply soluble plant food that is high in nitrogen every 2 weeks while growing.

Problems. Watercress is sometimes subject to fungal diseases, which cause rotting of the stems and death of the leaves. Remove infected plants.

HARVESTING
Picking. Pick leaves as required.

Storing. Freshly picked leaves will keep in fresh cold water or sealed plastic bags in the fridge for a couple of days.

Freezing. Do not freeze.

USES
Culinary. Watercress is rich in iron and vitamin C. Use it raw in salads, sandwiches, or as a garnish. The peppery taste adds flavor to other salad greens. The Chinese tend to cook watercress in tasty soups.

FEATURES

This is a popular garden vegetable because of its high yields, economic growing space, and lengthy cropping period. A fleshy, cream to white underground tap root grows to 8 inches with celery-like leaves protruding above-ground. The edible root contains a lot of sugar, most of which is lost during cooking, but it retains a distinctive sweet taste and aroma that is unusual for a vegetable. This is a traditional favorite for some vegetable growers and is a tasty and nutritious addition to any vegetable plot. It is not suited to container growing.

GROWING METHOD

Planting. Sow seeds in spring through to early summer in cold climates, in midwinter to mid-fall in temperate zones, and from fall through winter in tropical and subtropical areas. Seed is not usually viable over long periods, so obtain fresh stock each season. Plant seeds ¼–½ inch deep, in rows 16 inches apart in the open garden. Otherwise, raise in seed beds, keeping damp until seedlings appear. Plant out when seedlings are 4¾–6 inches high and space them 2 inches apart. Before planting, beds should be well turned to a depth of 10–12 inches to ensure a healthy tap root. Avoid deep cultivation while growing because it will damage roots. Hand weed, if necessary. In very hot areas, mulch to keep soil cool and to stop short root growth.

Watering. Water generously during early stages of growth but ease off as root thickens. Too much water induces root crack; too little leads to slow development and even stunting of root.

Fertilizing. Dig in complete fertilizer a week before sowing seeds or transplanting seedlings. Do not over-fertilize because too much nitrogen leads to heavy leaf growth at the expense of developing roots.

Problems. No serious diseases, but insects can be a nuisance. Control aphids, which turn leaves curly and reddish-brown, with sprays.

HARVESTING

Picking. Harvest after 4–5 months. Using a garden fork, lift the root gently out of the soil when there is a thickness of approximately 1¾–2 inches across the crown of the vegetable.

Storing. Parsnips can be kept in the ground for 2–3 months after reaching maturity; or refrigerate for 2–3 weeks.

Freezing. Peel and dice. Blanch for 2 minutes, chill, drain, then spread on a tray in a single layer and freeze for 30 minutes. Remove from tray, pack in plastic bags, then freeze for up to 6 months.

USES

Culinary. Parsnip can be served roasted, mashed, or added to casseroles and soups.

Pastinaca sativa
PARSNIP
Apiaceae

CONDITIONS

Climate. Prefers cool weather but grows in all climates.

Aspect. Full sun to partial shade

Soil. Well-drained, organically enriched, deep, sandy loams. Incorporate plenty of well-rotted animal manure to keep soil friable well ahead of planting. Use a garden bed that has been heavily fertilized and mulched for a previous crop.

Phaseolus vulgaris
BEAN
Fabaceae

CONDITIONS
Climate. This is a warm season vegetable that does not like frosts. Before planting, be sure that any cold snaps are over and the danger of frost has passed. In warmer, subtropical climates it can be grown throughout the year. In high temperatures of more than 80°F bean pods may not set.

Aspect. Prefers sunny spots where the soil is warm.

Soil. Soils should be rich in humus, well drained and moderately fertilized. Dig in plenty of organic matter if soil is too sandy. If soil has a low pH, add lime 1 month before sowing.

FEATURES
Annuals of both climbing and dwarf varieties of bean have edible leaves composed of three small leaflets, and edible flowers that come in a variety of colors. The immature pod is the part of the plant that we generally eat. It can be green, yellow, or purple, depending on variety, and comes in stringed and stringless forms. Climbing beans give a heavier crop over a longer period than dwarf varieties.

GROWING METHOD
Planting. Warm weather lovers, beans are best planted mid-spring through to late summer. Sow seeds directly into beds 1½–2 inches deep; climbing beans 6 inches apart, in rows 3½ feet apart; dwarf varieties 2½ inches apart, in rows 2 feet apart. Hill rows with soil during early growth to safeguard against windy conditions. When planting, set in trellises that are at least 8 feet tall. Tie vines as necessary to trellis. Weed carefully so as not to disturb the shallow roots. Mulch with compost to protect roots and to promote water retention. Some varieties are suitable for medium to large container growing—check with your local nursery.

Watering. Seeds sown in moist soils do not require watering until the seedlings appear; but water well in sandy soils. At flowering time, beans like humid conditions.

Fertilizing. Apply complete fertilizer that is not high in nitrogen as a 1¾ inch wide layer either side of young plants. Or, apply as a band, covered by soil, under newly sown seeds. Be sure to protect seeds from direct contact with fertilizer. Apply liquid fertilizer when flowering commences.

Problems. Aphids and red spider mite in midsummer to mid-fall, and bean fly, are the main pests. Beans are also susceptible to blight mosaic and anthracnose. Control pests and diseases by spraying or dusting with insecticides, especially on undersides of leaves. Remove dead plant material and seasonally rotate crops so as to avoid spreading disease.

HARVESTING
Picking. Dwarf beans will mature in about 10 weeks and climbing beans will be ready in 10–12 weeks. Pick frequently to increase flowering and yields. When picking pods, be careful not to damage the vines. The pods are ready to pick when they snap easily between the fingers and the seeds are not yet fully developed. Avoid harvesting in either very hot or cold spells.

Storing. Store in the crisper drawer in the refrigerator for up to 1 week.

Freezing. String, top, and tail. Blanch for 2 minutes, chill, drain, then spread on a tray in a single layer and freeze for 30 minutes. Remove, pack in plastic bags, then freeze for up to 6 months.

USES
Culinary. Steam, boil, cook in stir-fries, or blanch for use in salads.

FEATURES

Mainly climbing annuals with pretty flowers and green tendrils clinging to a supporting trellis, peas are an attractive addition to the home vegetable garden. There are many types of pea, some, such as the garden pea, are grown for the seeds contained in the fibrous pod and others, such as snow peas, or mangetout, and sugar snap peas, are grown for the pods themselves. Flowers and habit differ, but all varieties have similar requirements for successful growth.

GROWING METHOD

Planting. Sow seeds directly into garden from winter to early spring in cold climates; in fall through winter in warm zones; and in fall to early winter in warm, subtropical areas. Succession planting every 2–3 weeks extends cropping time. Plant 1½ inches deep, 2 inches apart in cooler climates where rainfall is plentiful (slightly deeper to 2 inches, in warmer regions), in rows 2 feet apart. Fill trenches with soil, firm down, then wet, but do not over-water. Protect seedlings from birds with wire netting. Trellis most varieties for easy cultivation and harvesting. Lightly cultivate beds to keep weeds down. After harvesting, dig whole plant into soil as green manure.

Watering. Water carefully as plants need adequate, but not excessive, water at soil level. Avoid watering over the top of mature leaves and flowers.

Fertilizing. Apply complete fertilizer to improve the soil fertility.

Problems. Rotate crops to inhibit fungal diseases, which peas are susceptible to, especially in wet weather. Discoloration of the leaves and pods and the appearance of blackish streaks on the stems indicate disease. If disease is present, remove all vines after harvesting (healthy or otherwise) and burn them. Fungicide dusting of seeds before sowing will avert seed rot and damping-off, especially in areas where winter sowings are in cold soils. Hose aphids off vines or destroy all infected foliage. Control grubs that attack pods with appropriate pesticide.

HARVESTING

Picking. Pick when the pods are full, firm, shining bright green, and 2–3½ inches long. Frequent harvesting from the bottom of the plant prolongs the cropping season. Harvest regular peas in spring through to late summer in cool zones, in late summer through to mid-fall in warm areas, and through winter into early spring in tropical areas. Harvest sugar snap and snow peas in spring through to the end of fall in cool zones, fall and spring in warm zones, and fall through to mid-spring in subtropical zones.

Storing. Fresh peas keep for 2–3 days in the refrigerator.

Freezing. Shell, wash, then blanch for 1 minute. Chill and drain, then spread on a tray in a single layer and freeze for 30 minutes. Remove, pack in plastic bags, then freeze for up to 6 months.

USES

Culinary. Boil peas or add them to soups and risottos. Eat snow peas raw in salads or use them in stir-fries.

Pisum sativum
PEA
Fabaceae

CONDITIONS

Climate. Most climates are suitable, but plantings should be confined to the cool months of the year for best results. Both flowers and pods are subject to frost damage, so avoid cropping in winter in frost-prone areas.

Aspect. Prefers sun to partial shade. In cooler zones, where summer growing is possible, shade protection during the hottest part of the day may be necessary.

Soil. Loose, well-drained soil. Beds must be enriched with organic matter. Treat acid soils with lime to bring them to a pH level of 6.5. It is also advisable to rotate crops because peas fix nitrogen in the soil through bacterial action in their root nodules and this will affect following pea crops negatively.

Raphanus sativus
RADISH
Brassicaceae

CONDITIONS
Climate. Grows in all climates.

Aspect. Radish likes to be in a moist, shady place. In high summer, protection from direct sunlight may be required for a few hours of the day.

Soil. Rich, deep, sandy loams with high moisture-holding capacity are needed for rapid growth. The ideal pH is 6.5. Add lime to soil, if necessary. Soil that has been manured and fertilized for a previous crop is ideal. Heavily mulch garden bed during hot weather.

FEATURES
The radish is a round to globular and sometimes cylindrical root vegetable with winter and summer varieties. The longer root form grows to 6 inches in length and is good for cooking. The smaller, rounder summer radish is usually eaten fresh in salads and is ideal for container growing. They are quick growers with sweet flesh, which turns bitter and hot to the taste if left in the ground too long. The thin skin ranges from red through to white. This is an easy vegetable for the home gardener to cultivate. Because of the quick-growing nature of radishes, they can be planted in alternate rows among slower-growing vegetables, such as lettuce.

GROWING METHOD
Planting. Plant in spring, summer, and early fall in colder regions; throughout the year except in early winter in warm temperate zones; and all year round in tropical to subtropical areas. Plant seed directly into the soil ¼ inch deep, 2 inches apart, in rows 6 inches apart. Or, dig a shallow furrow along the length of the planting row, lay fertilizer along the bottom, cover with a little soil and then plant seed. Fill in the furrow with light compost or seed-raising mix and water in. Seedlings take 1–2 weeks to appear. Thin to 2 inches apart (3½ inches for winter radish) at second leaf stage. Successive sowings every 2 or 3 weeks ensure a continuous crop. Weed by regular, shallow cultivation. The plant has a tendency to bolt or go to seed in hot summer weather.

Watering. Water thoroughly to keep soil moist during growing stage.

Fertilizing. Use a complete fertilizer for furrow planting, otherwise dig into garden bed. Feed with a recommended liquid fertilizer every week at the seedling stage. Once seedlings are established, do not add further manure.

Problems. Caterpillars of cabbage whites are the main pests to watch out for. Early spraying with appropriate insecticide is recommended. Clubroot can affect winter radish because this type of radish is left in the ground longer than other varieties. Aphids and other insects can be controlled by using pyrethrum or other approved sprays. Discontinue use of spray a week before harvesting.

HARVESTING
Picking. Pull the whole plant from the ground at around 3–5 weeks for salad radishes and 1½–2 months for the longer root form. It is a good idea to undertake test pullings to judge size and firmness of fruit when anticipated maturity time is reached. Harvest before the radish gets old and tough.

Storing. Refrigerate radishes, trimmed of greens, wrapped in plastic bags for up to 10 days.

Freezing. Do not freeze.

USES
Culinary. Eat summer radishes raw in salads; braise winter radishes with a knob of butter.

FEATURES

This is an oriental form of radish, often called by its Japanese name daikon, which means "big root". It is a member of the mustard family and various types are used in Japanese and Chinese cuisines. The leaves, stems, seed pods, and seedlings, as well as the tap root, are used in Asian food preparations. The shape of the swollen tap root varies from spherical to elongated and triangular, depending on the variety; its flesh is white to greenish. The plant itself has an erect nature, generally growing 1–2 feet tall, but reaching 3½ feet when left to flower. The non-branching stem supports a leafy rosette composed of large, sprawling leaves.

GROWING METHOD

Planting. Sow in fall in cool regions and twice a year in spring and fall in warm and tropical areas. Sow seeds thinly, directly into the garden bed, ½–¾ inch deep, in drills 1¾ inch deep. Seedlings will appear in 10–14 days. Thin so that young plants are at least 4 inches apart, depending on the variety. Really large rooting types will need up to 16 inches of space around each plant. As the seedlings grow, cover stems with soil from around the drill holes. Keep beds free of weeds and carefully avoid damage to roots. These plants have a tendency to bolt in warm conditions after cold snaps.

Watering. Water steadily and constantly and do not let soil dry out. As plants reach maturity, cut down on watering because excess water leads to cracking of roots.

Fertilizing. Preferably use previously fertilized beds. If necessary, use complete fertilizer beneath drill holes before planting.

Problems. Aphids, cabbage white caterpillars, nematodes, and black beetle cause root damage. Control with pyrethrum sprays. Hot, wet weather can give rise to soil diseases, such as bacterial soft rot, which affects the root at ground level gradually sending the whole root soft and mushy. To prevent, keep bed free of decaying vegetable matter. Destroy any diseased plants. Rotate crops at least every 3 years as a preventative measure.

HARVESTING

Picking. White radish matures within 8–10 weeks in most areas, but can be harvested at any stage of the growing cycle. Roots are ready when about 8 inches long (for elongated varieties) or when diameter is 2–4 inches. Skin should be smooth and white and the flesh firm. Crop during cool weather, pulling root whole from the ground.

Storing. Refrigerate, wrapped in plastic for several weeks. It can also be dried, pickled, fermented, or preserved in brine.

Freezing. Do not freeze.

USES

Culinary. Raw white radish can be diced and added to salads; cooked, use like a potato or turnip; added to soups, stews, or stir-fries.

Raphanus sativus var. *longipinnatus*
WHITE RADISH (DAIKON)
Brassicaceae

CONDITIONS

Climate. Best grown as a cool weather crop ideally in temperatures around 68°F. The most important thing to remember is to choose the variety most suited to your local climate.

Aspect. Prefers moist, shady spots.

Soil. Rich, light, and well-drained soils. Root shape tends to be modified by the character of the soil so avoid heavy clay soils, which prevent roots expanding. To counter this problem, the root in some adaptable varieties props itself above the soil level.

Sechium edule
CHAYOTE
Cucurbitaceae

CONDITIONS
Climate. Best suited to subtropical areas and warmer areas of temperate zones. Severe frosts will kill the vine, but in cooler areas the vine will die down over winter with new growth in spring.

Aspect. Prefers warm, sunny spots against a wall. During cool to cold snaps, it is possible for chayote to be grown in a pot. It can then be brought inside and replanted out when the weather warms up.

Soil. Deep, fertile, moist, well-drained soil. Dig in a lot of organic matter and fertilizer before planting.

FEATURES
Chayote is known by various names, among them choko. The greenish-white fruit looks rather like a flattened pear and is borne on a large, vigorous, rambling vine. It needs considerable support and produces both male and female flowers. Leaves are large and hairy to the touch. This plant requires plenty of space but is easy to grow and relatively trouble-free.

GROWING METHOD
Planting. Select a mature chayote showing signs of a germinating seed. During early spring in warm climates and in fall through to spring in tropical zones, plant the whole chayote 4 inches deep in damp soil at an angle, with the broad or shooting end downwards and the other end showing just above soil level. Plant near a fence or other strong supporting structure. To ensure success, plant 2 or 3 plants 3½ feet apart. Keep weeds down during the growing period. After harvesting and before winter sets in, cut the vine back to 3 or 4 shoots and mulch heavily to protect the tuberous root system.

Watering. Give plenty of water to keep vine growing, especially during the late summer cropping period.

Fertilizing. Several weeks before planting, prepare bed with complete fertilizer. Side dress with the same fertilizer in midsummer. During the second year of growth, fertilize around the new shoots during early spring.

Problems. Relatively free from pests and diseases. Aphids and squash beetle may be a problem. Spray or dust with appropriate insecticide.

HARVESTING
Picking. A warm 6-month growing season is needed for fruit to reach maturity. Two crops can be harvested in tropical zones in spring to early summer, and one in summer in warm areas. The fruit is at its best when light green in color and about 2 inches long. Large fruit, sometimes with prickly spines on the skin, is both coarse in texture and lacking in flavor when cooked.

Storing. Refrigerate for up to 2 weeks.

Freezing. Boil sliced chayotes until tender. Drain well, then mash and cool. Pack into plastic containers and freeze for up to 6 months.

USES
Culinary. Steam, boil, bake, or braise; grate young flesh raw in salads.

FEATURES

Known commonly as both eggplant and aubergine, this vegetable grows on small bushes to 5 feet tall with large, coarse, hairy, gray-green leaves. The star-shaped flowers are an attractive mauve and the plants produce about 8 fruit per bush. The fruit varies in shape and size including long and slender or egg-shaped varieties. They are generally dark purple to black or creamy white to mauve in color. Recently released varieties include small and rounded, reddish forms and pea-sized, green varieties from Asia. Eggplants can be grown successfully in containers.

GROWING METHOD

Planting. Plant during late spring in cool climates, spring through to early summer in temperate zones, and spring through to fall in tropical areas. To ensure a good striking rate, especially in cold areas, sow seeds in small pots or seed boxes at least 8 weeks before transplanting into the open garden during warm weather. Cold soil will shock the plant and set it back considerably. For this reason and because of the fear of soil-borne diseases, many people grow eggplants in containers where conditions are more controllable. Thin out and choose the hardiest seedlings for transplanting. Plant in furrows, 20–24 inches apart, in rows 2–3 feet apart. Keep the area around the plant free of weeds by shallow cultivation.

Watering. Do not over-water because the plant is susceptible to root rot. Maintain even moisture and temperature levels in soil by mulching. Increase watering as the plant matures.

Fertilizing. A few days before planting, dig complete fertilizer into topsoil. Fertilize furrows to a depth of 6 inches and width of 4 inches. Fill in furrow with soil to cover fertilizer before planting. Side dress with urea when first fruit has set.

Problems. Aphids, lace bugs, flea beetles, and spider mites are the main pests. Treat with appropriate sprays. Crop rotation may be necessary to lessen incidence of soil-borne wilt diseases. However, do not grow peppers or tomatoes in succession with eggplants. Control leaf spot and fruit rot with fungicide sprays.

HARVESTING

Picking. Pick the fruit in full color after about 3–4 months and before the seeds harden and turn brown. The skin should be tight, firm, and unwrinkled. Over-ripe fruit is coarse and bitter. Cut hard, woody stems with a sharp tool to prevent damage to fruit.

Storing. Refrigerate for 7–10 days. Eggplant is ideal for pickling.

Freezing. Cut into slices, sprinkle with salt, and allow to stand for 20 minutes. Drain off excess liquid and fry eggplant gently in butter until just tender. Cool, then pack into plastic containers and freeze for up to 3 months.

USES

Culinary. Eggplant can be served hot or cold, puréed, fried, stuffed, or battered.

Solanum melongena var. *esculentum*
EGGPLANT
Solanaceae

CONDITIONS

Climate. Definitely a warm climate vegetable, needing temperatures of 77°F and above during the growing season. Seeds will not germinate unless the soil is warm and the air temperature is above 68°F. Eggplant is extremely sensitive to frosts. Extended cool periods will retard growth.

Aspect. Requires full sun and protection from winds.

Soil. Light, rich, well-drained soil.

Solanum tuberosum
POTATO
Solanaceae

CONDITIONS

Climate. Potatoes can be grown in all climates. They need a frost-free season of 4–5 months to develop successfully.

Aspect. Grows best in full sun.

Soil. Well-drained, fertile, and friable soils with a pH of 5–5.5 are ideal. Beds should be raised if underlying ground is heavy clay. Add lime sparingly to reduce soil acidity. Too much lime increases incidence of scab disease, which infects skin.

FEATURES

Although originally from the high mountains of South America, potatoes do not do well in areas of extreme frost or extreme heat. The potato is an underground tuber that produces a stem with hairy, tomato-like leaves above-ground. Depending on the variety, the skin ranges in color from cream through reddish-brown to dark purple. The flesh is creamy-white to white and either floury or waxy in texture. An easy vegetable to cultivate, it also grows quite successfully in containers.

GROWING METHOD

Planting. Planting time does depend on variety used but, in general, plant when soils are warm: spring to early summer in cold regions; spring to end of summer in temperate zones; and summer through winter in warm tropical climates. Seed pieces are eyes cut from potato tubers with about 1¾ ounces of flesh attached. Lay seed pieces 14 inches apart, on fertilized furrows 2½ feet apart. Fill furrows with soil and rake topsoil evenly. Alternatively, for a cleaner crop, cover sprouting tubers with 8–12 inches of decomposing straw or mulch, and top with 4 inches of rich, friable soil. Keep moist. Hill growing plants for support, to exclude sunlight and to protect from insects. Keep weeds down by shallow cultivation.

Watering. Water regularly to promote smooth, bigger vegetables. Irrigate along channels between hilled rows. Reduce watering just before harvest, when plant tops die off.

Fertilizing. Before planting, dig furrows to 6 inches, then lay 3–3½ ounces of fertilizer along the base. Cover with 2 inches soil. Use a fertilizer high in phosphorus.

Problems. Potato tuber moth attacks exposed tubers, so be sure to cover vegetable with soil. Treat aphids and Colorado potato beetle with appropriate sprays. Blight is common in humid weather, causing leaves and stems to rot, the tuber flesh to become spotted, and the whole potato to soften and rot. Spray with a registered fungicide to prevent the disease. Remove and burn diseased plants.

HARVESTING

Picking. Harvest "new" potatoes 1 month after flowering, when the leaves have turned yellow. Leave "old" potatoes to mature in the ground—4–5 months. Lift after plant dies down.

Storing. Keep in a cool, dry, dark, well-ventilated place to prevent from sprouting. Exposure to light causes potatoes to turn green, become bitter, indigestible, and even poisonous.

Freezing. Scrub, boil until almost cooked, drain, cool, pack in freezer bags, then freeze for up to 6 months. Or, prepare fries and deep fry for 4 minutes until cooked but not brown. Drain and cool. Place on a tray in a single layer and freeze for 30 minutes. Remove from tray, pack in freezer bags, then freeze for up to 3 months. Mash and freeze for up to 3 months.

USES

Culinary. Roast, fry, or boil. Different varieties lend themselves to different cooking techniques.

FEATURES
Mature plants of spinach produce a rosette of dark green leaves 4–6½ inches long with a prominent midrib. The edible part of the vegetable is the leaves, which are either crinkled or smooth, depending on the variety and they grow in clusters at ground level.

GROWING METHOD
Planting. Plant from fall through winter in cold areas, late summer through fall in temperate zones, and summer through fall in subtropical climates. Sow seeds directly into the garden bed, ½ inch deep, 12 inches apart, in rows 14 inches apart. Lightly cover seeds with compost and water in so that soil is just moist. Seedlings emerge within 2–3 weeks. Successive sowings every 3 weeks will ensure a continuous crop. Keep weeds down by heavy mulching. Mulching will also keep the roots cool.

Watering. Soil should be moist, but avoid continual wetting of leaves.

Fertilizing. A week before planting, dig in a complete fertilizer. Regular side feedings of a nitrogen-rich fertilizer after the first appearance of seedlings will promote good leaf growth.

Problems. Cucumber mosaic virus will cause leaves to yellow and then curl up and die. Downy mildew causes pale patches on leaves. Leaf miners and mites are the main pests. All these should be controlled by an appropriate fungicide or insect sprays.

HARVESTING
Picking. Crops take 8–10 weeks to mature. Pick individual leaves as required or pull the whole plant from the ground.

Storing. Refrigerate for up to 1 week.

Freezing. Wash well and trim leaves. Blanch for 1 minute in a small quantity of water. Chill, drain, pack in plastic bags or containers, then freeze for up to 6 months.

USES
Culinary. Use younger leaves in salads; steam or boil older leaves or cook in stir-fries.

Spinacia oleracea
SPINACH
Chenopodiaceae

CONDITIONS
Climate. Best in cool climate, but grows in most areas. Ideal temperatures are 50–59°F.

Aspect. Prefers sun to partial shade and needs shelter from winds.

Soil. Prefers non-acidic, well-drained soils with a pH range of 6–7, enriched with decayed animal or poultry manure. Lime or dolomite will help neutralize acidic soil and should be dug in 2 weeks before planting.

Vicia faba
FAVA BEAN
Fabaceae

CONDITIONS
Climate. Grows very well in mild temperate and cool climates, where temperatures are below 68°F. Cool weather helps to set the pods. Pods will not develop in areas that have very hot summers.

Aspect. Likes full sunlight

Soil. Grow in beds of alkaline soil that are well-drained and rich in organic matter.

FEATURES
A hardy, winter annual growing to 5 feet tall, fava beans (also known as broad beans) have square stems producing small leaflets, which give the plant a bushy look. White flowers produce 6–8 inch pods that contain edible seeds. The seeds are large and may be eaten fresh, although they are often dried. Fava beans are particularly easy to grow in the home garden, but are not suited to container growing.

GROWING METHOD
Planting. Plant fall to winter in cooler zones and mild temperate zones and early fall in warm temperate climates. Sow seeds directly into beds 2 inches deep, 2 inches apart, in rows at least 3½ feet apart. When seedlings are well established, thin to 8 inches apart. If a good crop is evident, tips of growing shoots can be nipped out to hasten maturity. The crop requires only limited attention during the 4–5 month growing season.

Watering. Do not over-water fava beans. In combination with high temperatures, wet soil conditions lead to root diseases. Seeds planted in damp soil require no further watering until seedlings appear. As plant matures, water only when soil starts to dry out.

Fertilizing. When preparing beds, dig in complete fertilizer that has a good amount of phosphorus. Too much fertilizer, especially in the form of animal manures, leads to pod-setting failure. As with other legumes and pulses, fava beans add nitrogen to the soil through the action of nitrogen-fixing bacteria on their roots and so in a way produce their own fertilizer.

Problems. Control aphids and small mites with recommended insecticides or organically prepared garlic sprays. Diseases include rust, and tomato spotted wilt virus, which causes darkening of the growing tip, wilting, then death. Remove and burn diseased plants immediately. Protect remaining plants from aphids. Crop rotation over several seasons is recommended.

HARVESTING
Picking. Young pods, which can be eaten whole, can be harvested during early spring in most areas. Mature plants are ready for harvest 4–5 months after planting.

Storing. Refrigerate for up to 2 weeks.

Freezing. Shell, wash, then blanch in boiling water for 1½ minutes. Cool, place on a tray in a single layer, then freeze for 30 minutes. Remove from tray, pack in freezer bags, then freeze for up to 6 months.

USES
Culinary. When harvested young, the whole pod containing half-ripe seeds can be prepared and eaten as you would climbing beans. Remove older beans from pods and steam, boil, stir-fry, or cook for use in salads.

FEATURES

A member of the grass family, corn grows to a majestic 16½ feet tall, and produces 1–2 ears per stalk. The ears or cobs are completely covered with regularly arranged seeds, called kernels, which are white to yellow, although some heirloom varieties have red and black seeds or a combination of all these colors.

GROWING METHOD

Planting. Plant late spring to early summer in colder regions; in spring to midsummer in temperate zones; and all year round in subtropical and tropical climates, although fall is optimal. Prepare short rows, rather than long, 20–24 inches apart, to give an overall clumping effect to the garden bed. Dig seed trenches to a depth of 10 inches, layer with complete fertilizer, then cover with 4 inches soil. Space seeds about 10 inches apart. Soil should be damp and warm, at least 59°F. Seedlings should emerge within 14 days of seeds being sown. Remove weeds by light cultivation.

Watering. Keep soil evenly moist, especially in hot weather and after pollination when care should be taken not to wet tassels.

Fertilizing. Dig in plenty of poultry manure at least a fortnight before planting. Give applications of fertilizer high in nitrogen and phosphate when planting and apply side dressings throughout the growing period.

Problems. Many pests attack corn including corn earworm, corn borer, and cutworm, which penetrate the ears and damage the seed. Sap-sucking aphids are also a problem. At the first sign of trouble, spray with appropriate insecticide every 2 or 3 days when the plant is at the "green silk" stage. Birds may also attack the ears of corn. Cover at the ripening stage.

HARVESTING

Picking. Corn will reach maturity within 12–14 weeks of planting. The kernels will be plump and full of milk, which oozes out when the ripe cob is cut. If the fluid is clear, it means the cob is immature.

Storing. Store corn in the fridge, with the husks on, for up to 2 days.

Freezing. Remove leaves and silk and cut off top of cob. Wash, blanch for 5–7 minutes, chill, then drain. Wrap in plastic, place in plastic bags, then freeze for up to 6 months.

USES

Culinary. Corn can be boiled, steamed, barbecued, roasted, and even microwaved.

Zea mays var. *saccharata*
CORN
Poaceae

CONDITIONS

Climate. Prefers hot, warm frost-free climates.

Aspect. Needs full sun and wind breaks, if necessary.

Soil. Grows in a wide range of soils, but prefers deep, well-manured soil.

index

Page numbers in *italics* indicate a recipe. **Bold** face indicates an entry in the vegetable directory.

a

Abelmoschus esculentus   21, 28, 147, 155, 159, 182, **200**
acidic soil   22–3, 123
aerobic composting   100, 103
Agaricus spp.   68–9, 147, 155, 159, 179, **201**
aïoli   172
Ajuga spp.   111
alfalfa (*Medicago sativa*)   14, 29, 64, 81, 109
alfalfa green manure/mulch   109–112
algal growth   97, 99
alkaline soil   22–3
Allium spp.   91, 93
Allium ampeloprasum   6, 9, 10, 11, 14, 28, 63, 65, 66, 67, 87, 92, 93, 122, 123, 154, 159, 177, **202**
Allium ascalonicum   **203**
Allium cepa   6, 9, 10, 11, 14, 25, 62, 63, 65, 66, 67, 86, 87, 91, 92, 93, 118, 122, 123, 141, 146, 147, 155, 159, 182, **204**
Allium fistulosum   81, 92, 93, 122, 123, 151, 182
Allium sativum   9, 14, 63, 64, 65, 86, 92, 93, 122, 123, 146, 150, 151, 154, 159, 172, 172, **205**
Allium schoenoprasum   136
Allium tuberosum   44, 81, 137
Allium ursinum   173
Alocasia macrorrhiza   90, 140, 141, **206**
Alpinia galanga   90, 150
Althaea officinalis   175
Alternanthera sissoo   141
amaranth   see Chinese spinach
Amaranthus giganteus   140
Amaranthus hypochondriacus   44
Amaranthus tricolor   28, 63, 154, 158, **207**
anaerobic composting   100, 102, 112
angled luffa   see sin qua
anthracnose   120, **240**

Anthriscus cerefolium   136
aphids   115, 116, 118, 121
Apium graveolens   6, 14, 28, 33, 36, 37, 63, 65, 66, 67, 86, 88, 92, 153, 158, 169, **208**
aquaculture   see hydroponics
aquatic and moisture-loving vegetables   58–9
Armoracia rusticana   21, 67, 90, 186
armyworms   118
artichoke   6, 21, 28, 37, 62, 63, 90, 122, 138, 139, 153, 154, 157, 159, 164, 176, 176, **229**, **234**
arugula   (*Eruca vesicaria* subsp. *sativa*)   122, 137, 173, 190, **232**
arugula and Parmesan cheese   190
Asclepias spp.   174
Asian vegetables   14, 15, 131, 180–1
asparagus (*Asparagus officinalis*)   6, 14, 21, 24, 28, 38, 62, 65, 66, 81, 92, 153, 157, 164, **209**
aspect   26–7
avocado   120

b

baba ganouj   171
bamboo shoots (*Phyllostachys* spp.)   14, 80
barriers   115, 118
base dressing   98
Basella alba   49, 140
Basella rubra   49, 140
basil   64, 65, 67
bean (*Phaseolus vulgaris*)   21, 28, 30, 57, 62, 64, 65, 66, 67, 78, 79, 87, 88, 89, 119, 120, 122, 123, 124, 125, 144, 146, 147, 153, 157, 165, 165, **240**   see also fava bean; runner beans
bean teepees   38
beanettes   125
beefsteak plant   see shiso
beet (*Beta vulgaris*)   6, 11, 14, 15, 20, 31, 36, 63, 66, 67, 86, 89, 90, 122, 123, 147, 148, 150, 151, 153, 157, 166, **210**
beet mash   166
Belgian endive   (*Cichorium intybus*)   28, 80, 92, 136, 137, 156, 161, 170, **223**
bell cloches   134
Beta maritiima   58–9

Beta vulgaris   6, 11, 14, 15, 20, 31, 36, 63, 66, 67, 86, 89, 90, 122, 123, 147, 148, 150, 151, 153, 157, 166, **210**
Beta vulgaris var. *cicla*   136, 137, **211**
bhindi   see okra
bitter melon   180
black sage tea   116
blackjack   99
bok choy   14, 180
borage (*Borago officinalis*)   41, 173
Botrytis cinerea   120
braised fennel   172, 172
braised green beans   165
Brassica spp.   186
Brassica juncea   15, 136
Brassica napus   28, 63, 87, 90, 151, 155, 161, **212**
Brassica oleracea   136, 150, **213–18**
Brassica rapa   **219–220**
Brazilian spinach (*Alternanthera sissoo*)   141
broadcast sowing   77
broccoli (*Brassica oleracea*)   6, 21, 28, 62, 63, 67, 86, 89, 153, 154, 157, 166, 166, **218**   see also Chinese kale
brown mustard (*Brassica* spp.)   186
Brussels sprouts (*Brassica oleracea*)   14, 21, 28, 63, 66, 67, 86, 89, 122, 144, 153, 157, 166, **216**
Brussels sprouts with bacon   166
buckwheat   64
buckwheat green manure   109
burdock   90
bush okra (*Corchorus olitorius*)   140
bush squash   36

c

cabbage (*Brassica oleracea*)   6, 10, 14, 15, 21, 28, 34, 41, 62, 63, 65, 66, 67, 83, 86, 89, 118, 122, 123, 146, 153, 157, 167, 167, **215**   see also Chinese cabbage; red cabbage
cabbage whites   118, 215, 216, 217, 218, 242, 243
caesar salad   178
calcium   23, 98
Canadian wild onion   92
canola   21

Capsicum annuum   6, 21, 28, 46, 47, 50, 51, 63, 87, 88, 89, 122, 123, 130, 131, 138, 139, 147, 155, 160, 184, 184, 186, 187, **221**
cardoons   35, 37, 138, 139
carrot (*Daucus carota*)   6, 11, 12, 14, 28, 29, 31, 36, 47, 62, 63, 65, 66, 67, 84, 86, 88, 90, 122, 123, 141, 147, 150, 153, 158, 168, 168, **230**
cassava (*Manihot esculenta*)   90, 140, 141
caterpillars   66, 113, 115, 212, 213, 214, 217, 219, 220, 242
cauliflower (*Brassica oleracea*)   6, 21, 28, 63, 66, 67, 86, 118, 144, 153, 158, 168, **214**
cauliflower cheese   168
cayenne   186, 187
celeriac   86, 88, 90, 169
celeriac remoulade   169
celery (*Apium graveolens*)   6, 14, 28, 33, 36, 37, 63, 65, 66, 67, 86, 88, 92, 153, 158, 169, **208**
celery cabbage   see Chinese cabbage
Cercospora spp.   120
chamomile   41
chard   see *Beta vulgaris* var. *cicla*; Chinese chard; Swiss chard
chayote (*Sechium edule*)   28, 49, 154, 158, **244**
chemical sprays   116, 118, 119, 120, 121
Chenopodium album   11, 173
cherry tomatoes (*Lycopersicon esculentum*)   30
chervil (*Anthriscus cerefolium*)   136
chicken manure   97, 102
chickweed (*Stellaria media*)   173
chicory (*Cichorium endivia*)   6, 14, 21, 28, 36, 37, 131, 153, 156, 158, 170, **222**
chicory flower (*Cichorium intybus*)   137
chicory "Pane de Sucre" (*Cichorium endivia*)   137
children's vegetables   30–1
chili and soap spray   117
chili con queso   185
chilies (*Capsicum annuum*)   21, 43, 63, 88, 138, 139, 146, 147, 154, 158, 184, 185, 186, 187, **221**
Chinese bitter melon   see winter melon
Chinese cabbage (*Brassica rapa*)   28, 63, 154, 158, 180, **219**
Chinese chard   see bok choy

Chinese kale (*Brassica oleracea*)   15, 154, 158, 180, **213**
Chinese keys   see finger-root
Chinese leaves   see Chinese cabbage
Chinese okra   see sin qua
Chinese spinach (*Amaranthus tricolor*)   28, 44, 63, 154, 158, **207**
chives   41, 63, 64, 65, 66, 92, 93
choko   see chayote
Chorispora tenella   137
choy sum   180
chrysanthemum greens   180
Cichorium endivia   137, **222**
Cichorium intybus   28, 80, 92, 136, 137, 156, 161, 170, **223**
clay soil   33
climate   20, 27–8, 72–3, 77–8, 79, 94, 138–41
climbing beans   38, 41, 49, 50, 63
climbing peas   38, 41, 49, 50
climbing vegetables   49–51
cloches   12, 20, 122, 123, 128, 134
cold frames   76, 128, 132–3
coleslaw   167
collards   140
Colletotrichum spp.   120
Colocasia esculenta   **206**
companion planting   25, 38, 64–7
compost   54, 57, 100–8, 110, 112, 113, 114
compost bins   55, 102, 105, 106
compost heaps   101–2, 104–5
compost tumblers   105
conservatories   128, 130
container growing   42–3
containers for seed   74–6
cooking   162–97
cool climate plants   78
cool-season vegetables   28
Corchorus olitorius   140
corn (*Zea mays* var. *saccharata*)   6, 14, 21, 24, 27, 28, 37, 65, 67, 87, 89, 118, 122, 123, 131, 138, 139, 141, 147, 156, 161, 170, 170, **249**
corn fritters   170
corn salad (*Valerianella locusta*)   122, 173
courgette   see zucchini

Crambe maritima   59, 173
cranberry beans   42, 124, 165
crop covers   135
crop rotation   62–3, 118, 120
cross pollination   89
cucumber (*Cucumis sativus*)   6, 9, 21, 28, 43, 47, 49, 50, 51, 63, 65, 86, 121, 122, 123, 131, 154, 158, 171, 171, **224**
Cucumis sativus   6, 9, 21, 28, 43, 47, 49, 50, 51, 63, 65, 86, 121, 122, 123, 131, 154, 158, 171, 171, **224**
Cucurbita spp.   6, 21, 28, 63, 71, 87, 121, 146, 147, 154, 155, 159, 160, 178, 178, 189, 189, **227–8**
Cucurbita pepo var. *melopepo*   21, 36, 37, 42, 49, 63, 65, 67, 121, 122, 123, 139, 156, 161, 197, 197, **225, 226**
cultivating   52–69
curly endive (*Cichorium endivia*)   137
curly kale   36
currant tomato   140, 141
curried parsnip soup   183
cut and come again vegetables   136–7
cutworms   66, 115, 118, 221, 222, 249
Cymbopogon citratus   80
Cynara scolymus   21, 63, 153, 157, **229**

d

daikon   see white radish
dandelion (*Taraxacum officinale*)   21, 64, 90, 175
Daucus carota   6, 11, 12, 14, 28, 29, 31, 36, 47, 62, 63, 65, 66, 67, 84, 86, 88, 90, 122, 123, 141, 147, 150, 153, 158, 168, 168, **230**
day lily (*Hemerocallis llilioasphodelus*)   45
deep bed system   54–5
deep cultivation   52–4
digging over   114, 123
dill   10, 66, 67, 115
Dioscorea spp.   49, 90, 140, 141, 151
Diplotaxis erucoides   173
Diplotaxis tenuifoliia   173
direct sowing   76–7
diseases   25, 54, 82, 96, 99, 113, 114, 120–1, 131
dolomite   98
double digging   56–7
drainage   32–3, 52

drill sowing   78
drip irrigation   25, 129
drought-tolerant vegetables   138, 139
dry areas   138–9
dry season   140
drying vegetables   147, 153
dulse (*Palmaria palmata*)   58
dwarf bean   63, 153, 157

e

earthing up   92
edible bulb planting   91–2
edible flowers   6, 12, 15, 29, 44–5, 197
edible landscaping   34
edible tuber planting   90
edible weeds   173–5
eelworms   65, 67, 118
eggplant (*Solanum melongena* var. *esculentum*)   6, 15, 21, 28, 37, 51, 63, 67, 78, 86, 89, 122, 123, 131, 138, 139, 154, 158, 171, 171, **245**
Eleocharis dulcis   33, 59, 92, 156, 161, **231**
endive   see chicory
Equisetum spp.   116
Eruca vesicaria subsp. *sativa*   137, **232**
Ethiopian mustard   140
eucalyptus tea   116

f

fat hen (*Chenopodium album*)   11, 173
fava bean (*Vicia faba*)   6, 10, 21, 28, 36, 63, 67, 73, 86, 122, 123, 124, 153, 157, 165, **248**
fennel (*Foeniculum vulgare*)   14, 22, 28, 151, 154, 159, 172, 172, 174, **233**
fertilizer/fertilizing   82, 84, 96–9, 123
Ficus carica   44
fiddleheads   80, 173
field-stored vegetables   148, 153, 154, 155
Finger-root   180
fingerling potato (*Solanum tuberosum*)   151
flowers   6, 12, 15, 29, 44–5, 197
Foeniculum vulgare   14, 22, 28, 151, 154, 159, 172, 172, 174, **233**
freezing vegetables   144, 153, 154, 155, 156, 157–61

French bean   see bean
French marigold (*Tagetes patula*)   64, 65
frisée   see curly endive
fuchsias   65
fungal diseases   96, 99, 120, 121, 129, 238
fungicides   116
fuzzy melon   see hairy melon

g

gai choy   14, 63, 181
gai larn   see Chinese broccoli
galangal (*Alpinia galanga*)   90, 150
garden design   34–51
garden sheds   55, 123
garlic (*Allium sativum*)   9, 14, 63, 64, 65, 86, 92, 93, 122, 123, 146, 150, 151, 154, 159, 172, 172, **205**
   see also wild garlic
garlic chives (*Allium tuberosum*)   44, 81, 137
garlic spray   116, 117
geranium (*Pelargonium* spp.)   44
germination   72, 76, 78, 79, 82, 94
ginger   90, 154, 159
ginseng   90
gladioli   65
globe artichoke (*Cynara scolymus*)   21, 63, 153, 157, **229**
grapes   65
green cayenne   186
green manure   109
greenhouses   12, 46, 55, 128–30, 131
growing bags   50–1
growing media problems   82
gumbo   see okra

h

hairy melon   181
Hamburg parsley   90
harvest time   122, 123, 144–61
heirloom vegetables   15, 38, 89, 138
Helianthus annuus   29, 30, 37, 44, 65
Helianthus tuberosus   21, 63, 90, 122, 154, 159, 176, **234**
Hemerocallis lilioasphodelus   45

Hibiscus esculentus   see *Abelmoschus esculentus*
history   8–14, 39
hops   see wild hops
horseradish (*Armoracia rusticana*)   21, 67, 90, 186
hot foods   186–7
hot frames   132
housekeeping   114
Humulus lupulus   173
humus   23
hydroponics   14, 20, 43, 46–7
hyssop   65, 66

i

indoor sowing   122
in-ground-stored vegetables   148, 153, 154, 155
inorganic mulch   110
insect pests   64, 66, 67, 113, 114, 115, 116–17, 118, 119, 122, 123, 131, 135
insect pollinators   64
insect predators   64, 116, 118, 119
insecticidal soap   116, 118
interplanting   38, 87
IPCC   28
Ipomoea aquatica   136, 181
Ipomoea batatas   28, 49, 90, 141, 150, 156, 161, 192, **235**
Italian parsley (*Petroselinum crispum* var. *neapolitanum*)   137

j

jasmine (*Jaminum* spp.)   45
Jerusalem artichoke (*Helianthus tuberosus*)   21, 63, 90, 122, 154, 159, 176, 176, **234**
jicama   14, 90, 140, 141, 176
jute mallow (*Corchorus olitorius*)   140

k

kale   14, 25, 36, 41, 87, 122, 128, 136, 140, 177
kang kong   see ong choy
katuk (*Sauropus androgynous*)   140
kelp   58
kidney beans   87, 125
kitchen waste   101

kohlrabi (*Brassica oleracea*)   14, 28, 41, 63, 65, 87, 90, 122, 150, 154, 159, 177, **217**
kombu   58
kumara   see sweet potato

l

Lactuca sativa   6, 14, 15, 20, 21, 28, 36, 41, 42, 43, 50, 62, 63, 65, 66, 67, 78, 82, 83, 87, 122, 123, 131, 141, 154, 159, 178, 178, **236**
lady's fingers   see okra
lamb's-quarters   see fat hen
lavender (*Lavandula* spp.)   45, 64
leaf spot   120, 208, 211, 236, 237, 245
leek (*Allium ampeloprasum*)   6, 9, 10, 11, 14, 28, 63, 65, 66, 67, 87, 92, 93, 122, 123, 154, 159, 177, **202**
leeks à la grecque   177
legumes   21, 124–5
lemongrass (*Cymbopogon citratus*)   80
lettuce (*Lactuca sativa*)   6, 14, 15, 20, 21, 28, 36, 41, 42, 43, 50, 62, 63, 65, 66, 67, 78, 82, 83, 87, 122, 123, 131, 141, 154, 159, 178, 178, **236**
lima beans   21, 125
lime   23, 123
limestone   98
liquid fertilizer   98, 99, 112
living mulch   111
lotus   14, 59
lucerne   see alfalfa
lupin green manure   109
Lupinus angustifolia   109
Lycopersicon esculentum   6, 11, 14, 15, 20, 21, 24, 28, 30, 37, 38, 43, 46, 47, 49, 50, 62, 63, 64, 65, 66, 67, 87, 89, 119, 122, 123, 127, 131, 138, 139, 140, 141, 146, 156, 161, 194–5, **237**

m

magnesium   23, 98
maintenance   94–125
Malabar spinach (*Basella alba*)   49, 140
mangetout   see snow pea
Manihot esculenta   90, 140, 141
manure   54, 57, 97, 99, 102, 109, 123
marigolds (*Tagetes* spp.)   64, 65, 67, 118

marinated zucchini   197
market gardens   11
marrow (*Cucurbita* spp.)   21, 63, 87, 121, 146, 154, 159, 178, 178, **228**
marsh mallow (*Althaea officinalis*)   175
Medicago sativa   14, 29, 64, 81, 109
melons   21, 36, 63, 65
Mexican beans   138
milkweed (*Sonchus oleraceus*)   174
mint   65, 66
mixed mushroom stir-fry   69
mizuna (*Brassica juncea*)   15, 136
mosaic disease   121
mulch   54, 110–12, 113, 138, 141
mung bean (*Vigna radiata*)   14, 81, 165
mushroom (*Agaricus* spp.)   68–9, 147, 155, 159, 179, **201**
mushroom compost   102
mustard greens   14, 63, 181

n

napa cabbage   see Chinese cabbage
Nasturtium officinale   21, 29, 47, 59, 175, **238**
nasturtiums (*Tropaeolum majus*)   29, 38, 41, 43, 45, 65, 66, 67, 115
navets   196
Nelumbo nucifera   14, 59
nematodes   65, 67, 118, 201, 230, 243
New Zealand spinach (*Tetragonia tetragonioides*)   140
nicola potato (*Solanum tuberosum*)   150
nitrogen   23, 97, 102, 107, 109, 110, 111–12
nitrogen-fixing plants   64
no-dig gardening   48
NPK ratio   97
nutriculture   see hydroponics

o

okra (*Abelmoschus esculentus*)   21, 28, 147, 155, 159, 182, **200**
ong choy   136, 181
onion (*Allium cepa*)   6, 9, 10, 11, 14, 25, 62, 63, 65, 66, 67, 86, 87, 91, 92, 93, 118, 122, 123, 141, 146, 147, 150, 155, 159, 182, **204**

onion chives (*Allium schoenoprasum*)   136
onion spray   117
organic fertilizers   29, 46, 54, 97
organic gardening   23, 54, 112, 113, 114
organic mulch   110
organic sprays   116–17
oriental mustard   see gai choy
ornamental kale (*Brassica oleracea*)   41

p

palm hearts   21
Palmaria palmata   58
parsley   11, 41, 63, 66, 90, 137
parsnip (*Pastinaca sativa*)   6, 14, 28, 63, 67, 82, 87, 88, 90, 122, 123, 150, 152, 155, 159, 183, 183, **239**
paths   55
pea (*Pisum sativum*)   6, 10, 20, 21, 28, 29, 43, 62, 63, 64, 66, 67, 78, 79, 87, 88, 89, 122, 123, 124, 125, 144, 146, 147, 155, 160, 183, **241**
peanuts   90
Peking cabbage   see Chinese cabbage
Pelargonium spp.   44
pennyroyal   111
pepper (*Capsicum annuum*)   6, 21, 28, 46, 47, 50, 51, 63, 87, 88, 89, 122, 123, 130, 131, 138, 139, 147, 155, 160, 184, 184, 186, 187, **221**
peppercorn (*Piper nigrum*)   186
perilla   see shiso
perpetual vegetables   15
pests   25, 28, 50, 54, 64, 65, 66, 67, 82, 113, 114, 115–19, 122, 123, 131, 135
Petroselinum crispum var. *neapolitanum*   137
pH range   22–3
Phacelia tanecetifolia   109
Phaseolus vulgaris   26, 28, 30, 57, 62, 64, 65, 66, 67, 78, 79, 87, 88, 89, 119, 120, 122, 123, 124, 125, 144, 146, 147, 153, 157, 165, 165, **240**
Phyllostachys spp.   14, 80
pickling   154
Picrasma quassioides   116
pigweed (*Portulaca oleracea*)   173, 174
pinching out   123
Piper nigrum   186

Pisum sativum   6, 10, 20, 21, 28, 29, 43, 62, 63, 64, 66, 67, 78, 79, 87, 88, 89, 122, 123, 124, 125, 144, 146, 147, 155, 160, 183, **241**
Pisum sativum var. *macrocarpon*   6, 21, 29, 30, 31, 43, 80, 125, 155, 160, 183
Pisum sativum var. *sativum*   31
plantain (*Plantago major*)   174
plant protection   126–7
plant spacing   86–7
Plantago major   174
planting depth   73, 82
polytunnels   50, 130–1
Porphyra spp.   58
portable frames   128
Portulaca oleracea   173, 174
potager gardens   11, 39, 41
potassium   97, 98, 107
potato (*Solanum tuberosum*)   6, 11, 13, 14, 21, 28, 36, 42–3, 62, 65, 66, 67, 86, 90, 91, 122, 123, 150, 151, 155, 160, 188, **246**
potatoes Anna   188
poultry manure   97, 102
powdery mildew   121
pricking out   83–4
propagation   70–93, 132
pumpkin   see winter squash
purple kale (*Brassica oleracea*)   136
purple mustard (*Chorispora tenella*)   137
purslane (*Portulaca oleracea*)   173, 174
pyrethrum spray   116, 118

q

quassia tea   116

r

radicchio (*Cichorium intybus*)   136, 170
radish (*Raphanus sativus*)   14, 15, 21, 28, 30, 50, 63, 66, 87, 90, 122, 123, 150, 155, 156, 160, 186, 189, **242**
raised bed gardening   26, 27, 40, 41
raita   171
ramp   92
rapeseed oil   116

Raphanus sativus   14, 15, 21, 28, 30, 50, 63, 66, 87, 90, 122, 123, 150, 155, 156, 160, 186, 189, **242**
Raphanus sativus var. *longipinnatus*   14, 150, 156, 161, 187, **243**
red cabbage   36, 42, 167
red chard (*Beta vulgaris* var. *cicla*)   137
red clover   109
red kidney beans   125
red onion (*Allium cepa*)   150
refrigeration of seed   72, 79
rhubarb   122, 123
ridged loofah   see sin qua
roast broccoli   166
roasted Jerusalem artichoke   176
root knot nematodes   see eelworms
rose (*Rosa* spp.)   45
rosemary (*Rosmarinus officinalis*)   45
row covers   135
Rumex acetosa   173
runner beans   11, 41, 49, 50, 122, 125, 165
rust   121, 248
rutabaga (*Brassica napus*)   28, 63, 87, 90, 151, 155, 161, **212**
rye green manure   109

s

sage   66
salad vegetables   122, 123
salicornia   58
Salvia spp.   44
Salvia mellifera   116
sand storage   149, 153
Sauropus androgynous   140
sautéed garlicky spinach   191
scale   116
scallions (*Allium fistulosum*)   81, 92, 93, 122, 123, 151, 182
scorzonera   90
sea beet (*Beta maritiima*)   58–9
sea kale (*Crambe maritima*)   59, 173
sea lettuce (*Ulva lactuca*)   58
season extension   126–41
seasonal tasks   114, 122–3

seaweed   58, 101
seaweed fertilizer   97, 98, 99, 112, 131
seaweed meal   98
Sechium edule   28, 49, 154, 158, **244**
seed   20, 70, 72–3, 94, 132, 133, 138
seed depth and spacing   73, 82, 86
seed potatoes   91, 122
seed-raising basics   70
seed-raising mixes   73–4, 94
seed saving   88
seed sowing   74–8, 86–7
seed storage   79
seed viability   79, 82
shade cloth   130
shallots (*Allium cepa*, *A. ascalonium*)   14, 28, 63, 92, 93, 122, 123, 151, 155, 160, 190, **203**
shiso   181
shoots and sprouts   80–1
silverbeet   see Swiss chard
sin qua   181
site analysis   26
slugs   82, 216
snails   82, 119, 216, 222
snake beans   see yard long beans
snap peas (*Pisum sativum* var. *sativum*)   31
snow pea (*Pisum sativum* var. *macrocarpon*)   6, 21, 29, 30, 31, 43, 80, 125, 155, 160, 183
society garlic (*Tulbaghia violacea*)   45
soil
    clay   33
    cultivation of   52–69
    double digging of   56–7
    drought-prone   139
    germination problems &   82
    pH range of   22–3
    poor   20, 26
    raised bed gardening &   26, 27, 41
    structure of   54
    tropics &   140, 141
soilless culture   see hydroponics
Solanum melongena var. *esculentum*   6, 15, 21, 28, 37, 51, 63, 67, 78, 86, 89, 122, 123, 131, 138, 139, 154, 158, 171, 171, **245**

Solanum tuberosum 6, 11, 13, 14, 21, 28, 36, 42–3, 62, 65, 66, 67, 86, 90, 91, 122, 123, 150, 151, 155, 160, 188, **246**
sorrel 11, 173
southernwood tea 116
sowing 74–8, 86–7, 122
soybean dip 193
soybeans 14, 21, 49, 192–3
spinach (*Spinacia oleracea*) 6, 11, 14, 20, 28, 31, 36, 41, 63, 78, 83, 122, 123, 155, 160, 191, 191, **247** see also Chinese spinach; New Zealand spinach
squash 28, 38, 63, 65, 67, 89, 155, 161, 191, **225**
staking 122, 123
Stellaria media 173
storage 122, 123
  clamps for 152
  crop selection for 146
  freezing for 144, 153, 154, 155, 156, 157–61
  harvesting & 146–7
  methods for 144, 149, 152, 153–6
  root vegetables & 148–9
  sand for 149
straw compost 57
strawberries 65, 67
string bean see bean
stuffed marrow 178
subsoil 56
succession planting 85
successive sowing 86
sugar cane mulch 110
sugar snap peas 155, 161, 183
summer squash (*Cucurbita pepo* var. *melopepo*) **225** see also squash
sunflowers (*Helianthus annuus*) 29, 30, 37, 44, 65
support and protection 50–1
swamp cabbage see ong choy
swatow mustard cabbage see gai choy
swede see rutabaga
sweet corn see corn
sweet potato (*Ipomoea batatas*) 28, 49, 90, 141, 150, 156, 161, 192, **235**
Swiss chard (*Beta vulgaris* var. *cicla*) 15, 20, 28, 36, 37, 41, 62, 63, 67, 122, 136, 156, 194, **211**

t

Tagetes spp. 64, 65, 67, 118
tampala spinach (*Amaranthus giganteus*) 140
tansy 66
Taraxacum officinale 21, 64, 90, 175
taro (*Alocasia macrorrhiza*) 90, 140, 141, **206**
tatsoi 15, 181
teas, insect repellent 116
teepees 38, 43
terracing 32
Tetragonia tetragonioides 140
Thai winter squash coconut soup 189
thinnings 83, 173
thyme 64, 66
tofu 193
tomatillo 194
tomato (*Lycopersicon esculentum*) 6, 11, 14, 15, 20, 21, 24, 28, 30, 37, 38, 43, 46, 47, 49, 50, 62, 63, 64, 65, 66, 67, 87, 89, 119, 122, 123, 127, 131, 138, 139, 140, 141, 146, 156, 161, 194–5, **237**
tomato salad 195
tomato seed 88
tomato support systems 50–1
top dressing 98, 123
topography 32
topsoil 56, 57
trace elements 23, 98
transplanting 85–6
traps 115
trench composting 108
Triticum aestivum 45
Tropaeolum majus 29, 38, 41, 43, 45, 65, 66, 67, 115
tropical vegetable gardening 140–1
Tulbaghia violacea 45
tunnel cloches 134
turnip (*Brassica rapa*) 6, 11, 14, 15, 21, 28, 62, 63, 65, 75, 87, 90, 122, 123, 156, 161, 196, **220**

u

Ulva lactuca 58

v

Valerianella locusta 122, 173
vegetable directory 198–249vegetable families 21
vegetable garden calendar 122–3
vegetable gourd see sin qua
vegetable patches 18–20
vegetable storage clamp 152
vegetable timbales 47
Vichy carrots 168
Vicia faba 6, 10, 21, 28, 36, 63, 73, 86, 122, 123, 124, 153, 157, 165, **248**
Vigna radiata 14, 81, 165
viral diseases 114, 225, 226, 227, 228

w

Waldorf salad 169
wall arugula (*Diplotaxis tenuifoliia*) 173
warm climate plants 78
warm-season vegetables 28
warrigal greens (*Tetragonia tetragonioides*) 140
water chestnuts (*Eleocharis dulcis*) 33, 59, 92, 156, 161, **231**
water convolvulus see ong choy
water lotus (*Nelumbo nucifera*) 59
water spinach (*Ipomoea aquatica*) 136, 181
watercress (*Nasturtium officinale*) 21, 29, 47, 59, 175, **238**
watering
  dry areas & 139
  greenhouse 129, 131
  overview of 94, 96
  recycling & 139
  seeds & 84, 94
wax gourd see winter melon
weather screens 20
weeds 112, 118, 121, 122, 140, 141
weeds, edible 173–5
wet season 140
wheat (*Triticum aestivum*) 45
white chard (*Beta vulgaris* var. *cicla*) 137
white frilled kale (*Brassica oleracea*) 136
white gourd see winter melon
white grub 119

white radish (*Raphanus sativus* var. *longipinnatus*) 14, 109, 156, 161, **243**
whitefly 116, 119, 131
wild arugula (*Diplotaxis erucoides*) 173
wild fennel (*Foeniculum vulgare*) 174
wild garlic (*Allium ursinum*) 173
wild hops (*Humulus lupulus*) 173
wild mustard 174, 175
wild rice (*Zizania palustris*) 58
wild sorrel (*Rumex acetosa*) 173
wild tomatoes 140, 141
wind 26, 134, 139
window gardens 38
winter cabbage 128
winter melon 181
winter squash (*Cucurbita* spp.) 6, 21, 28, 63, 71, 121, 147, 155, 160, 189, 189, **227** wong bok see Chinese cabbage
worms 48, 52, 54, 57, 100, 101
wormwood 65
wormwood tea/spray 116

x

xeric vegetables 138

y

yam (*Dioscorea* spp.) 49, 90, 140, 141, 151
yam beans see jicama
yard long beans 165
yellow chard (*Beta vulgaris* var. *cicla*) 137
yellow mustard (*Brassica* spp.) 186

z

Zea mays var. *saccharata* 6, 14, 21, 24, 27, 28, 37, 65, 67, 87, 89, 118, 122, 123, 131, 138, 139, 141, 147, 156, 161, 170, 170, **249**
zinnias 115
Zizania palustris 58
zucchini (*Cucurbita pepo* var. *melopepo*) 21, 36, 37, 42, 49, 63, 65, 67, 121, 122, 123, 139, 156, 161, 197, 197, **226**
zucchini flowers 197

Acknowledgments

The publisher would like to thank The Digger's Club for generously supplying vegetables for photography.

Photographic credits

John Coco 28 (top).

Ben Dearnley/Jared Fowler 21 (top), 24 (btm), 27 (btm), 29 (btm), 33 (top R and btm), 37 (btm), 38 (btm), 42 (btm), 46–7, 49 (btm), 54 (btm), 58 (L), 58 (top R and btm), 59, 68 (top R), 69 (top L and btm L), 70-1, 72–3 (btm), 75 (L), 79 (btm), 89 (btm), 90 (top), 91 (L), 92 (btm L), 93 (top L and btm), 109, 133 (L), 139, 140 (R), 141, 146 (R), 164–73, 176 (btm L and R), 177–83, 184 (top), 185, 188–9, 190 (btm), 192 (top), 194, 195 (btm), 196, 197 (top R), 231.

Joe Filshie front cover, 56 (R), 93 (top R), 111 (btm).

Denise Greig 42 (top).

Ian Hofstetter 22 (btm), 62 (btm), 184 (btm), 191, 195 (top), 197 (top L).

Chris L. Jones back cover, 34–5, 92 (btm R), 126–7, 130, 138 (top), 142–3, 162–3, 190 (top R).

Brian McInerney 87 (btm).

Luis Martin 101 (btm), 104 (L).

© **Murdoch Books Photo Library** 20 (btm), 29 (top), 63 (L), 83 (btm), 84 (btm L), 86, 88 (btm), 115 (top), 117 (btm), 128, 131, 134, 149 (L), 152 (R), 176 (top), 190 (top L), 192 (btm), 200–30, 232–3, 235–41.

Robin Powell 6–7, 8, 9, 10, 12, 13, 15, 16–17, 36, 37 (top).

Rob Reichenfeld 193.

Lorna Rose 4, 20 (top), 25 (top), 26 (top), 28 (btm), 38 (top), 39, 41, 48 (top), 49 (top), 58 (top L), 62 (top and center), 64, 73 (top), 79 (top), 89 (top), 90 (btm), 92 (top), 97 (top), 102, 105 (top), 106, 111 (top), 113 (top), 115 (btm), 140 (L), 234.

Sue Stubbs 14, 22 (top), 23, 30–1, 43–5, 48 (btm), 60–1, 63 (R), 65, 68 (top L), 69 (R), 72 (top), 74, 75 (R), 76, 80–1, 83 (top), 84 (top), 85 (btm), 87, 88 (top), 91 (R), 94–6, 100, 101 (top), 103, 110, 112, 114, 116, 117 (top), 124–5, 136–7, 144–5, 148, 150–1, 174–5, 186–7, 198–9, 242.

Mark Winwood 18–19, 24 (top), 32, 33 (top L), 40, 50–3, 56 (R), 57, 58 (R), 77–8, 85 (top and center), 98–9, 105 (btm), 107–8, 129, 132, 133 (R), 135, 138 (btm), 146 (L), 147, 149 (R), 152 (L).

Although every care has been taken to trace and acknowledge copyright, the publisher apologizes for any accidental infringement where copyright has proved untraceable. The publisher would be pleased to come to a suitable arrangement with the rightful owner in each case.